COBIT 5

for Information Security

COBIT® 5

ISACA®

With more than 100,000 constituents in 180 countries, ISACA (*www.isaca.org*) is a leading global provider of knowledge, certifications, community, advocacy and education on information systems (IS) assurance and security, enterprise governance and management of IT, and IT-related risk and compliance. Founded in 1969, the nonprofit, independent ISACA hosts international conferences, publishes the *ISACA® Journal*, and develops international IS auditing and control standards, which help its constituents ensure trust in, and value from, information systems. It also advances and attests IT skills and knowledge through the globally respected Certified Information Systems Auditor® (CISA®), Certified Information Security Manager® (CISM®), Certified in the Governance of Enterprise IT® (CGEIT®) and Certified in Risk and Information Systems Control™ (CRISC™) designations.

ISACA continually updates and expands the practical guidance and product family based on the COBIT® framework. COBIT helps IT professionals and enterprise leaders fulfill their IT governance and management responsibilities, particularly in the areas of assurance, security, risk and control, and deliver value to the business.

Disclaimer

ISACA has designed this publication, *COBIT® 5 for Information Security* (the 'Work'), primarily as an educational resource for security professionals. ISACA makes no claim that use of any of the Work will assure a successful outcome. The Work should not be considered inclusive of all proper information, procedures and tests or exclusive of other information, procedures and tests that are reasonably directed to obtaining the same results. In determining the propriety of any specific information, procedure or test, security professionals should apply their own professional judgement to the specific circumstances presented by the particular systems or information technology environment.

ISACA

3701 Algonquin Road, Suite 1010
Rolling Meadows, IL 60008 USA
Phone: +1.847.253.1545
Fax: +1.847.253.1443
Email: *info@isaca.org*
Web site: *www.isaca.org*

Feedback: *www.isaca.org/cobit*
Participate in the ISACA Knowledge Center: *www.isaca.org/knowledge-center*
Follow ISACA on Twitter: *https://twitter.com/ISACANews*
Join the COBIT conversation on Twitter: #COBIT
Join ISACA on LinkedIn: ISACA (Official), *http://linkd.in/ISACAOfficial*
Like ISACA on Facebook: *www.facebook.com/ISACAHQ*

COBIT® 5 for Information Security
ISBN 978-1-60420-254-0
Printed in the United States of America

2

ACKNOWLEDGEMENTS

ISACA wishes to recognise:

COBIT 5 for Information Security Task Force
Christos K. Dimitriadis, Ph.D., CISA, CISM, CRISC, INTRALOT S.A., Greece, Chairman
Manuel Aceves Mercenario, CISA, CISM, CGEIT, CRISC, CISSP, FCITSM, Cerberian Consulting, S.A. de C.V., Mexico
Mark Chaplin, Information Security Forum, UK
Meenu Gupta, CISA, CISM, CBP, CIPP, CISSP, Mittal Technologies, USA
Jo Stewart-Rattray, CISA, CISM, CGEIT, CRISC, CSEPS, RSM Bird Cameron, Australia
Rolf M. von Roessing, CISA, CISM, CGEIT, CISSP, FBCI, Forfa AG, Switzerland

Development Team
Floris Ampe, CISA, CGEIT, CRISC, CIA, ISO 27000, PwC, Belgium
Stefanie Grijp, PwC, Belgium
Ariel Litvin, CRISC, CCSK, PwC, Israel
Bart Peeters, CISA, PwC, Belgium
Christopher Wilken, CISA, CGEIT, PwC, USA

Workshop Participants
Elisabeth Judit Antonsson, CISM, Nordea Bank, Sweden
Garry Barnes, CISA, CISM, CGEIT, CRISC, Stratsec, Australia
Todd Fitzgerald, CISA, CISM, CGEIT, CRISC, CISSP, PMP, ManpowerGroup, USA
Erik P. Friebolin, CISA, CISM, CRISC, CISSP, ITIL, PCI-QSA, USA
Ramses Gallego, CISM, CGEIT, CCSK, CISSP, SCPM, ITIL, 6 Sigma, Quest Software, Spain
Roger Gallego, Entelgy Consulting S.A., Spain
Norman Kromberg, CISA, CGEIT, CRISC, CQA, NBE, Alliance Data, USA
Aureo Monteiro Tavares da Silva, CISM, CGEIT, Pelissari, Brazil
Naiden Nedelchev, Ph.D., CISM, CGEIT, CEH, ITIL V2 Manager, Mobiltel EAD, Bulgaria
Steve Orrin, Intel Corp., USA
Christian Palomino, CISA, CISM, CGEIT, Melia Hotels International, Spain
Vernon Richard Poole, CISM, CGEIT, CRISC, Sapphire, UK
Jeffrey Roth, CISA, CGEIT, CISSP, Parsons, USA
Craig Silverthorne, CISA, CISM, CGEIT, CRISC, CPA, IBM Global Business Services, USA
Cathie Skoog, CISM, CGEIT, CRISC, IBM, USA
Robert E. Stroud, CGEIT, CRISC, CA Technologies, USA
Marc Vael, Ph.D., CISA, CISM, CGEIT, CISSP, Valuendo, Belgium
Mike Villegas, CISA, CEH, CISSP, GSEC, Newegg, Inc., USA

Expert Reviewers
Sanjiv Agarwala, CISA, CISM, CGEIT, CISSP, ITIL, MBCI, Oxygen Consulting Services Pvt. Ltd., India
Jean-Luc Allard, CISA, CISM, MISIS scri, Belgium
Elisabeth Judit Antonsson, CISM, Nordea Bank, Sweden
Garry Barnes, CISA, CISM, CGEIT,ww CRISC, Stratsec, Australia
Allan Boardman, CISA, CISM, CGEIT, CRISC, ACA, CA (SA), CISSP, Morgan Stanley, UK
Jeimy J. Cano, Ph.D., CFE, CMAS, Ecopetrol S.A, Colombia
Cilliam Cuadra, CISA, CISM, CRISC, Banco Nacional de Costa Rica, Costa Rica
Erick Dahan, CISA, CISM, CISSP, PSP Investments, Canada
Heidi L. Erchinger, CISA, CRISC, CISSP, System Security Solutions Inc., USA
Todd Fitzgerald, CISA, CISM, CGEIT, CRISC, CISSP, PMP, ManpowerGroup, USA
Erik P. Friebolin, CISA, CISM, CRISC, CISSP, ITIL, PCI-QSA, USA
Joerg Fritsch, CISM, CRISC, NATO, The Netherlands
Timothy M. Grace, CISA, CISM, CRISC, CIA, MorganFranklin Corp., USA
Jimmy Heschl, CISA, CISM, CGEIT, ITIL Expert, bwin.party digital entertainment plc, Austria
Jerry M. Kathingo, CISM, Infosec Consulting Company, Kenya
Luc Kordel, CISA, CISM, CISSP, CIA, RFA, Belfius Bank, Belgium
Kyeong Hee Oh, CISA, CISM, Fullbitsoft, Korea
Gary Langham, CISA, CISM, CGEIT, CISSP, CPFA, Australia
Yves Le Roux, CISM, CISSP, CA Technologies, France

ACKNOWLEDGEMENTS *(CONT.)*

Expert Reviewers *(cont.)*
Oscar Mauricio Moreno Lopez, CISA, CISM, CGEIT, CISSP, ITIL(f), F&M Technology, Colombia
Tamanu Lowkie, CISM, CAP, CISSP, PMP, USA
Aureo Monteiro Tavares da Silva, CISM, CGEIT, Pelissari, Brazil
Naiden Nedelchev, Ph.D., CISM, CGEIT, CEH, ITIL V2 Manager, Mobiltel EAD, Bulgaria
Hitoshi Ota, CISA, CISM, CGEIT, CRISC, CIA, Mizuho Corporate Bank, Japan
Christian Palomino, CISA, CISM, CGEIT, Melia Hotels International, Spain
Maria Patricia Prandini, CISA, CRISC, Universidad de Buenos Aires, Argentina
Abdul Rafeq, CISA, CGEIT, CIA, FCA, A. Rafeq & Associates, India
R.V. Ramani, CISM, CGEIT, Paramount Computer Systems, United Arab Emirates
Jeffrey Roth, CISA, CGEIT, CISSP, Parsons, USA
Cheryl Santor, CISSP, CNA, CNE, Metropolitan Water District of SoCal, USA
Tim Sattler, CISA, CISM, CRISC, CCSK, CISSP, Jungheinrich AG, Germany
Gurvinder Pal Singh, CISA, CISM, CRISC, Australia
Jonathan D. Sternberg, CISA, CISM, CRISC, CISSP, FFSI, FLMI, Northwestern Mutual, USA
John G. Tannahill, CISM, CGEIT, CRISC, CA, John Tannahill & Associates, Canada
Darlene Tester, JD, CISM, CHSS, CISSP, Bluestem Brands Inc., USA
Smita Totade, Ph.D., CISA, CISM, CGEIT, CRISC, FIEI, National Insurance Academy, India
Marc Vael, Ph.D., CISA, CISM, CGEIT, CISSP, Valuendo, Belgium
Bruce R. Wilkins, CISA, CISM, CGEIT, CRISC, CISSP, TWM Associates, Inc., USA
Hui Zhu, CISA, CISM, CGEIT, BlueImpact, Canada

ISACA Board of Directors
Kenneth L. Vander Wal, CISA, CPA, Ernst & Young LLP (retired), USA, International President
Christos K. Dimitriadis, Ph.D., CISA, CISM, CRISC, INTRALOT S.A., Greece, Vice President
Gregory T. Grocholski, CISA, The Dow Chemical Co., USA, Vice President
Tony Hayes, CGEIT, AFCHSE, CHE, FACS, FCPA, FIIA, Queensland Government, Australia, Vice President
Niraj Kapasi, CISA, Kapasi Bangad Tech Consulting Pvt. Ltd., India, Vice President
Jeff Spivey, CRISC, CPP, PSP, Security Risk Management, Inc., USA, Vice President
Jo Stewart-Rattray, CISA, CISM, CGEIT, CRISC, CSEPS, RSM Bird Cameron, Australia, Vice President
Emil D'Angelo, CISA, CISM, Bank of Tokyo-Mitsubishi UFJ Ltd. (retired), USA, Past International President
Lynn C. Lawton, CISA, CRISC, FBCS CITP, FCA, FIIA, KPMG Ltd., Russian Federation, Past International President
Allan Boardman, CISA, CISM, CGEIT, CRISC, ACA, CA (SA), CISSP, Morgan Stanley, UK, Director
Marc Vael, Ph.D., CISA, CISM, CGEIT, CISSP, Valuendo, Belgium, Director

Knowledge Board
Marc Vael, Ph.D., CISA, CISM, CGEIT, CISSP, Valuendo, Belgium, Chairman
Michael A. Berardi Jr., CISA, CGEIT, Bank of America, USA
John Ho Chi, CISA, CISM, CRISC, CBCP, CFE, Ernst & Young LLP, Singapore
Phillip J. Lageschulte, CGEIT, CPA, KPMG LLP, USA
Jon Singleton, CISA, FCA, Auditor General of Manitoba (retired), Canada
Patrick Stachtchenko, CISA, CGEIT, Stachtchenko & Associates SAS, France

Framework Committee
Patrick Stachtchenko, CISA, CGEIT, Stachtchenko & Associates SAS, France, Chairman
Steven A. Babb, CGEIT, CRISC, Betfair, UK
Sushil Chatterji, CGEIT, Edutech Enterprises, Singapore
Sergio Fleginsky, CISA, Akzo Nobel, Uruguay
John W. Lainhart, IV, CISA, CISM, CGEIT, CRISC, IBM Global Business Services, USA
Anthony P. Noble, CISA, CCP, Viacom, USA
Derek J. Oliver, Ph.D., DBA, CISA, CISM, CRISC, CITP, FBCS, FISM, MInstISP, Ravenswood Consultants Ltd., UK
Rolf M. von Roessing, CISA, CISM, CGEIT, CISSP, FBCI, Forfa AG, Switzerland

ACKNOWLEDGEMENTS *(CONT.)*

ISACA and IT Governance Institute® (ITGI®) Affiliates and Sponsors
Information Security Forum
Institute of Management Accountants Inc.
ISACA chapters
ITGI France
ITGI Japan
Norwich University
Socitum Performance Management Group
Solvay Brussels School of Economics and Management
Strategic Technology Management Institute (STMI) of the National University of Singapore
University of Antwerp Management School

ASIS International
Hewlett-Packard
IBM
Symantec Corp.
TruArx Inc.

Page intentionally left blank

TABLE OF CONTENTS

Page intentionally left blank

LIST OF FIGURES

EXECUTIVE SUMMARY

Introduction

Information is a key resource for all enterprises and, from the time information is created to the moment it is destroyed, technology plays a significant role. Technology is increasingly advanced and has become pervasive in enterprises and the social, public and business environments.

COBIT 5 provides a comprehensive framework that assists enterprises in achieving their objectives for the governance and management of enterprise IT. Simply stated, it helps enterprises create optimal value from information technology (IT) by maintaining a balance between realising benefits and optimising risk levels and resource use. COBIT 5 enables IT to be governed and managed in a holistic manner for the entire enterprise, taking into account the full end-to-end business and IT functional areas of responsibility, considering the IT-related interests of internal and external stakeholders.

COBIT 5 for Information Security, highlighted in **figure 1**, builds on the COBIT 5 framework in that it focuses on information security and provides more detailed and more practical guidance for information security professionals and other interested parties at all levels of the enterprise (see **figure 2**).

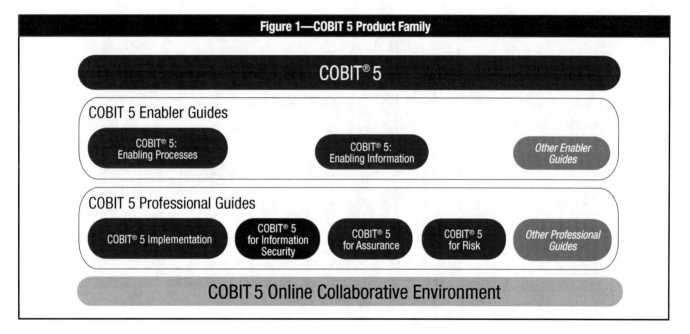

Figure 1—COBIT 5 Product Family

Drivers

In COBIT 5, the processes APO13 *Manage security*, DSS04 *Manage continuity* and DSS05 *Manage security services* provide basic guidance on how to define, operate and monitor a system for general security management. However, the assumption made in this publication is that information security is pervasive throughout the entire enterprise, with information security aspects in every activity and process performed. Therefore, *COBIT 5 for Information Security* provides the next generation of ISACA's guidance on the enterprise governance and management of information security.

The major drivers for the development of *COBIT 5 for Information Security* include:
• The need to describe information security in an enterprise context including:
 – The full end-to-end business and IT functional responsibilities of information security
 – All aspects that lead to effective governance and management of information security, such as organisational structures, policies and culture
 – The relationship and link of information security to enterprise objectives
• An ever-increasing need for the enterprise to:
 – Maintain information risk at an acceptable level and to protect information against unauthorised disclosure, unauthorised or inadvertent modifications, and possible intrusions.
 – Ensure that services and systems are continuously available to internal and external stakeholders, leading to user satisfaction with IT engagement and services.
 – Comply with the growing number of relevant laws and regulations as well as contractual requirements and internal policies on information and systems security and protection, and provide transparency on the level of compliance.
 – Achieve all of the above while containing the cost of IT services and technology protection.

Figure 2—COBIT 5 as it Relates to Information Security

Information Security-specific Organisational Structures

- Chief information security officer (CISO)
- Information security steering committee (ISSC)
- Information security manager (ISM)
- Other related roles and structures

Section II, Chapter 4
Detailed Guidance: Appendix C

Desired Information Security-specific Culture, Ethics and Behaviour

- Information security is practiced in daily operations.
- People respect the policies and principles.
- People are provided with sufficient and detailed guidance, and are encouraged to participate in and challenge the current situation.
- Everyone is accountable for protection.
- Stakeholders identify and respond to threats to the enterprise.
- Management proactively supports and anticipates innovations.
- Business management engages in continuous cross-functional collaboration.
- Executive management recognises the business value.

Section II, Chapter 5
Detailed Guidance: Appendix D

Information Security-specific Principles, Policies and Frameworks

Policy Framework

Input
- Mandatory Information Security Standards, Frameworks and Models
- Generic Information Security Standards, Frameworks and Models

- Information Security Principles
- Information Security Policy
- Specific Information Security Policies
- Information Security Procedures
- Information Security Requirements and Documentation

Section II, Chapter 2
Detailed Guidance: Appendix A

Information Security-specific People, Skills and Competencies

- Information security governance
- Information security strategy formulation
- Information risk management
- Information security architecture development
- Information security operations
- Information assessment and testing and compliance

Section II, Chapter 8
Detailed Guidance: Appendix G

COBIT 5 ENABLERS

- Culture, Ethics and Behaviour
- Organisational Structures
- Processes
- Principles, Policies and Frameworks
- People, Skills and Competencies
- Services, Infrastructure and Applications
- Information

RESOURCES

Information Security-specific Services, Infrastructure and Applications

- Provide a security architecture.
- Provide security awareness.
- Provide secure development.
- Provide security assessments.
- Provide adequately secured and configured systems.
- Provide user access and access rights.
- Provide adequate protection against external attacks and intrusion attempts.
- Provide adequate incident response.
- Provide security testing.
- Provide monitoring and alert services.

Section II, Chapter 7
Detailed Guidance: Appendix F

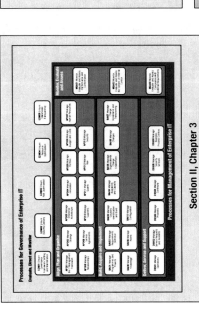

Processes for Management of Enterprise IT

Section II, Chapter 3
Detailed Guidance: Appendix B

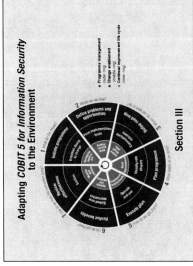

Adapting COBIT 5 for Information Security to the Environment

- Programme management (outer ring)
- Change enablement (middle ring)
- Continual improvement life cycle (inner ring)

Section III

Information Security-specific Information Types

- Information security strategy
- Information security budget
- Information security plan
- Policies
- Information security requirements
- Awareness material
- Information security review reports
- Information risk profile
- Information security dashboard

Section II, Chapter 6
Detailed Guidance: Appendix E

- The need to connect to, and, where relevant, align with, other major frameworks and standards in the marketplace. The (non-exhaustive) mapping (**appendix H**) will help stakeholders understand how various frameworks, good practices and standards are positioned relative to each other and how they can be used together and complement each other under the umbrella of *COBIT 5 for Information Security*.
- The need to link together all major ISACA research, frameworks and guidance, with a primary focus on the Business Model for Information Security (BMIS) and COBIT, but also considering Val IT, Risk IT, the IT Assurance Framework (ITAF), the publication titled *Board Briefing on IT Governance* and the Taking Governance Forward (TGF) resource.

In addition to these major drivers for the development of *COBIT 5 for Information Security* is the fact that information security is essential in the day-to-day operations of enterprises. Breaches in information security can lead to a substantial impact within the enterprise through, for example, financial or operational damages. In addition, the enterprise can be exposed to external impacts such as reputational or legal risk, which can jeopardise customer or employee relations or even endanger the survival of the enterprise.

The need for stronger, better and more systematic approaches for information security is illustrated in the following examples:
- A national critical infrastructure depends on information systems, and successful intrusions can result in a significant impact to economies or human safety.
- Non-public financial information can be used for economic gain.
- Disclosure of confidential information can generate embarrassment to enterprises, cause damage to reputations or jeopardise business relations.
- Intrusion in commercial networks, for example, to obtain credit card or other payment-related data, can lead to substantial reputational and financial damage due to fines, as well as increased scrutiny from regulatory bodies.
- Industrial espionage can enable trade secrets to be imitated and increase competition for manufacturing enterprises.
- Leakage of national or military intelligence can result in damage to political relationships.
- Personal data leaks can result in financial loss and unnecessary efforts to rebuild an individual's financial reputation.
- Significant unplanned costs (both financial and operational) related to containing, investigating and remediating security breaches can impact any enterprise that has suffered a breach.

Benefits

Using *COBIT 5 for Information Security* brings a number of information security-related capabilities to the enterprise, which can result in a number of enterprise benefits such as:
- Reduced complexity and increased cost-effectiveness due to improved and easier integration of information security standards, good practices and/or sector-specific guidelines
- Increased user satisfaction with information security arrangements and outcomes
- Improved integration of information security in the enterprise
- Informed risk decisions and risk awareness
- Improved prevention, detection and recovery
- Reduced (impact of) information security incidents
- Enhanced support for innovation and competitiveness
- Improved management of costs related to the information security function
- Better understanding of information security

These benefits are obtained by leveraging the *COBIT 5 for Information Security* capabilities shown in **figure 3**.

| **Figure 3—*COBIT 5 for Information Security* Capabilities** ||
COBIT 5 for Information Security Capability	Description
Up-to-date view on governance	*COBIT 5 for Information Security* provides the most up-to-date view on information security governance and management through alignment with COBIT 5, International Organization for Standardization (ISO)/International Electrotechnical Commission (IEC) 38500 and other IT governance initiatives. During the development of *COBIT 5 for Information Security*, the most important guidance and standards were analysed. *COBIT 5 for Information Security* aligns with other major frameworks, standards and models in the marketplace, such as the ISO/IEC 27000 series, the Information Security Forum (ISF) Standard of Good Practice, and BMIS. Additionally, ISACA's information security governance offerings, *Information Security Governance: Guidance for Information Security Managers* and *Information Security Governance: Guidance for Boards of Directors and Executive Management, 2nd Edition* were analysed during the development of *COBIT 5 for Information Security*.
Clear distinction between governance and management	COBIT 5 clarifies the roles of governance and management and provides a clear distinction between them, with a revised process model reflecting this distinction and showing how they relate to each other.
End-to-end view	*COBIT 5 for Information Security* is a process model that integrates both business and IT functional responsibilities. It provides a clear distinction between information security governance and information security management practices, outlining responsibilities at various levels of the enterprise, encompassing all process steps from the beginning to the end.
Holistic guidance	The *COBIT 5 for Information Security* framework brings together comprehensive and holistic guidance on information security. Holistic means that attention is paid not only to processes, but to all enablers, including information, structures, culture, policies and their interdependence.

COBIT 5 for Information Security is based on the COBIT 5 framework, from which all information security-relevant information has been filtered and complemented with more detailed and specific guidance, therefore ensuring consistency with the COBIT 5 product architecture. COBIT 5 starts from stakeholder expectations and concerns related to enterprise IT. All guidance can be related back to stakeholder issues, and thus information security assists to support the mission of the business and achievement of business goals.

Target Audience

COBIT 5 for Information Security is intended for all stakeholders of information security. Chief information security officers (CISOs), information security managers (ISMs) and other information security professionals are the most obvious target audience. However, information security is the responsibility of all stakeholders of the enterprise, including all staff members, and other stakeholders, including third parties. Therefore, this publication may be of interest to all stakeholders in the enterprise.

Conventions Used and Overview

COBIT 5 for Information Security refers to a number of enablers such as roles and job titles, committees and boards, processes, and policies. The unique characteristics of each enterprise will cause these enablers to be used in many different ways to provide information security in an optimal manner. *COBIT 5 for Information Security* uses guidance and examples to provide a pervasive view that explains each concept of COBIT 5 from an information security perspective.

To guide the reader through the vast collection of information, *COBIT 5 for Information Security* follows a set structure consisting of three sections and eight appendices.

Each section contains several chapters. Within a chapter, as required, signposting is used to guide the reader throughout the explanation. In addition, blue and grey information boxes are used:
• A blue box calls out attention points relevant for information security.
• A grey box highlights material that is given to link the information with other relevant items. The sections also refer to the appendices for more specific information.

Each section and its interconnections with other sections is described as follows:
- **Section I**—Elaborates on **information security** and describes briefly how the COBIT 5 architecture can be tailored to information security-specific needs. This section provides a conceptual baseline that is followed throughout the rest of the publication.
- **Section II**—Elaborates on **the use of COBIT 5 enablers for implementing information security**. Governance of enterprise IT is systemic and supported by a set of enablers. In this section, the concept of the security-specific enablers is introduced and explained using practical examples. Detailed guidance regarding these enablers is provided in the appendices.
- **Section III**—Elaborates on how **to adapt *COBIT 5 for Information Security* to the enterprise environment**. This section contains guidance on how information security initiatives can be implemented and contains a mapping with other standards and frameworks in the area of information security and *COBIT 5 for Information Security*.

The **appendices** contain detailed guidance based on the enablers introduced in section II:
- **Appendix A**—Detailed guidance regarding the principles, policies and frameworks enabler
- **Appendix B**—Detailed guidance regarding the processes enabler
- **Appendix C**—Detailed guidance regarding the organisational structures enabler
- **Appendix D**—Detailed guidance regarding the culture, ethics and behaviour enabler
- **Appendix E**—Detailed guidance regarding the information enabler
- **Appendix F**—Detailed guidance regarding the services, infrastructure and applications enabler
- **Appendix G**—Detailed guidance regarding the people, skills and competencies enabler
- **Appendix H**—Detailed mappings of *COBIT 5 for Information Security* to other information security standards

The **Acronyms** and **Glossary** sections clarify the abbreviations and terms used exclusively in this publication. For standardised terms, please refer to the ISACA Glossary of Terms located at *www.isaca.org/Glossary*.

Page intentionally left blank

SECTION I. INFORMATION SECURITY

CHAPTER 1
INFORMATION SECURITY DEFINED

ISACA defines information security as something that:

> *Ensures that within the enterprise, information is protected against disclosure to unauthorised users (confidentiality), improper modification (integrity) and non-access when required (availability).*

- Confidentiality means preserving authorised restrictions on access and disclosure, including means for protecting privacy and proprietary information.
- Integrity means guarding against improper information modification or destruction, and includes ensuring information non-repudiation and authenticity.
- Availability means ensuring timely and reliable access to and use of information.

Although several other definitions of the term exist, this definition provides the very basics of information security as it covers the confidentiality, integrity and availability (CIA) concept. It is important to note that while the CIA concept is globally accepted, there are broader uses of the term 'integrity' in the wider business context. COBIT 5 covers this term in the information enabler as information goals of completeness and accuracy. *COBIT 5 for Information Security* is limited to the security view of this term and builds on this definition to describe how information security can be applied in real life, taking into account the COBIT 5 principles.

Information security is a business enabler that is strictly bound to stakeholder trust, either by addressing business risk or by creating value for an enterprise, such as competitive advantage. At a time when the significance of information and related technologies is increasing in every aspect of business and public life, the need to mitigate information risk, which includes protecting information and related IT assets from ever-changing threats, is constantly intensifying. Increasing regulation within the business landscape adds to the awareness of the board of directors of the criticality of information security for information and IT-related assets.

Page intentionally left blank

COBIT 5 FOR INFORMATION SECURITY

Page intentionally left blank

CHAPTER 2
COBIT 5 PRINCIPLES

2.1 Overview

COBIT 5 for Information Security is based on the same principles as the COBIT 5 framework (**figure 4**).

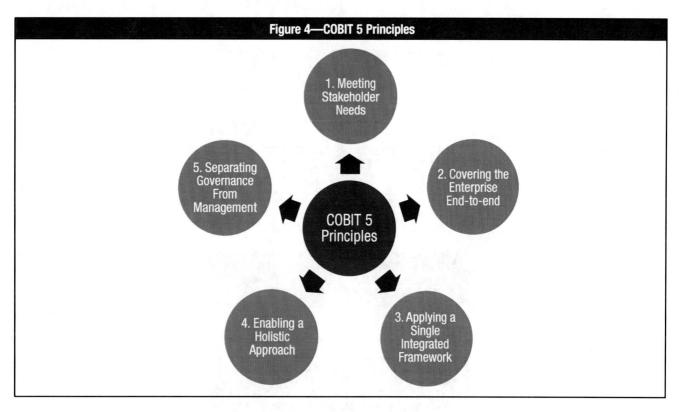

Figure 4—COBIT 5 Principles

The following text describes briefly each principle and its relevance to information security.

2.2 Principle 1. Meeting Stakeholder Needs

Enterprises exist to create value for their stakeholders—including stakeholders for information security—by maintaining a balance between the realisation of benefits and the optimisation of risk and use of resources. Optimisation of risk is considered most relevant for information security.

Since every enterprise has different objectives, an enterprise should use the goals cascade to customise COBIT 5 to suit its own context. In the goals cascade, depicted in **figure 5**, stakeholder needs, which are influenced by a number of drivers, are translated and specified into operational enterprise goals to be satisfied. These enterprise goals in turn require IT-related goals to be achieved, and finally translate into goals for the different enablers.

Information security is one major stakeholder need, and this translates into information security-related goals for the enterprise, for IT and ultimately for the supporting enablers.

In *COBIT 5 for Information Security*, information security-specific goals for processes are defined in support of the information security-related stakeholder needs. Likewise, specific information security-related goals are defined for the other enablers (section II).

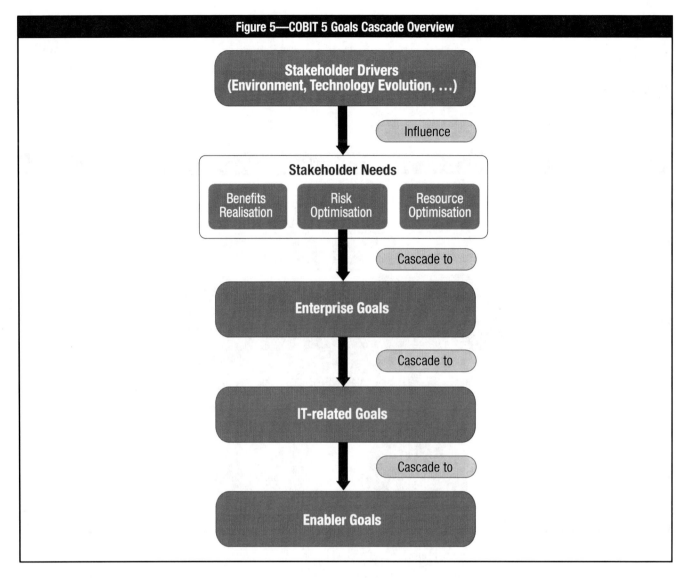

Figure 5—COBIT 5 Goals Cascade Overview

2.3 Principle 2. Covering the Enterprise End-to-end

COBIT 5 integrates governance of enterprise IT into enterprise governance by:
• Covering all functions and processes within the enterprise. COBIT 5 does not focus on only the 'IT function', but instead treats information and related technologies as assets that need to be dealt with just like any other asset by everyone in the enterprise.
• Considering all IT-related governance and management enablers to be enterprisewide and end-to-end, i.e., inclusive of everything and everyone, internal and external, that is relevant to governance and management of enterprise information and related IT. Applying this principle to information security, *COBIT 5 for Information Security* covers all stakeholders, functions and processes within the enterprise that are relevant for information security.

2.4 Principle 3. Applying a Single, Integrated Framework

There are many IT-related standards and best practices, each providing guidance on a subset of IT-related activities. COBIT 5 is complete in enterprise coverage, providing a basis to integrate effectively other frameworks, standards and practices used. As a single, integrated framework, it serves as a consistent and integrated source of guidance in a non-technical, technology-agnostic common language. COBIT 5 aligns with other relevant standards and frameworks, and thus allows the enterprise to use it as the overarching governance and management framework for enterprise IT.

More specifically, *COBIT 5 for Information Security* brings together knowledge previously dispersed over different ISACA frameworks and models (COBIT, BMIS, Risk IT, Val IT) with guidance from other major information security-related standards such as the ISO/IEC 27000 series, the ISF Standard of Good Practice for Information Security and U.S. National Institute of Standards and Technology (NIST) SP800-53A.

2.5 Principle 4. Enabling a Holistic Approach

Efficient and effective governance and management of enterprise IT and information require a holistic approach, taking into account several interacting components. COBIT 5 defines a set of enablers to support the implementation of a comprehensive governance and management system for enterprise IT and information. Enablers are factors that, individually and collectively, influence whether something will work—in this case, governance and management over enterprise IT and, related to that, information security governance. Enablers are driven by the goals cascade, i.e., higher-level IT-related goals define what the different enablers should achieve.

The COBIT 5 framework defines seven categories of enablers (**figure 6**).

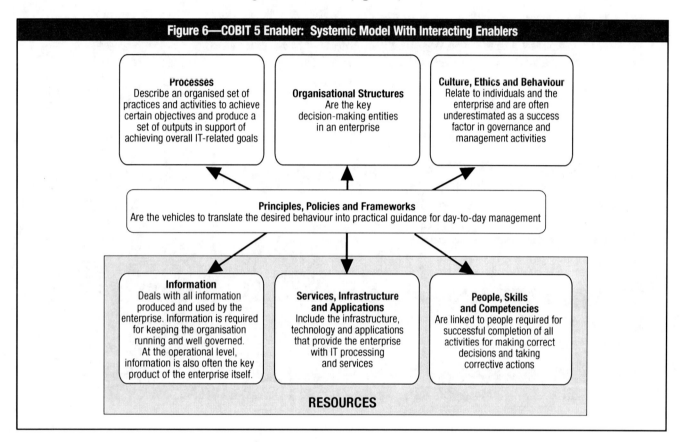

In section II, all interconnected enablers required for adequate information security are treated and discussed, presenting a true holistic and systemic approach towards information security.

2.6 Principle 5. Separating Governance From Management

The COBIT 5 framework makes a clear distinction between governance and management. These two disciplines encompass different types of activities, require different organisational structures and serve different purposes. COBIT 5's view on this key distinction follows.

Governance

> **Governance ensures that stakeholder needs, conditions and options are evaluated to determine balanced, agreed-on enterprise objectives to be achieved; setting direction through prioritisation and decision making; and monitoring performance and compliance against agreed-on direction and objectives.**

In most enterprises, governance is the responsibility of the board of directors under the leadership of the chairperson.

Management

> **Management plans, builds, runs and monitors activities in alignment with the direction set by the governance body to achieve the enterprise objectives.**

In most enterprises, management is the responsibility of the executive management under the leadership of the chief executive officer (CEO).

In practice, the different roles of information security governance and management are made visible by the COBIT 5 process reference model, which includes governance processes and management processes, each set with its own responsibilities. This is depicted in **figure 7** and further elaborated in section II.

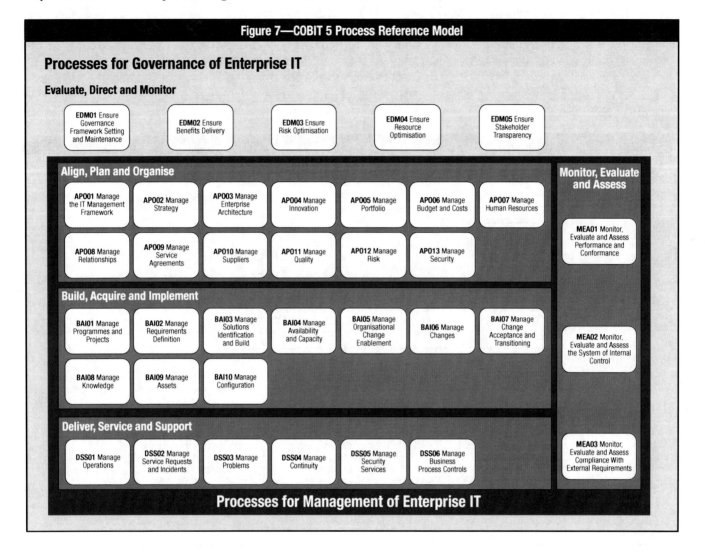

Figure 7—COBIT 5 Process Reference Model

SECTION II. USING COBIT 5 ENABLERS FOR IMPLEMENTING INFORMATION SECURITY IN PRACTICE

CHAPTER 1
INTRODUCTION

This section describes how the COBIT 5 enablers, as introduced in section I, can be applied in practical situations and how these enablers can be used to implement effective and efficient information security governance and management in the enterprise.

1.1 The Generic Enabler Model

The enablers defined in COBIT 5 have a set of common dimensions (**figure 8**). This set:
• Provides a simple and structured way to deal with enablers
• Allows an entity to manage its complex interactions
• Facilitates successful outcomes of the enablers

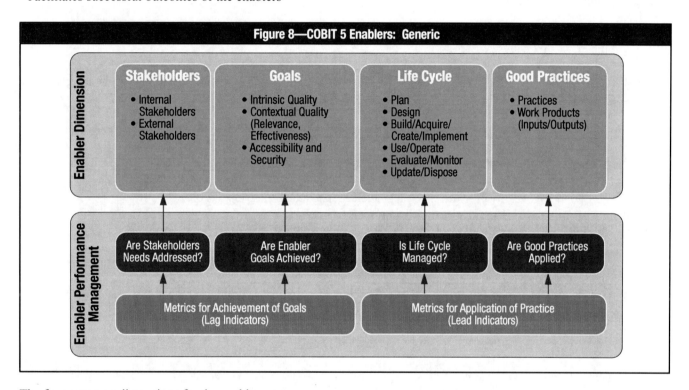

Figure 8—COBIT 5 Enablers: Generic

The four common dimensions for the enablers are:
• **Stakeholders**—Each enabler has stakeholders (parties who play an active role and/or have an interest in the enabler). For example, processes have different parties who execute process activities and/or who have an interest in the process outcomes; organisational structures have stakeholders, each with his/her own roles and interests, that are part of the structures. Stakeholders can be internal or external to the enterprise, all having their own, sometimes conflicting, interests and needs. Stakeholder needs translate to enterprise goals, which in turn translate to IT-related goals for the enterprise.
• **Goals**—Each enabler has a number of goals (expected outcomes) and enablers provide value by achieving these goals. The enabler goals are the final step in the COBIT 5 goals cascade.

Goals can be further divided into different categories:
– **Intrinsic quality**—The extent to which enablers provide accurate, objective and reputable results
– **Contextual quality**—The extent to which outcomes of the enablers are fit for purpose given the context in which they operate. For example, outcomes should be relevant, complete, current, appropriate, consistent, understandable and easy to use.
– **Access and security**—The extent to which enablers are accessible (available when and if needed) and secured (access is restricted to those entitled and needing it)

- **Life cycle**—Each enabler has a life cycle, from inception through an operational/useful life until disposal. The phases of the life cycle consist of:
  - Plan (includes concepts development and concepts selection)
  - Design
  - Build/acquire/create/implement
  - Use/operate
  - Evaluate/monitor
  - Update/dispose
- **Good practices**—For each of the enablers, good practices can be defined. Good practices support the achievement of the enabler goals and provide examples or suggestions on how best to implement the enabler and what work products or inputs and outputs are required. Once these good practices are properly tuned and successfully integrated within the enterprise, they can become, through follow-up of the changing business needs and proper monitoring, best practices for the enterprise.

1.2 Enabler Performance Management

Enterprises expect positive outcomes from the application and use of enablers. To manage performance of the enablers, the following questions must be monitored and answered—based on metrics—on a regular basis:
- Are stakeholder needs addressed?
- Are enabler goals achieved?
- Is the enabler life cycle managed?
- Are good practices applied?

The first two bullets deal with the actual outcome of the enabler. The metrics used to measure to what extent the goals are achieved can be called 'lag indicators'.

The last two bullets deal with the actual functioning of the enabler itself, and metrics for this can be called 'lead indicators'.

1.3 *COBIT 5 for Information Security* and Enablers

COBIT 5 for Information Security provides specific guidance related to all enablers:
1. Information security **policies, principles and frameworks**
2. **Processes**, including information security-specific details and activities
3. Information security-specific **organisational structures**
4. In terms of **culture, ethics and behaviour**, factors determining the success of information security governance and management
5. Information security-specific **information** types for enabling information security governance and management within the enterprise
6. **Service capabilities** required to provide information security and related functions to an enterprise
7. **People, skills and competencies** specific for information security

For each enabler considered in this chapter, all components will be discussed as relevant or when the generic description needs to be made more specific. The chapters of this section follow the same order as listed above.

In addition to an information security-specific description of the enabler components, detailed guidance regarding these enablers can be found in appendices A through G.

CHAPTER 2
ENABLER: PRINCIPLES, POLICIES AND FRAMEWORKS

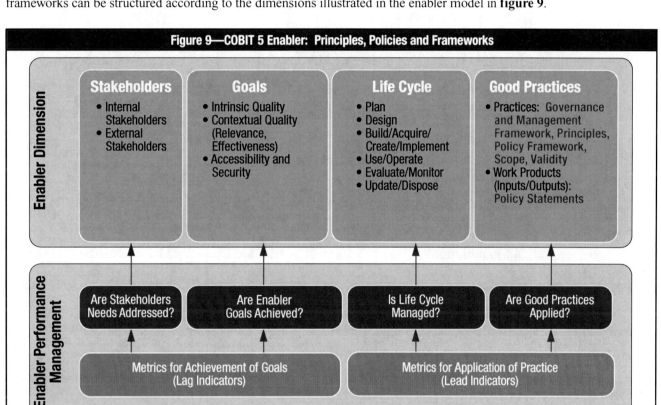

Principles, policies and frameworks refer to the communication mechanisms put in place to convey the direction and instructions of the governing bodies and management. The following items are covered in this chapter:
1. Principles, policies and framework model
2. Information security principles
3. Information security policies
4. Adapting policies to the enterprise's environment
5. Policy life cycle

2.1 Principles, Policies and Framework Model

Principles, policies and frameworks are the vehicles to translate the desired behaviour of enterprise staff members towards information security into formal, yet practical, guidelines for day-to-day management. These principles, policies and frameworks can be structured according to the dimensions illustrated in the enabler model in **figure 9**.

Figure 9 shows at a high level the different components of principles, policies and frameworks as they are defined within this publication. This process model is an extension of the generic enabler model explained in **figure 8**.

The principles, policies and frameworks model indicates that:
• **Stakeholders** for principles, policies and frameworks include the board and executive management, compliance officers, risk managers, internal and external auditors, service providers and customers, and regulatory agencies. The stakes are twofold: some stakeholders define and set policies, others need to align to and comply with policies.
• Principles, policies and frameworks are instruments used to communicate the rules of the enterprise in support of the **governance objectives and enterprise values**, as defined by the board and executive management. Principles should be limited in number and expressed in simple language. Policies provide more detailed guidance on how to put principles into practice; they influence how decision making aligns with the principles.
• Policies have a **life cycle** that must support the achievement of the defined goals. Frameworks are key because they provide a structure to define consistent guidance, for example, a policy framework defines the structure in which a consistent set of policies can be created and maintained, and it provides an easy point of navigation within and between individual policies.

• **Good practices** require all policies to be part of an overall policy framework, providing a (hierarchical) structure into which the policies should fit and clearly making the link to the underlying principles.

The policy framework needs to define the:
• Approvers of the enterprise policies
• Consequences of failing to comply with the policy
• Means for handling exceptions
• Manner in which compliance with the policy will be checked and measured

Accountability for developing and maintaining the framework and related policies is attributed to the chair of the information security steering committee (ISSC). The framework can be used as a placeholder in which to fit all policies/procedures and link them with the identified principles. In practice, the framework advises the information security professional and/or other users of the information security policies how to consult the available guidance, as depicted in **figure 10**.

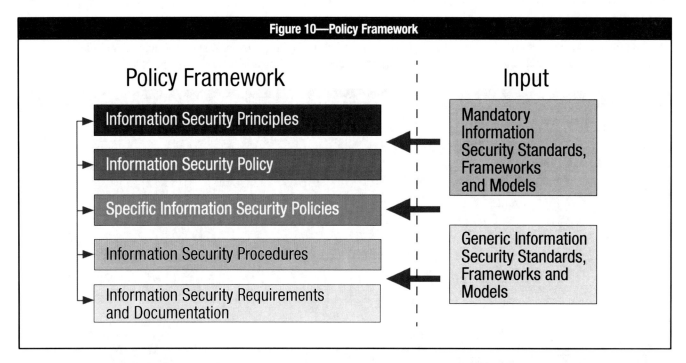

Figure 10—Policy Framework

The detailed information security requirements and documentation must be consulted first in case of an operational issue. Should the proper operational and/or technical guidance not exist, the user can consult the information security procedures and consequently the **related specific information security policies**. These policies cover a subsidiary area of information security and provide tactical guidance. The information security policy consists of high-level direction on information security. A user can consult this **general policy** when no detailed policy exists. Finally, the user needs to apply the **general principles** when the general information security policy is unclear on the topic.

When a user has identified the need for more detailed guidance, this should always be communicated to the information security manager.

For the development of the specific guidance for the enterprise, the ISSC (or delegated function) can use the information security standards. In this context, the use of generic and mandatory standards, frameworks and models as input for the policy framework can be distinguished. Depending on the situation, mandatory standards, frameworks and models are required to be taken into account when developing the principles, policies, procedures and requirements. For example, when enterprises make the business decision to become ISO/IEC 27001-certified, those organisations are required to comply with the ISO/IEC 27001 standard. Enterprises that provide and accept credit cards need to comply with Payment Card Industry Data Security Standards (PCI DSS). In these cases, the related standards used become mandatory due to the business decisions made. Alternatively, the ISSC may want to use information security standards and guidelines as generic good practices to efficiently develop the principles, policies, procedures and requirements required.

2.2 Information Security Principles

Information security principles communicate the rules of the enterprise in support of the governance objectives and enterprise values, as defined by the board and executive management. These principles need to be:
• Limited in number
• Expressed in simple language and state, as clearly as possible, the core values of the enterprise

In 2010, three leading global information security organisations—ISACA, ISF and International Information System Security Certification Consortium [(ISC)²]—joined forces to develop 12 independent, non-proprietary principles that will help information security professionals add value to their organisations by successfully supporting the business and promoting good information security practices. These principles are structured in support of three tasks:
1. Support the business:
   • **Focus on the business** to ensure that information security is integrated into essential business activities.
   • **Deliver quality and value to stakeholders** to ensure that information security delivers value and meets business requirements.
   • **Comply with relevant legal and regulatory requirements** to ensure that statutory obligations are met, stakeholder expectations are managed, and civil or criminal penalties are avoided.
   • **Provide timely and accurate information on information security performance** to support business requirements and manage information risk.
   • **Evaluate current and future information threats** to analyse and assess emerging information security threats so that informed, timely action to mitigate risk can be taken.
   • **Promote continuous improvement in information security** to reduce costs, improve efficiency and effectiveness, and promote a culture of continuous improvement in information security.
2. Defend the business:
   • **Adopt a risk-based approach** to ensure that risk is treated in a consistent and effective manner.
   • **Protect classified information** to prevent disclosure to unauthorised individuals.
   • **Concentrate on critical business applications** to prioritise scarce information security resources by protecting the business applications in which a security incident would have the greatest business impact.
   • **Develop systems securely** to build quality, cost-effective systems on which business people can rely.
3. Promote responsible information security behaviour:
   • **Act in a professional and ethical manner** to ensure that information security-related activities are performed in a reliable, responsible and effective manner.
   • **Foster an information security-positive culture** to provide a positive security influence on the behaviour of end users, reduce the likelihood of security incidents occurring, and limit their potential business impact.

These principles are generic and applicable to all enterprises. In developing information security principles unique to the enterprise, this list can be used as inspiration.

For each of these principles, the objective and the description have been provided in **appendix A**.

2.3 Information Security Policies

Policies provide more detailed guidance on how to put principles into practice and how they will influence decision making. Not all relevant policies are written and owned by the information security function. A number of policies are described in this publication, and the policy driver within the enterprise is specified. The policies are structured in three groups:
• The information security policy written by the information security function, but driven by the board of directors
• Specific information security policies driven by the information security function
• Other policies that can be related to information security, but are driven by other functions in the enterprise. In these policies, information security should influence the development to ensure the achievement of the information security requirements.

The following list of relevant policies is illustrative and not exhaustive:
• Information security policy
• Access control policy
• Personnel information security policy
• Physical and environmental information security policy
• Incident management policy
• Business continuity and disaster recovery policy
• Asset management policy
• Rules of behaviour (acceptable use)

- Information systems acquisition, software development and maintenance policy
- Vendor management policy
- Communications and operation management policy
- Compliance policy
- Risk management policy

For each of these policies, the following attributes are described in **appendix A**:
- **Scope**
- **Validity** (except for information security policies driven by other functions within the enterprise)
  – **Applicable**—To which areas of the enterprise is this policy applicable?
  – **Update and revalidation**—Who is responsible for maintaining the policy and what is the frequency of revalidation?
  – **Distribution**—How should policies be distributed throughout the enterprise?
- **Goals** (except for information security policies driven by other functions within the enterprise)

2.4 Adapting Policies to the Enterprise's Environment

These policies, and consequently the policy framework, should be aligned with the principles and the overall enterprise objectives, strategy and risk appetite. As part of risk governance activities, the enterprise's risk appetite is defined, and the risk appetite should be reflected in the policies. A risk-averse enterprise will have different policies than a risk-taking organisation. This is due to the nature of the enterprise, the environment in which it operates and its risk stance.

Policies should take into account the specific situation in which the enterprise exists. The content of the enterprise policies will change depending on the context of the organisation and the environment in which it operates. This specific situation is made up by factors such as:
- Applicable regulations unique to the enterprise
- Business operational and functional requirements
- Intellectual property and competitive data protection needs
- Existing high-level policies and the corporate culture
- Unique IT enterprise architecture designs
- Governmental regulations such as the Federal Information Security Management Act (FISMA) in the United States
- Industry standards (PCI DSS)

In the detailed guidance, some suggestions are made regarding the possible content of an information security policy:
- Coverage within the enterprise
- Information security life cycle budget and cost management
- Information security strategic plans and portfolio management
- Vision, goals and metrics
- Innovation and best practices
- Value creation
- Stakeholder communication and reporting
- Technology and architecture governance
- Information security culture and awareness
- Ownership attributed to the relevant stakeholders regarding critical information
- Vendors and third parties

This list can provide guidance to develop a unique policy adapted and aligned to the specific situation. The policy can exist in one large document, containing all relevant elements, or one guiding document, containing high-level guidance with links to the more detailed policies. Either way is acceptable as long as the format is clearly described in a policy framework.

2.5 Policy Life Cycle

As defined in APO01.03 *Maintain the enablers of the management system*, policies need to be managed throughout their life cycle. Policy evaluation and update are required on a regular basis, and a trigger mechanism for updates outside the life cycle should be implemented as well.

Evolution and emerging technology in policies:
The evolution regarding the use of mobile devices, social media, cloud computing, shadow IT or the business use of non-central IT should trigger the need to review and update a policy. In addition, changes in local regulatory compliance requirements necessitate review and update of existing policies, or perhaps the need for new policies.

In addition, review of policies outside the information security function is required in many enterprises. Potential privacy issues, for example, may trigger the involvement of the legal and human resources functions in the approval of policies. The ISSC remains ultimately accountable for the development of policies and their update. This steering committee may require the approval of executive management when the overall information security policy is adapted. For more technical policies, the steering committee can decide independently. For smaller enterprises, policies can exist even if they are not documented or formally approved.

Page intentionally left blank

CHAPTER 3
ENABLER: PROCESSES

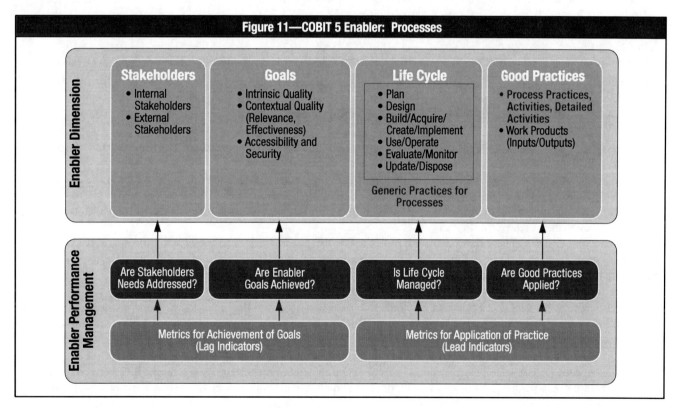

This chapter contains all COBIT 5 processes rendered specifically for information
security, including details such as information security goals and metrics, and information
security-specific activities. The COBIT 5 process content is reduced to what is relevant for
information security and expanded to align with external information security sources.
As such, this is an information security-specific complement to the *COBIT® 5: Enabling Processes* publication.

The following items will be discussed:
1. The process model
2. Governance and management processes
3. Information security governance and management processes
4 Linking processes to other enablers

Processes describe an organised set of practices and activities to achieve certain objectives and produce a set of outputs in
support of achieving overall IT-related goals, as described previously.

3.1 The Process Model

Figure 11 shows at a high level the different components of a process as it is defined within *COBIT 5 for
Information Security*.

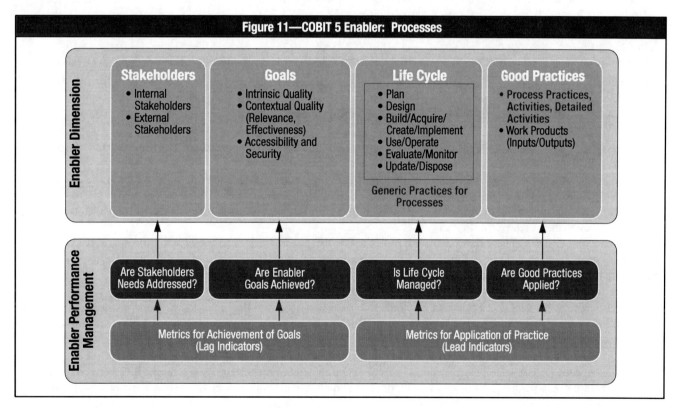

Figure 11—COBIT 5 Enabler: Processes

Enabler Dimension

Stakeholders
- Internal Stakeholders
- External Stakeholders

Goals
- Intrinsic Quality
- Contextual Quality (Relevance, Effectiveness)
- Accessibility and Security

Life Cycle
- Plan
- Design
- Build/Acquire/Create/Implement
- Use/Operate
- Evaluate/Monitor
- Update/Dispose

Generic Practices for Processes

Good Practices
- Process Practices, Activities, Detailed Activities
- Work Products (Inputs/Outputs)

Enabler Performance Management

Are Stakeholders Needs Addressed?
Are Enabler Goals Achieved?
Is Life Cycle Managed?
Are Good Practices Applied?

Metrics for Achievement of Goals (Lag Indicators)
Metrics for Application of Practice (Lead Indicators)

This process model is an extension of the generic enabler model explained in **figure 8**. COBIT 5 defines a process as
**'a collection of practices influenced by the enterprise's policies and procedures that takes inputs from a number
of sources (including other processes), manipulates the inputs and produces outputs (e.g., products, services)'**. The
process model indicates that:
- Processes have internal (e.g., board, management, staff, volunteers, regulators) and external (e.g., customers, business
partners, shareholders) **stakeholders**, each possessing role and responsibility levels (documented in responsible,
accountable, consulted, informed [RACI] charts).

They can be categorised as intrinsic goals, contextual goals, or accessibility and security goals. At each level of the goals
cascade, metrics are defined to measure the extent to which goals are achieved. In addition, performance management
of the enabler describes the extent to which good practice is applied. Associated metrics can be defined to help with the
management of the enabler.

- Each process has a **life cycle** which is defined, created, operated, monitored and adjusted/updated, or retired. Generic process practices such as those defined in the COBIT process assessment model[1] based on ISO/IEC 15504 can assist with defining, running, monitoring and optimising processes.
- **Internal good practices** are described in growing levels of detail: practices, activities and detailed activities. **External good practices** can exist in any form or level of detail, and mostly refer to other standards and frameworks. Users can refer to these practices at all times, knowing that *COBIT 5 for Information Security* is aligned with these standards and models where relevant, and mapping information will be made available.

> The alignment between *COBIT 5 for Information Security* and other standards and models is described in more detail in section III of this publication.

The detailed process-related and information security-specific information for the COBIT 5 governance and management processes includes:
- **Process identification**—On the first page of each process description, the following information is identified:
  – Process label—Consisting of the domain prefix (EDM, APO, BAI, DSS, MEA) and the process number
  – Process name—A short description, indicating the main subject of the process
  – Area—Governance or management
  – Domain name
- **Process description**—This short paragraph describes the process in more detail and contains an:
  – Overview of what the process does, i.e., the purpose of the process
  – Overview at a very high level of how the process accomplishes the purpose
- **Process purpose statement**—A description of the overall purpose of the process
- **Process goals and metrics**—For each process, a limited number of **information security-specific** process goals are included, and for each process goal a limited number of information security-specific example metrics is listed, reflecting the clear relationship between the goals and the metrics.
- **Detailed description of the process practices**—This description contains for each practice:
  – Practice title and description
  – **Information security-specific** practice inputs and outputs (work products), with indication of origin and destination
  – **Information security-specific** process activities

3.2 Governance and Management Processes

As mentioned previously, one of the guiding principles in COBIT 5 is the distinction made between governance and management. In line with this principle, each enterprise is expected to implement a number of governance processes and a number of management processes to provide comprehensive governance and management of information security.

When considering processes for governance and management in the context of the enterprise, the difference between types of processes lies in the objectives of the processes:
- **Governance processes**—These processes deal with the governance objectives of benefits realisation, risk optimisation and resource optimisation. They include practices and activities aimed at evaluating strategic options, providing direction to information security and monitoring the outcome (as represented in COBIT 5's Evaluate, Direct and Monitor [EDM] domain, in line with the ISO/IEC 38500 standard concepts).
- **Management processes**—These processes include practices and activities designed to cover the responsibility areas of planning, building, running and monitoring (PBRM) information security. The management processes provide end-to-end coverage of information security.

The outcomes of the two types of processes are different and are intended for different audiences. However, internally, all processes require planning, building or implementation, execution and monitoring activities within the process itself.

3.3 Information Security Governance and Management Processes

> **Figure 7** shows the complete set of 37 governance and management processes within COBIT 5. The details of all information security-specific processes, according to the process model described previously, are included as **appendix B**.

---

[1] ISACA, *COBIT® Process Assessment Model (PAM): Using COBIT 4.1*, USA, 2011, *www.isaca.org/cobit-pam*

3.4 Linking Processes to Other Enablers

As described in section I, all enablers are interconnected and interact dynamically; i.e., to achieve the main enterprise objectives, the enterprise must always consider an interconnected set of enablers. Therefore, each enabler:
• Needs the input of other enablers to be fully effective (e.g., processes need information, organisational structures need skills and behaviour)
• Delivers output to the benefit of other enablers (e.g., processes deliver information, skills and behaviour make processes efficient)

For every process, a box is provided at the bottom of the process description, describing the related enablers, as in the following example:

For more information regarding the related enablers, please consult:
• Appendix D. Detailed Guidance: Culture, Ethics and Behaviour

Page intentionally left blank

CHAPTER 4
ENABLER: ORGANISATIONAL STRUCTURES

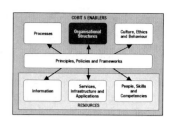

This chapter discusses organisational structures relevant for information security. Organisational structures are the key decision-making entities in an enterprise. The following items are covered:

1. The organisational structures model
2. Examples of information security roles and structures that are commonly found
3. Accountability over information security within the enterprise

4.1 Organisational Structures Model

Organisational structures are defined as the key decision-making entities in an organisation. These entities can be structured according to the dimensions illustrated in the enabler model shown in **figure 12**.

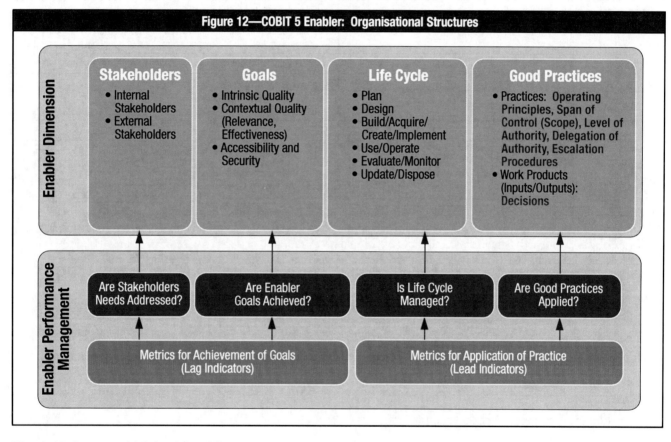

Figure 12 shows at a high level the different components of organisational structure as it is defined within this publication. This process model is an extension of the generic enabler model explained in **figure 8**.

The organisational structures model indicates that:
• Organisational structures **stakeholder** roles (which include decision making, influencing and advising) vary, as do the stakes (i.e., the interest they have in the decisions made by the structure).
• The **goals** for the organisational structures enabler itself include having a proper mandate, well-defined operating principles and application of other good practices. The outcome of the organisational structures enabler should include a number of good activities and decisions.
• An organisational structure has a **life cycle**. It is created, exists and is adjusted, and finally it can be disbanded. During its inception, a mandate—a reason and purpose for its existence—must be defined.
• A number of **good practices** for organisational structures can be distinguished, which are described in detail in **appendix C**.

Stakeholders are the first component in the organisational structures enabler model. From an information security point of view, stakeholders are organised into two categories:
• Information security-**specific** roles and structures—These roles and structures are internal to the information security function.
• Information security-**related** roles and structures—These roles and structures are not organised or filled by members of the information security function, but information security issues and topics are discussed or handled by these roles and structures (e.g., users and business process owners).

4.2 Information Security Roles and Structures

Within a typical enterprise, the information security roles and structures depicted in **figure 13**, rows 1, 2 and 3, are commonly found.

Figure 13—Information Security-specific Roles/Structures	
Role/Structure	**Mandate**
Chief information security officer (CISO) (defined in COBIT 5)	Overall responsibility of the enterprise information security programme
Information security steering committee (ISSC)	Ensuring through monitoring and review that good practices in information security are applied effectively and consistently throughout the enterprise
Information security manager (ISM) (defined in COBIT 5)	Overall responsibility for the management of information security efforts
Enterprise risk management (ERM) committee	Responsible for the decision making of the enterprise to assess, control, optimise, finance and monitor risk from all sources for the purpose of increasing the enterprise's short- and long-term value to its stakeholders
Information custodians/business owners	Liaison between the business and information security functions

In **appendix C**, detailed descriptions of these groups and roles can be found. For each of these, the following good practices have been described:
• **Composition**—An appropriate skill set should be required of all members of the organisational group.
• **Mandate, operating principles, span of control and authority level**—These elements describe the practical arrangements of how the structure will operate, the boundaries of the organisational structure's decision rights, the responsibilities and accountabilities, and the escalation path or required actions in case of problems.
• **High-level RACI chart**—RACI charts link process activities to organisational structures and/or individual roles in the organisation. They describe the level of involvement of each role for each process practice: responsible, accountable, consulted or informed.
• **Inputs/Outputs**—A structure requires inputs (typically information) before it can take informed decisions, and it produces outputs, for example, decisions, other information or requests for additional inputs.

Additional information security-specific roles can be created depending on the enterprise. Examples of typical roles in an information security team are:
• Information security administrators
• Information security architects
• Information security compliance and auditing officers

In smaller enterprises, however, the tasks covered by these roles can be carried out by the information security manager. In addition to the information security-specific roles and structures, two examples of related structures are described in the last two rows in **figure 13**.

Additional practical guidance regarding these structures can be found in **appendix C**.

These roles and structures are appropriate for an enterprise that not only handles sensitive information, but also has reached a certain size and organisational complexity. For larger enterprises or enterprises that require a more robust focus on information security, an elaborated information security organisation is appropriate, and additional groups and roles can be added.

Special attention should be paid to the relationship between information security and IT within enterprises. In cases in which information security reports directly to IT, there may be a conflict of interest. IT, by its nature, provides service to the enterprise, while information security manages risk related to the protection of information. This dichotomy could lead to IT overriding information security practices in the name of customer service. Therefore, a certain degree of independence between IT and information security should be established.

4.3 Accountability Over Information Security

It is important to note that the position of the information security function(s) in an enterprise is a key factor in determining the organisation's ability to protect information. This position can be the difference between information security being proactively aligned with business initiatives and it being only an afterthought where risk needs to be mitigated, thereby often limiting risk treatment options.

> **The board of directors carries final accountability for all matters, including information security.**
> This accountability can and should be delegated to the appropriate level within the enterprise. Considering that information security is a critical business issue, enterprises should always assign final accountability over information security to a senior member of executive management. Failing to do so can expose the board to claims of negligence from regulators or other stakeholders, should incidents occur.

The actual decision for delegating the overall accountability depends on the specific situation of the enterprise. **Figure 14** contains some potential advantages and disadvantages of information security reporting to a given role, which can be taken into account when making the decision.

Figure 14—Advantages and Disadvantages of Potential Paths for Information Security Reporting		
Role	**Advantages**	**Disadvantages**
Chief executive officer (CEO)	Information risk is elevated to the highest level in the enterprise.	Information risk needs to be presented in a format that is understandable to the CEO. Given the multitude of responsibilities of the CEO, information risk might be monitored and managed at too high a level of abstraction or might not be fully understood in its relevant details.
Chief information officer (CIO)	Information security issues and solutions can be aligned with all IT initiatives.	Information risk may not be addressed due to other IT initiatives and deadlines taking precedence over information security. There is a potential conflict of interest. The work performed by information security professionals may be IT-focussed and not information security-focussed. In other words, there may be an insufficient business focus.
Chief financial officer (CFO)	Information security issues can be addressed from a financial business impact point of view.	Information risk may not be addressed due to financial initiatives and deadlines taking precedence over information security. There is a potential conflict of interest.
Chief risk officer (CRO)	Information risk is elevated to a position that can also look at risk from strategic, financial, operational, reputational and compliance perspectives.	This role does not exist in most enterprises. It is most often found in financial service organisations. In enterprises in which a CRO is not present, organisational risk decisions may be decided by the CEO or board of directors.
Chief technology officer (CTO)	Information security can be partnered and included in future technology road maps.	Information risk may not be addressed due to technology directions taking precedence over information security.
Chief operating officer (COO)	Information security issues and solutions can be addressed from the standpoint of impact to the business' operations.	Information risk may not be addressed due to operational initiatives and deadlines taking precedence over information security.
Board of directors (indirect report)	Information risk is elevated to the highest level in the enterprise.	Information risk needs to be presented in a format that is understandable to board members, and hence may become too high-level to be relevant.

Page intentionally left blank

CHAPTER 5
ENABLER: CULTURE, ETHICS AND BEHAVIOUR

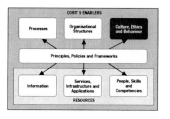

Behaviour of individuals and enterprises is often underestimated as a success factor in information security governance and management arrangements. The following items are covered in this chapter:
1. The culture model
2. The culture life cycle
3. Leadership and champions who can influence behaviour
4. Desirable behaviour that should be encouraged within any enterprise

5.1 Culture Model

Culture, ethics and behaviour can be structured according to the dimensions illustrated in **figure 15**

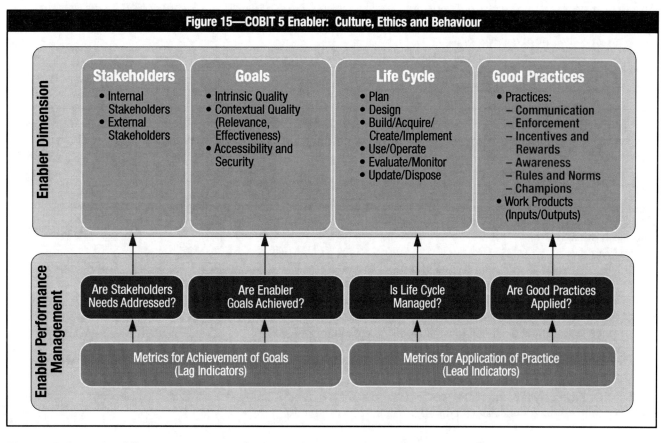

Figure 15 shows the different components of culture, ethics and behaviour as they are defined within this publication. This process model is an extension of the generic enabler model explained in **figure 8**.

The culture, ethics and behaviour model indicates that:
• Culture, ethics and behaviour **stakeholders** comprise the entire enterprise, but also include external stakeholders such as regulators, external auditors and supervisory bodies. Stakes are two-fold: some stakeholders, for example, legal officers, risk managers, HR managers, remuneration boards and officers, deal with defining, implementing and enforcing desired behaviours; others need to align with the defined rules and norms.

Consequently, when influencing culture, both stakeholders need to be taken into account. For example, not only do internal staff members need to be made aware of the information security situation, but so do external consultants, suppliers and other external parties.
• The **goals** for this enabler relate to organisational ethics (determined by the values that the enterprise wants to live by), individual ethics (determined by the personal values of each individual in the enterprise) and individual behaviours.
• Organisational cultures, ethical stance, individual behaviours, etc., have **life cycles**. Starting from an existing culture, an enterprise can identify required changes and work towards their implementation. Several tools—described in the good practices—can be used.

- **Good practices** for creating, encouraging and maintaining desired behaviour throughout the enterprise include:
  - Communication throughout the enterprise of desired behaviours and the underlying corporate values
  - Awareness of desired behaviour (strengthened by the example behaviour exercised by senior management and other champions)
  - Incentives to encourage and deterrents to enforce desired behaviour, rules and norms (which provide more guidance on desired organisational behaviour and link very clearly to the principles and policies an enterprise puts in place)

Human behaviour is one of the key factors determining the success of any enterprise. Behaviours of all members of the enterprise collectively determine the culture of the enterprise. Many factors drive behaviour: external factors such as beliefs, ethnicity, socio-economic background, geographic location and personal experiences, and interpersonal relationships in enterprises, personal objectives and ambitions.

Culture is defined in BMIS[2] as 'a pattern of behaviours, beliefs, assumptions, attitudes and ways of doing things'. The ISACA *Creating a Culture of Information Security*[3] publication extends the thought leadership around culture and information security and describes information security culture as:

> *All enterprises have a culture of information security. In most cases, it lacks intentionality and is inconsistent to the extent that it exists at all; in others, it is robust and guides the daily activities of employees and others who come in contact with the enterprise.*

5.2 Culture Life Cycle

As culture transcends the enterprise, it also evolves in time. Behaviours are adapted, and cultural awareness regarding information security can increase or decrease. It is important to understand the existing culture so that positive changes to enable a security culture can be made. Many measurement methodologies exist to measure culture. In addition to measuring the enterprise culture, the effectiveness of information security measures themselves should also be measured to evaluate the underlying security culture.

To have a proper view of information security culture, the behaviours of the stakeholders need to be measured over time. Examples of such measurements include:
- Strength of passwords
- Swipe card use
- Number of laptop locks distributed and used by employees
- Public/open discussion of confidential information
- Lack of approach to security (password sharing, tailgating, etc.)
- User password protection in practice
- Adherence to system and application change management practices
- Completion of visitor logs and visitor accountability
- Percent of proper marking and labelling of information (electronic and hard copy)

As static data, these metrics have little value. Only when their evolution through time is examined can these simple metrics provide a solid evaluation mechanism for information security culture.

5.3 Leadership and Champions

To influence culture, the enterprise needs champions to carry the changes throughout the enterprise. Champions are those people in the enterprise who are eager to speak up and set examples for others. Champions may be the senior executives of an enterprise, but the activity is not limited to that group within the organisation. Staff members can be champions as well, as long as they actively provide the background for change and enforcement of a culture. *Creating a Culture of Information Security* provides a number of common candidates who can serve as information security champion:
- Risk managers
- Information security professionals
- C-level executives: CEO, COO, CFO, CIO
- Head of HR

[2] ISACA, *The Business Model for Information Security* (BMIS), USA, 2010
[3] ISACA, *Creating a Culture of Security*, USA, 2011

Leadership—the decision makers—in this information security context can be equally important. Champions are needed to influence leadership to make decisions taking into account the information security requirements. It is obvious that leadership and champions can overlap; however, they are mentioned in a different context. Leadership is categorised as:
• Executive management
• Business management
• CISO/ISM

5.4 Desirable Behaviour

A number of desirable behaviours have been identified that positively influence the culture towards information security and its actual implementation in day-to-day life. These include:
• Information security is practiced in daily operations.
• People respect the importance of information security policies and principles.
• People are provided with sufficient and detailed information security guidance, and are encouraged to participate in and challenge the current information security situation.
• Everyone is accountable for the protection of information within the enterprise.
• Stakeholders are aware of how to identify and respond to threats to the enterprise.
• Management proactively supports and anticipates new information security innovations and communicates this to the enterprise. The enterprise is receptive to account for and deal with new information security challenges.
• Business management engages in continuous cross-functional collaboration to allow for efficient and effective information security programmes.
• Executive management recognises the business value of information security.

For each of the behaviours defined, the following attributes are described in **appendix D**:
• **Organisational ethics**—Determined by the values by which the enterprise wants to live
• **Individual ethics**—Determined by the personal values of each individual in the enterprise, and, to an important extent, depend on external factors such as beliefs, ethnicity, socio-economic background, geographic location and personal experiences
• **Leadership**—Ways that leadership can influence desired behaviour:
  – How communication, enforcement and rules and norms can be used to influence behaviour
  – Incentives and rewards can be used to influence behaviour
  – Raising awareness

More in-depth information on information security culture can be found in BMIS and Creating a *Culture of Information Security* at *www.isaca.org.*

Page intentionally left blank

CHAPTER 6
ENABLER: INFORMATION

This chapter contains guidance on how information embedded in the organisation can be used to govern and manage information security within the enterprise. The following items are discussed:
1. The information model
2. Examples of common information types
3. Information stakeholders and how to identify the impacted parties within the enterprise
4. Information life cycle, describing the different phases of information management in this context

Information is widespread throughout all enterprises and is required to keep the organisation running and well governed. At the operational level, information is often the key product of the enterprise.

6.1 Information Model

Information (and, by consequence, communication) is not only the main subject of information security, but a key enabler for information security. Information as an information security enabler means that management can use information as a decision base (e.g., the ISSC can use the information security profile to develop an information security strategy).

Figure 16 shows at a high level the different components of information as it is defined within this publication. This process model is an extension of the generic enabler model explained in **figure 8**.

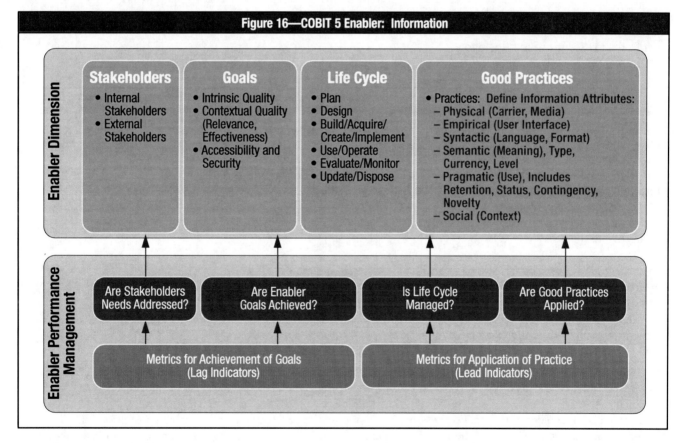

Figure 16—COBIT 5 Enabler: Information

The information model indicates that:
• The internal and external **stakeholders** must be identified and their key areas of responsibility defined; i.e., why they care about, or are interested in, the information must be clear.
• The **goals** of information are divided in three subdimensions of quality:
  – **Intrinsic quality**—The extent to which data values are in conformance with the actual or true values
  – **Contextual and representational quality**—The extent to which information is applicable to the task of the information user and is presented in an intelligible and clear manner, recognising that information quality depends on the context of use
  – **Security/accessibility quality**—The extent to which information is available or obtainable

• The full **life cycle** of information needs to be considered, and different approaches may be required for information in different phases of the life cycle (plan, design, build/acquire, use/operate, monitor and dispose).
• **Good practices** define information as consisting of six layers, presenting a continuum of attributes ranging from the physical world of information, where attributes are linked to information technologies and media for information capturing, storing, processing, distribution and presentation, to the social world of information use, sense-making and action.

6.2 Information Types

The following list contains examples of information types that are common in an information security governance and management context. These information types vary from strategy to an operational dashboard, each serving its specific purpose in the governance and management of information security.

The list is not meant to be exhaustive, but it does provide an idea of how deep information security extends throughout an enterprise. Depending on the enterprise, this list may need to be extended or limited.

Examples of information types are:
• Information security strategy
• Information security budget
• Information security plan
• Policies
• Information security requirements, which may include:
  – Information security configuration requirements
  – Service level agreement (SLA)/operating level agreement (OLA) information security requirements
• Awareness material
• Information security review reports, which include:
  – Information security audit findings
  – Information security maturity report
  – Information security-related risk management:
    · Threat analysis
    · Vulnerability (information security) assessment reports
• Information security service catalogue
• Information risk profile, which includes:
  – Information risk register
  – Breaches and loss reports (consolidated incident report)
• Information security dashboard (or equivalent), which includes:
  – Information security incidents
  – Information security problems
  – Information security metrics

For each of the information types, more detailed guidance is provided in **appendix E**, including:
• **Goals**—Descriptions of a number of goals to be achieved, using the three categories defined in the information model
• **Life cycle**—A specific description of the life cycle requirements in addition to a general approach as described in the information life cycle information in subsection 6.4 Information Life Cycle
• **Good practices** for this type of information—A description of typical contents and structure

6.3 Information Stakeholders

Identifying the stakeholder of information is essential to optimise the development and distribution of information throughout the enterprise. This subsection provides an approach to summarise the originators and destinations of each common information type.

For example, the stakeholders for information security-related information within a typical small or medium enterprise (SME) could be structured as shown in **figure 17**, including:
• Stakeholder description—A streamlined version of the generic list of organisational structures of COBIT 5, complemented with a number of additional external stakeholders for this specific domain. This list reflects the less complex structure of an SME compared to large organisations.

• Information types as described in subsection 6.2 Information Types
• An indication of the nature of the relationship of the stakeholder for each information type:
  – A—Approver
  – O—Originator
  – I—Informed of information type
  – U—User of information type

Figure 17—Example Stakeholders for Information Security-related Information (Small/Medium Enterprise)	Information Type									
Stakeholder	Information Security Strategy	Information Security Budget	Information Security Plan	Policies	Information Security Requirements	Awareness Material	Information Security Review Reports	Information Security Service Catalogue	Information Risk Profile	Information Security Dashboard
Internal: Enterprise										
Board	U			I		U	I		A	
Chief executive officer (CEO)	U			A		U	I		U	
Chief financial officer (CFO)		A		U		U			U	
Chief information security officer (CISO)	O	U	O	O	A	A	A	A	U	U
Information security steering committee (ISSC)	A	O	A	U	U	I	U	I	U	U
Business process owner				U	O	U		U	U	
Head of human resources (HR)				U		U				
Internal: IT										
Chief information officer (CIO)/IT manager	U	O	U	U	U	U	I		U	U
Information security manager (ISM)	U	U	U	O	U	O	O	O	O	O
External										
Investors						I				
Insurers						I	I		I	
Regulators		I				I	I			
Business Partners						I	I			
Vendors/Suppliers						I				
External Auditors		I				I	I		I	I

A template containing all information types and all potential stakeholders based on COBIT 5 is provided in **appendix E**.

6.4 Information Life Cycle

Information security-specific types of information, such as the examples provided in subsection 6.2 Information Types, are also bound by a life cycle. In addition, the information security function has an important facilitating role to play in this life cycle. This duality in the context of information (as facilitator of the life cycle and user of information) leads to an increasing importance of information security within the enterprise.

The management of knowledge is described in process BAI08 of *COBIT 5: Enabling Processes*. This process elaborates on the life cycle that information is required to follow to be securely and efficiently managed in the enterprise. The full life cycle of information needs to be considered to ensure its correctness and optimal use. Additionally, different approaches may be required for information in different phases of the life cycle. The following phases can be distinguished:
• **Plan/design/build/acquire**—Information is identified, acquired and classified in this phase. Activities in this phase may refer to the development of standards and definitions (e.g., data definitions, data collection procedures), the

creation of data records, the purchase of data, and the loading of external files.
• **Use/operate**—This phase includes:
  – **Store**—The phase in which information is held electronically or in hard copy (or even just in human memory). Activities in this phase may refer to the storage of information in electronic form (e.g., electronic files, databases, data warehouses) or as hard copy (e.g., paper documents).
  – **Share**—The phase in which information is made available for use through a distribution method. Activities in this phase may refer to the processes involved in getting the information to places where it can be accessed and used (e.g., distributing documents by email). For electronically held information, this life cycle phase may largely overlap with the store phase (e.g., sharing information through database access, file/document servers).
  – **Use**—The phase in which information is used to accomplish goals. Activities in this phase may refer to different kinds of information usage (e.g., managerial decision making, running automated processes), and may also include activities such as information retrieval and converting information from one form to another.
• **Monitor**—The phase in which it is ensured that the information resource continues to work properly (i.e., it continues to be valuable). Activities in this phase may refer to keeping information up to date as well as other kinds of information management activities (e.g., enhancing, cleansing, merging and removing duplicate information data in data warehouses).
• **Disposal**—The phase in which an information resource is discarded when it is no longer of use. Activities in this phase may refer to information archiving or destroying.

The phases of the information life cycle are aligned with the BAI08 process practices.

A specific description of the life cycle requirements and a general approach are provided in the detailed guidance in **appendix E**.

CHAPTER 7
ENABLER: SERVICES, INFRASTRUCTURE AND APPLICATIONS

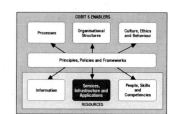

Services, infrastructure and applications provide the enterprise with information and information processing and services. The following items are covered in this chapter:
1. The services, infrastructure and applications model
2. Information security services, infrastructure and applications commonly found in enterprises

7.1 Services, Infrastructure and Applications Model

Services, infrastructure and applications can be structured according to the dimensions illustrated in **figure 18**.

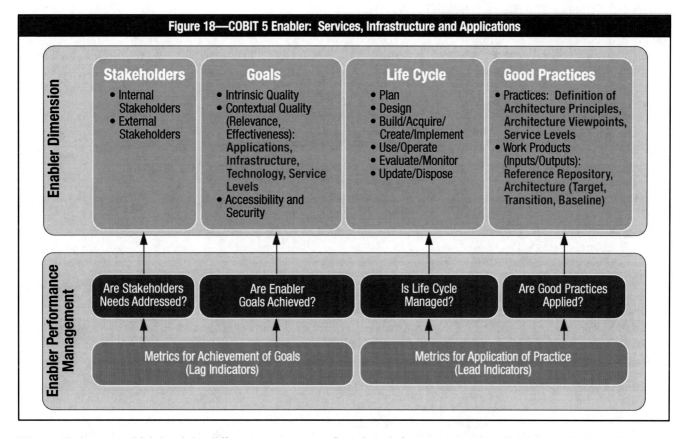

Figure 18—COBIT 5 Enabler: Services, Infrastructure and Applications

Figure 18 shows at a high level the different components of services, infrastructure and applications, as they are defined within this publication. This process model is an extension of the generic enabler model explained in **figure 8**.

The services, infrastructure and applications model indicates that:
• Service capabilities (the combined term for services, infrastructure and applications) **stakeholders** can be internal and external. Services can be delivered by internal or external parties (e.g., internal IT departments, operations managers, outsourcing providers); and users of services can also be internal (e.g., business users) and external to the enterprise (e.g., partners, clients, suppliers). The stakes of each of the stakeholders need to be identified and will focus on delivering adequate services or on receiving requested services from providers.
• **Goals** of the service level capability are expressed in terms of services (applications, infrastructure and technology) and service levels, considering which services and service levels are most economical for the enterprise. Again, goals relate to the services and how they are provided, as well as their outcomes, that is, the contribution towards successfully supported business processes. This is described in more detail in **appendix F**.
• Service capabilities have a **life cycle**. The future or planned service capabilities are typically described in a target architecture. It covers the building blocks, such as future applications and the target infrastructure model, and also describes the linkages and relationships amongst these building blocks.

- **Good practices** for service capabilities include:
  - Definition of architecture principles (overall guidelines that govern the implementation and use of IT-related resources within the enterprise)
  - Definition of the most appropriate architecture viewpoints (to meet the needs of different stakeholders)
  - Possession of an architecture repository (which can be used to store different types of architectural outputs) and service levels that need to be defined and achieved by the service providers

External good practices for architecture frameworks and service capabilities exist. They are guidelines, templates or standards that can be used to fast-track the creation of architecture deliverables.

7.2 Information Security Services, Infrastructure and Applications

Service capabilities are required to provide information security and related functions to an enterprise. Services not only require appropriate infrastructure and applications, but are provided through a combination of other enablers such as processes, information and organisational structures.

The following list contains some examples of potential security-related services as they could appear in a service catalogue. Typically, these services link to one or more COBIT 5 processes and their practices and activities, and require information (inputs and outputs) and organisational structures (RACI charts, specific security functions or roles). The following list provides a service-oriented view on security-related activities, and is not intended to duplicate or replicate security processes:
- Provide a security architecture.
- Provide security awareness.
- Provide secure development (development in line with security standards).
- Provide security assessments.
- Provide adequately secured and configured systems, in line with security requirements and security architecture.
- Provide user access and access rights in line with business requirements.
- Provide adequate protection against malware, external attacks and intrusion attempts.
- Provide adequate incident response.
- Provide security testing.
- Provide monitoring and alert services for security-related events.

For each of these service capabilities, the building blocks of services have been described in **appendix F**:
- **Detailed description** of the service, providing business functionality
- **Attributes**, describing for each service the inputs and supporting technologies (including applications and infrastructure)
- **Goals**, describing the quality and compliance goals for each service capability and the related metrics

CHAPTER 8
ENABLER: PEOPLE, SKILLS AND COMPETENCIES

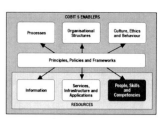

People must demonstrate the appropriate skills and competencies to ensure that all activities are completed successfully and correct decisions are made. The following items are discussed in this chapter:
1. The skill and competencies model
2. Information security-related skills and competencies

8.1 People, Skills and Competencies Model

People, skills and competencies can be structured according to the dimensions illustrated in the enabler model in **figure 19**.

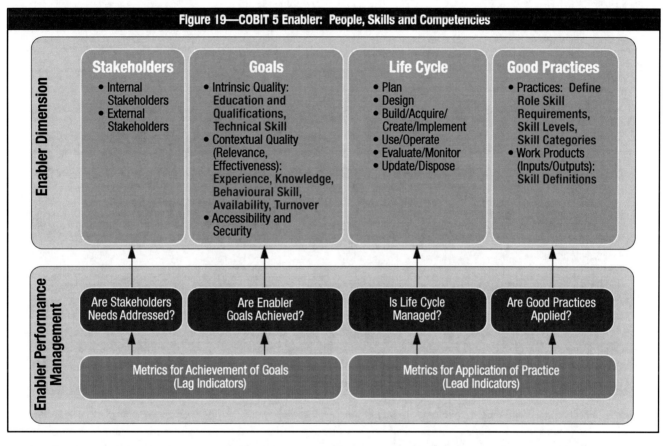

Figure 19 shows the different components of people, skills and competencies as defined within this publication. This process model is an extension of the generic enabler model explained in **figure 8**.

The people, skills and competencies model indicates that:
• Different **stakeholders** can assume different roles (e.g., business manager, project manager, partner, competitor, recruiter, trainer, developer, technical IT specialist, ISM, CISO, regulator) and each role requires a distinct skill set.
• **Goals for skills and competencies** relate to education and qualification levels, technical skills, experience levels, knowledge, and behavioural skills required to successfully provide and perform process activities, organisational roles, etc. **Goals for people** include correct levels of staff availability and turnover rate.
• Skills and competencies have a **life cycle**. An enterprise should know what its current skill base is and plan for what it needs to be. This is influenced by, amongst other factors, the strategy and goals of the enterprise. Skills need to be developed (e.g., through training), acquired (e.g., through recruitment) and deployed in the various roles within the organisation structure, and may need to be disposed of (e.g., if an activity is automated or outsourced). Periodically, the enterprise should assess the skill base to understand the evolution that has occurred.
• **Good practices** for skills and competencies include defining the need for objective skill requirements for each role assumed by the various stakeholders. This can be described through different skill levels in different skill categories, for which a skill definition should be available. The skill categories correspond to the IT-related activities undertaken; in this case, information security-related functions.

This chapter describes the skills and competencies at the most optimal skill level possible. In reality, however, enterprises may not always require the optimal skill level, or may not be able to employ resources demonstrating the optimal skill level.

8.2 Information Security-related Skills and Competencies

To effectively operate an information security function within an enterprise, individuals with appropriate knowledge and experience (e.g., skills and competencies) must exercise that function.

In **figure 20** some typical security-related skills and competencies are listed. While these skills can also translate to a specific position in larger enterprises (e.g., information security architecture skills may equal an information security architect position), this is not always the case in smaller enterprises.

Figure 20—Information Security Skills/Competencies
Skills/Competencies
Information security governance
Information security strategy formulation
Information risk management
Information security architecture development
Information security operations
Information assessment and testing and compliance

For each of the skills and competencies noted in **figure 20**, the following attributes are described in **appendix G**:
- **Skill definition**
- **Goals**—As defined previously
- **Related enablers**—Skills and competencies are required to perform process activities and take decisions in organisational structures. Conversely, some processes are aimed at supporting the life cycle of skills and competencies.

The added value of certification in information security:
The attributes for skills and competencies align with the practices analyses of ISACA's Certified Information Systems Auditor (CISA), Certified Information Security Manager (CISM), Certified in the Governance of Enterprise Information Technology (CGEIT), Certified in Risk and Information Systems Control (CRISC), and (ISC)² Certified Information System Security Professional (CISSP) certification. Because certification is an objective means to prove to employers that professionals have adequate base knowledge within a topic domain, a CISM certification or equivalent designation is suggested for all skills defined previously.

Skills and competencies follow a life cycle. An information security function must identify its current skill base, and align this skill base to the required skill set. This is influenced by (amongst other issues) the information security strategy and goals. Skills need to be developed (e.g., through classroom and hands-on training) or acquired (e.g., through recruitment) and deployed in the various roles within the structure. Skills may need to be realigned if, for example, an activity is automated or outsourced. Periodically, for example, on an annual basis, the enterprise needs to assess its skill base to understand the evolution that has occurred; this assessment will feed into the planning process for the next period. The assessment can also feed into the reward and recognition process for human resources.

Note that the attributes describing the skills and competencies are a set of criteria and not a prescriptive job description. Decisions for employment should be made on all of the previously described factors along with the individual's overall fit in the enterprise.

Section III. Adapting *COBIT 5 for Information Security* to the Enterprise Environment

Chapter 1
Introduction

Information security is valuable to an enterprise only when it is sufficiently adapted to the unique situation in which the enterprise exists and operates. This unique situation is created by numerous elements that make it challenging to change the environment. Section II describes information security-specific enablers that can be used to further enhance the maturity/capability/performance of information security within an enterprise. Adapting these information security-specific enablers to the enterprise's environment is the challenge that will be described in this section.

ISACA provides practical and comprehensive implementation guidance concerning governance of enterprise IT in its publication *COBIT® 5 Implementation*,[4] which is based on a continuous improvement life cycle. This guide is not intended to be a prescriptive approach, but rather a guide for information security professionals who need to integrate security within the overall operational framework of an enterprise. The guide is also supported by an implementation tool kit containing a variety of resources that will be continually enhanced. Its content includes:
• Self-assessment, measurement and diagnostic tools
• Presentations aimed at various audiences
• Related articles and further explanations

The purpose of this section is to introduce the implementation and continual improvement life cycle at a high level and to describe this generic guidance from an information security perspective. In addition, the relationship to existing information security frameworks, good practices and standards is described in the second part of this section.

---

[4] ISACA, *COBIT 5 Implementation*, USA, 2012, *www.isaca.org/cobit*

Page intentionally left blank

CHAPTER 2
IMPLEMENTING INFORMATION SECURITY INITIATIVES

2.1 Considering the Enterprise's Information Security Context

Every enterprise needs to define and implement its own information security enablers depending on factors in the enterprise's specific internal and external environment, such as:
• Ethics and culture relating to information security
• Applicable laws, regulations and policies
• Applicable contractual regulations
• Existing policies and practices
• Maturity level of the current information security enablers
• Information security capabilities and available resources
• Industry practices
• Existing and mandatory standards and frameworks regarding information security

The enterprise's information security requirements need to be defined based on:
• Business plan and strategic intentions
• Management style
• Information risk profile
• Risk appetite

Therefore, the approach for implementing information security initiatives will be different for every enterprise, and the context needs to be understood and considered to adapt *COBIT 5 for Information Security* effectively. It is equally important to leverage and build on the existing information security-specific enablers.

> **COBIT 5 for Information Security connecting to other frameworks, good practices and standards:**
> *COBIT 5 for Information Security* is underpinned by other information security frameworks, good practices and standards. These should provide the information security professional with details on specific topics to further optimise the enablers described in this publication. Connecting *COBIT 5 for Information Security* to these underpinning frameworks, good practices and standards is described in the following part of this section.

In general, key success factors for a successful implementation of information security enablers include:
• The direction and mandate for the information security initiative, as well as visible ongoing commitment and support provided by top management
• The information security initiative to understand the business and IT objectives supported by all parties
• Effective communication and enablement of the necessary changes ensured
• *COBIT 5 for Information Security* and other supporting good practices and standards tailored to fit the unique context of the enterprise
• Focus on quick wins and prioritising the most beneficial improvements that are easiest to implement
• Adequate funding and resource commitment
• Adequately skilled human resources who can implement the enablers

2.2 Creating the Appropriate Environment

It is important for information security initiatives leveraging COBIT to be properly governed and managed. Major IT-related initiatives often fail due to inadequate direction, support and oversight by stakeholders; the implementation of information security enablers leveraging this publication is no different. Support and direction from key stakeholders are critical to ensure that improvements are achieved and sustained. In a weak enterprise environment (such as an unclear overall information security strategy), this support and participation are even more important.

The use of enablers (leveraging *COBIT 5 for Information Security*) should be a solution addressing real business needs and issues rather than an end in itself. Information security requirements based on current pain points and drivers should be identified and accepted by management as areas that need to be addressed. High-level health checks, diagnostics or capability assessments based on this publication are tools that can be used to raise awareness, create consensus and generate a commitment to act. The commitment and buy-in of the relevant stakeholders need to be solicited from the beginning. To achieve this, implementation objectives and benefits need to be clearly expressed in business terms and summarised in an outline business case.

Once commitment has been obtained, adequate resources need to be provided to support the information security programme. Key programme roles and responsibilities should be defined and assigned. Care should be taken to maintain commitment from all affected stakeholders on an ongoing basis.

Appropriate structures and processes for oversight and direction should be established and maintained. These structures and processes should also ensure ongoing alignment with enterprisewide governance, risk management approaches and the business strategy.

Visible support and commitment should be provided by key stakeholders, such as the senior executives, to set the 'tone at the top' and ensure commitment for the information security programme at all levels.

2.3 Recognising Pain Points and Trigger Events

There are a number of factors that may indicate a need for improved information security enablers. By using pain points or trigger events as the launch point for implementation initiatives, the business case for information security enabler improvements can be related to practical, everyday issues. This should improve buy-in and create a sense of urgency within the enterprise, which is necessary to kick off the implementation.

In addition, quick wins can be identified and value-adds can be demonstrated in those areas that are most visible or recognisable in the enterprise. This provides a platform for introducing further changes and can assist in gaining widespread senior executive commitment and support for more pervasive changes.

Examples of some of the typical pain points for which new or revised information security enablers can be a solution are:
• Information security incidents within the enterprise or with competitors such as:
  – Data loss or theft caused by unauthorised users breaking into systems
  – Denial of service as a result of cyberattacks
  – (Un)intentional modification of critical information
• Failure to meet legal, regulatory or contractual requirements such as privacy rules
• The inability to cope with the adoption of new technology due to information security restrictions
• Audit findings regularly related to poor information security capabilities

In addition to these pain points, other events in the enterprise's internal and external environment can signal or trigger a focus on the governance and management of enterprise IT. Examples of these include:
• New regulatory, compliance or contractual requirements
• Significant technology changes or paradigm shifts
• External audit or consultant assessments
• Mergers, acquisitions or other large organisational changes

2.4 Enabling Change

Successful implementation depends on managing change in an effective manner. In many enterprises, there is a significant focus on the technical aspects of an information security programme, but not enough emphasis on managing the human, behavioural and cultural aspects of change and on motivating stakeholders to buy into that change.

It should not be assumed that the various stakeholders involved in, or impacted by, new or revised information security enablers will readily accept and adopt any proposed changes. The possibility of ignorance and/or resistance to change needs to be addressed through a structured and proactive approach. In support of that, optimal awareness of the implementation programme should be achieved through a communication plan that defines for each phase of the programme what will be communicated, in what way and by whom.

Sustainable improvement can be achieved by gaining the commitment of the stakeholders through persuasion and advocacy or, where possible, by enforcing compliance with legislation, regulations or contractual agreements. In other words, human and behavioural and cultural issues need to be considered to create a culture in which stakeholders are active participants in meeting the information security goals of the enterprise.

Information security culture and change:
The practices of the culture, ethics and behaviour enabler presented in section II are by far the most important tools to reduce any resistance to change. Influencing behaviour through effective communication, identifying the correct and relevant incentives and rewards, and enforcing adherence to changes are important factors to take into account. Investing in influencing practices will enable the acceptance of the changes made. Of course this will require time and patience from the information security team members.

2.5 A Life Cycle Approach

The implementation life cycle provides a way for enterprises to address the complexity and challenges typically encountered during implementations using COBIT to address information security. There are three interrelated components in the life cycle (see the circles in **figure 21**):
• The core continual improvement life cycle—Reflecting that this is not a one-off project
• The enablement of change—Addressing the behavioural and cultural aspects
• The management of the programme

As discussed previously, the appropriate environment needs to be created to ensure the success of the implementation or improvement initiative. The life cycle and its seven phases are illustrated in **figure 21**.

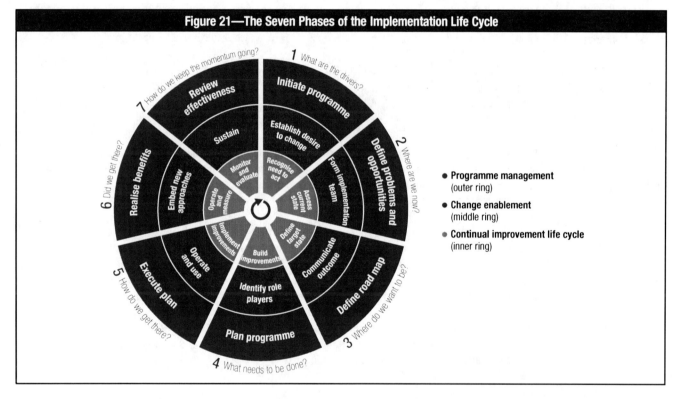

Figure 21—The Seven Phases of the Implementation Life Cycle

• Programme management (outer ring)
• Change enablement (middle ring)
• Continual improvement life cycle (inner ring)

The purpose of **phase 1** is to understand the breadth and depth of the envisioned change, the various stakeholders that are affected, the nature of the impact on and involvement required from each stakeholder group, as well as the current readiness and ability to adapt to change.

Information security environment:
The information security-related pain points and trigger events should be thoroughly assessed. Operational practices presented in the information enabler of section II can be very useful for this assessment. Information security review reports, including information security audit findings and risk reports, or the information security dashboard can provide important input on information security incidents, problems and risk. Discussions with executive management should provide a platform to establish a desire to change by presenting issues and reports in a clear and understandable manner.

Phase 2 is focussed on defining the scope of the implementation or improvement initiative. High-level diagnostics can be useful for scoping and understanding high-priority areas on which to focus. An assessment of the current state of the phase is then performed, and issues or deficiencies are identified by carrying out a process capability assessment. Large-scale initiatives should be structured as multiple iterations of the life cycle. For any implementation initiative exceeding six months, there is a risk of losing momentum, focus and buy-in from stakeholders.

> **Information security scoping:**
> To scope the information security initiative, the current state of all information security enablers should be assessed and verified. For processes, scoping can be based on the information security goals to the associated IT processes (as documented in the detailed process guidance in section II). It would also be useful to consider how risk scenarios may highlight key processes on which to focus.

During **phase 3**, an improvement target is set, followed by a more detailed analysis leveraging this publication and other guidance (see section III, 2.2 Creating the Appropriate Environment) to identify gaps and potential solutions. Some solutions may be quick wins and others more challenging and longer-term activities. Priority should be given to initiatives that are easier to achieve and those likely to yield the greatest benefits.

> **Using information security guidance:**
> In the following part of this section, additional guidance is provided on connecting commonly used information security frameworks, good practices and standards. An important phase in the implementation life cycle is setting the correct target and determining how the relevant information security frameworks, good practices and standards can assist the enterprise in achieving its target.
>
> Quick wins (initiatives with high impact and low effort) for an information security initiative are often challenging. The constant balancing act between ensuring information security and enabling the enterprise should be taken into account when defining these quick wins. Visible change is required for a quick win to rapidly demonstrate added value to the enterprise.

Phase 4 plans practical solutions by defining projects supported by justifiable business cases. A change plan for implementation is also developed. A well-developed business case helps to ensure that the project's benefits are identified and monitored. Measures can be defined and monitoring established by using *COBIT 5 for Information Security* goals and metrics to ensure that business alignment is achieved and maintained and performance can be measured.

Phase 5 implements the proposed solutions into day-to-day practices. To be successful, engagement and demonstrated commitment of top management are required, as well as ownership by the affected business and IT stakeholders.

Phase 6 focusses on the sustainable operation of new or improved enablers and monitoring the achievement of expected benefits. In other words, this phase is meant to determine whether the goals are reached and are sustainable.

During **phase 7**, the overall success of the initiative is reviewed, further information security requirements for the enterprise are identified, and the need for continual improvement is reinforced. Over time, the life cycle should be followed iteratively while building a sustainable approach to information security.

CHAPTER 3
USING *COBIT 5 FOR INFORMATION SECURITY* TO CONNECT OTHER FRAMEWORKS, MODELS, GOOD PRACTICES AND STANDARDS

COBIT 5 for Information Security aims to be an 'umbrella' framework to connect to other information security frameworks, good practices and standards. *COBIT 5 for Information Security* describes the pervasiveness of information security throughout the enterprise and provides an overarching framework of enablers, but other publications can be helpful as well as they elaborate on specific topics (e.g., information security practices or configuration settings). The relevant information security frameworks, good practices and standards need to be adapted to suit specific requirements of the enterprise's specific environment. The reader can then decide, based on the specific needs of the enterprise, which framework or combination of frameworks is best to use, also taking into account the legacy situation in the enterprise, the availability of the framework and other factors. For this, the mapping of *COBIT 5 for Information Security* to related standards in **appendix H** will help find a suitable framework according to relevant needs.

Examples of relevant information security frameworks and models, good practices and standards include:
• The *Business Model for Information Security* (BMIS), ISACA, USA, 2010
• The 2011 Standard of Good Practice for Information Security, Information Security Forum (ISF), UK, 2011
• Common Security Framework (CSF), Health Information Trust Alliance (HITRUST), USA, 2009
• Expression des Besoins et Identification des Objectifs de Sécurité (EBIOS), Direction Centrale de la Sécurité des Systèmes d'Information (DCSSI), Ministry of Defense, France, 2000
• Health Insurance Portability and Accountability Act (HIPAA)/Health Information Technology for Economic and Clinical Health (HITECH), USA, 1996 and 2009, respectively
• ISO/IEC 27000 series, Switzerland, 2009-2012
• National Institute of Standards and Technology (NIST) Special Publication (SP) 800-53A, *Guide for Assessing the Information Security Controls in Federal Information Systems and Organizations*, Building Effective Security Assessment Plans, Department of Commerce, USA, 2010
• Operationally Critical Threat, Asset, and Vulnerability Evaluation[SM] (OCTAVE®), Carnegie Mellon Software Engineering Institute (SEI), USA, 2001
• Payment Card Industry Data Security Standards (PCI DSS) v2.0, PCI Security Standards Council, USA, 2010

In addition, once proper guidance has been identified, *COBIT 5 for Information Security* can be used to structure the contents of these publications and perform a gap analysis, as described in phase 3 of the implementation life cycle.

However, it is important to note that standards related to information security and related topics are plentiful and keep evolving; this chapter therefore reflects the most common standards available.

In **appendix H** a detailed comparison and assessment template is presented for the following publications:
• *The 2011 Standard of Good Practice for Information Security*, Information Security Forum (ISF), UK, 2011, *www.securityforum.org/?page=publicdownload2011sogp*
• ISO/IEC 27001 and 27002, Switzerland, 2005, *www.iso.org/iso/store.htm*
• NIST SP 800-53A, *Guide for Assessing the Information Security Controls in Federal Information Systems and Organizations, Building Effective Security Assessment Plans*, Department of Commerce, USA, 2010, *http://csrc.nist.gov/publications/PubsSPs.html*

Page intentionally left blank

APPENDIX A
DETAILED GUIDANCE: PRINCIPLES, POLICIES AND FRAMEWORKS ENABLER

This appendix provides details regarding the information security principles and policies presented in section II. The information security principles communicate the rules of the organisation in support of the governance objectives and enterprise values, as defined by the board and executive management. These principles are developed in more detail in subsection A.1 in this appendix.

Additionally, policies provide more detailed guidance on how to put principles into practice and how they will influence decision making. Example policies include:
• Information security policy
• Access control policy
• Personnel information security policy
• Physical and environmental information security policy
• Incident management policy
• Business continuity and disaster recovery policy
• Asset management policy
• Rules of behaviour (acceptable use)
• Information systems acquisition, software development and maintenance policy
• Vendor management policy
• Communications and operation management policy
• Compliance policy
• Risk management policy

For each of the policies presented in section II, the following attributes are described in this appendix:
• **Scope**
• **Validity** (except for information security policies driven by other functions within the organisation)
  – **Applicable**—To which areas of the organisation is this policy applicable?
  – **Update and revalidation**—Who is responsible for maintaining the policy and what is the frequency of revalidation?
  – **Distribution**—How should policies be distributed throughout the enterprise?
• **Goals** (except for information security policies driven by other functions within the enterprise)

A.1 Information Security Principles

In 2010, three leading global information security organisations—ISACA, ISF and (ISC)[2]—joined forces to develop 12 independent, non-proprietary principles that will help information security professionals add value to their organisations by successfully supporting the business and promoting good information security practices (*www.isaca.org/Knowledge-Center/Standards/Pages/Security-Principles.aspx*). These principles are structured in support of three tasks:
• Support the business.
• Defend the business.
• Promote responsible information security behaviour.

These principles, in **figure 22**, are generic and applicable to all enterprises. This list can be used as a basis for developing information security principles unique to the enterprise.

Figure 22—Information Security Principles		
Principle	Objective	Description
1. Support the business.		
Focus on the business.	Ensure that information security is integrated into essential business activities.	Individuals within the information security community should forge relationships with business leaders and show how information security can complement key business and risk management processes. They should adopt an advisory approach to information security by supporting business objectives through resource allocation, programmes and projects. High-level, enterprise-focussed advice should be provided to protect information and help manage information risk both now and in the future.

	Figure 22—Information Security Principles (cont.)	
Principle	**Objective**	**Description**
1. Support the business. *(cont.)*		
Deliver quality and value to stakeholders.	Ensure that information security delivers value and meets business requirements.	Internal and external stakeholders should be engaged through regular communication so that their changing requirements for information security can continue to be met. Promoting the value of information security (both financial and non-financial) helps to gain support for decision making, which can in turn help the success of the vision for information security.
Comply with relevant legal and regulatory requirements.	Ensure that statutory obligations are met, stakeholder expectations are managed, and civil or criminal penalties are avoided.	Compliance obligations should be identified, translated into requirements specific to information security and communicated to all relevant individuals. The penalties associated with non-compliance should be clearly understood. Controls should be monitored, analysed and brought up to date to meet new or updated legal or regulatory requirements.
Provide timely and accurate information on information security performance.	Support business requirements and manage information risk.	Requirements for providing information on information security performance should be clearly defined, supported by the most relevant and accurate information security metrics (such as compliance, incidents, control status and costs), and aligned to business objectives. Information should be captured in a periodic, consistent and rigorous manner so that the information remains accurate and results can be presented to meet the objectives of relevant stakeholders.
Evaluate current and future information threats.	Analyse and assess emerging information security threats so that informed, timely action to mitigate risk can be taken.	Major trends and specific information security threats should be categorised in a comprehensive, standard framework covering a wide range of topics such as political, legal, economic, socio-cultural and technical issues. Individuals should share and build on their knowledge of upcoming threats to proactively address their causes, rather than just the symptoms.
Promote continuous improvement in information security.	Reduce costs, improve efficiency and effectiveness, and promote a culture of continuous improvement in information security.	Constantly changing organisational business models—coupled with evolving threats—require information security techniques to be adapted and their level of effectiveness improved on an ongoing basis. Knowledge of the latest information security techniques should be maintained by learning from incidents and liaising with independent research organisations.
2. Defend the business.		
Adopt a risk-based approach.	Ensure that risk is treated in a consistent and effective manner.	Options for addressing information risk should be reviewed so that informed, documented decisions are made about the treatment of risk. Risk treatment involves choosing one or more options, which typically include: • Accepting risk (by a member of management signing off that he/she has accepted the risk and no further action is required) • Avoiding risk (e.g., by deciding not to pursue a particular initiative) • Transferring risk (e.g., by outsourcing or taking out insurance) • Mitigating risk (typically by applying appropriate information security measures, e.g., access controls, network monitoring and incident management)
Protect classified information.	Prevent disclosure of classified (e.g., confidential or sensitive) information to unauthorised individuals.	Information should be identified and then classified according to its level of confidentiality (e.g., secret, restricted, internal and public). Classified information should be protected accordingly throughout all stages of the information life cycle—from creation to destruction—using appropriate controls such as encryption and access restrictions.
Concentrate on critical business applications.	Prioritise scarce information security resources by protecting the business applications on which an information security incident would have the greatest business impact.	Understanding the business impact of a loss of integrity or availability of important information handled by business applications (processed, stored or transmitted) will help to establish level of criticality. Information security resource requirements can then be determined and priority placed on protecting the applications that are most critical to the success of the organisation.
Develop systems securely.	Build quality, cost-effective systems on which business people can rely (e.g., that are consistently robust, accurate and reliable).	Information security should be integral to the scope, design, build and testing phases of the system development life cycle (SDLC). Good information security practices (e.g., rigorous testing for information security weaknesses; peer review; and ability to cope with error, exception and emergency conditions) should play a key role at all stages of the development process.

Figure 22—Information Security Principles *(cont.)*		
Principle	**Objective**	**Description**
3. Promote responsible information security behaviour.		
Act in a professional and ethical manner.	Ensure that information security-related activities are performed in a reliable, responsible and effective manner.	Information security relies heavily on the ability of professionals within the industry to perform their roles responsibly and with a clear understanding of how their integrity has a direct impact on the information they are charged with protecting. Information security professionals need to be committed to a high standard of quality in their work while demonstrating consistent and ethical behaviour and respect for business needs, other individuals and confidential (often personal) information.
Foster an information security-positive culture.	Provide a positive information security influence on the behaviour of end users, reduce the likelihood of information security incidents occurring, and limit their potential business impact.	Emphasis should be placed on making information security a key part of business as usual, raising information security awareness amongst users and ensuring that they have the skills required to protect critical or classified information and systems. Individuals should be made aware of the risk to information in their care and empowered to take the necessary steps to protect it.

A.2 Information Security Policy

This section covers information security policy at a high level, describing the scope of the policy and the people involved. The information contained in this section should be adapted as necessary to the specific needs of an enterprise.

Scope
The appearance and length of an information security policy varies greatly amongst enterprises. Some enterprises consider a one-page overview to be a sufficient information security policy. In this case, the policy could be considered a directive statement, and it should clearly describe links to other specific policies. In other enterprises, the information security policy is fully developed, containing nearly all the detailed guidance needed to put the principles into practice. It is important to understand what the information stakeholders expect in terms of coverage and to adapt to this expectation. The information in appendix E, on the information enabler, should be helpful in this regard.

Regardless of its size or degree of detail, the information security policy needs a clearly defined scope. This involves:
• A definition of information security for the enterprise
• The responsibilities associated with information security
• The vision regarding information security, accompanied by appropriate goals and metrics and an explanation of how the vision is supported by the information security culture and awareness
• Explanation of how the information security policy aligns with other high-level policies
• Elaboration on specific information security topics such as data management; information risk assessment; and compliance with legal, regulatory and contractual obligations
• Potentially, the information security life cycle budget and cost management. Information security strategic plans and portfolio management can be added as well.

This list is not exhaustive; more topics may be in scope depending on the business. It is important to innovate constantly and reuse best practices, which can be progressed via communication, reporting, and the required governance of technology and the architecture. The specific organisation and the interaction with involved stakeholders should be taken into account as well.

The policy should be actively communicated to the entire enterprise, and distributed to all employees, contractors, temporary employees and third-party vendors. Stakeholders need to know the information principles, high-level requirements, and roles and responsibilities for information security. The responsibility for updating and revalidating the information security policy lies with the information security function (CISO/ISM).

A.3 Specific Information Security Policies Driven by the Information Security Function

This subsection covers a number of examples of policies that are driven by different information security functions. The functions covered include access control, personnel information, physical and environmental information, and security incidents. For each of these policies, a description is provided, illustrating the scope and goals of the policy and the distribution to the proper audience.

Access Control Policy
The access control policy provides proper access to internal and external stakeholders to accomplish business goals. This can be measured by metrics such as the:
• Number of access violations that exceed the amount allowed
• Amount of work disruption due to insufficient access rights
• Number of segregation of duties incidents or audit findings

Additionally, the access control policy should ensure that emergency access is appropriately permitted and revoked in a timely manner. Metrics related to this goal include the:
• Number of emergency access requests
• Number of active emergency accounts in excess of approved time limits

The access control policy should cover the following topics, amongst others:
• Physical and logical access provisioning life cycle
• Least privilege/need to know
• Segregation of duties
• Emergency access

This policy is meant for all corresponding business units, vendors and third parties. Updates and revalidation should involve HR, data and system owners, and information security. A new or updated policy should be distributed to all corresponding business units, vendors and third parties.

Personnel Information Security Policy
The personnel information security policy objective includes, amongst others, the following goals:
• Execute regular background checks of all employees and people at key positions. This goal can be measured by counting the number of completed background checks for key personnel. This can be amplified with the number of overdue background check renewals based on a predetermined frequency.
• Acquire information about key personnel in information security positions. This can be followed up by counting the number of personnel in key positions that have not rotated according to a predefined frequency.
• Develop a succession plan for all key information security positions. A possible measure is to list all the critical information security positions that lack backup personnel.
• Verify whether all information security personnel have the necessary current and pertinent skills, and related certifications. A shortage in the number of critical information security positions with proper or qualified staffing could reflect the status of the goal.

This policy is meant for all corresponding business units, vendors and third parties. Updates and revalidation should involve HR, the privacy officer, the legal department, information security and facility security. A new or updated policy needs to be distributed to employees, contract personnel, vendors as indicated under contract, and temporary employees.

Physical and Environmental Information Security Policy
The objective of this policy is to provide direction regarding:
• Securing physical locations
• Environmental controls that provide capabilities to support operations

Securing the physical location can be measured by the number of identified exploitable vulnerabilities and/or incidents attributed to physical location threats (criminal, transportation and industrial hazards, natural threats). The environmental controls can be verified by measuring the number of identified exploitable vulnerabilities and/or incidents attributed to environmental control systems.

Indirectly, the policy contributes to optimising insurance costs. A related metric may be the trending of insurance costs related to loss due to physical, criminal and environmental threats.

The scope of the policy can include:
• Facility selection:
  – Criteria for selection
  – Construction attributes
• Environmental control standards
• Physical access control standards (employee, vendor, visitor)
• Information security monitoring and physical intrusion detection

This policy is meant for employees, all business units, the vendors holding organisational assets, and all visitors. Updates and revalidation should involve facilities, the legal department, information security and the data and system owners. A new or updated policy should be distributed to employees, contract personnel, vendors as indicated under contract, and temporary employees.

Security Incident Response Policy

The scope of this policy covers the need to respond to incidents in a timely manner to recover business activities. The policy should include:
• A definition of an information security incident
• A statement of how incidents will be handled
• Requirements for the establishment of the incident response team, with organisational roles and responsibilities
• Requirements for the creation of a tested incident response plan, which will provide documented procedures and guidelines for:
  – Criticality of incidents
  – Reporting and escalation process
  – Recovery (including):
    · Recovery time objectives (RTOs) for return to the trusted state
    · Investigation and preservation of process
    · Testing and training
  – Post-incident meetings to document root cause analysis and document enhancements of information security practices to prevent future similar events
• Incident documentation and closing

This policy is meant for all corresponding business units and key employees. Updates and revalidation should involve the information security function. A new or updated policy should be distributed to key employees.

A.4 Specific Information Security Policies Driven by Other Functions Within the Enterprise

This section discusses policies that are relevant in an information security context, but are not developed or owned by the information security function. For these policies, the input of the information security function is required. In **figure 23**, a possible scope relevant for the information security function is described.

Figure 23—Specific Information Security Policies Driven by Other Functions Within the Organisation: Scope	
Policy	**Scope for the Information Security Function**
Business continuity and disaster recovery policy	• Business impact analysis (BIA) • Business contingency plans with trusted recovery • Recovery requirements for critical systems • Defined thresholds and triggers for contingencies, escalation of incidents • Disaster recovery plan (DRP) • Training and testing
Asset management policy	• Data classification • Data ownership • System classification and ownership • Resource utilisation and prioritisation • Asset life cycle management • Asset protection measures

Rules of behaviour (acceptable use)	• At-work acceptable use and behaviour:
	  – Expectation of privacy
	  – Use of enterprise systems and assets
	  – Internet
	  – Email
	  – Instant messaging
	  – Remote access
	  – Mobile devices and camera use
	  – Printer, scanner and fax usage
	  – Use of personal computers for enterprise activities
	• Off-site acceptable use and behaviour:
	  – Social networks
	  – Blogs

Figure 23—Specific Information Security Policies Driven by Other Functions Within the Organisation: Scope (cont.)	
Policy	**Scope for the Information Security Function**
Information systems acquisition, software development and maintenance policy	• Information security in the life cycle process • Information security requirements definition process • Information security within the procurement/acquisition process • Secure coding practices • Integration of information security with change management and configuration management

Vendor management policy	• Contract management:
	  – Information security terms and conditions
	  – Information security evaluation
	  – Monitoring of contracts for information security compliance

Communication and operation management policy	• IT information security architecture and application design:
	  – Steering committee
	  – Standards
	  – Guidelines
	• SLA:
	  – Internal operations
	  – External operations
	• IT information security operational procedures

Compliance policy	• IT information security compliance assessment process:
	  – Regulatory
	  – Contractual
	  – Enterprise
	• Development of metrics
	• Assessment repositories:
	  – Audience
	  – Content
	  – Structure
	  – Follow-up

Risk management policy	• Organisational risk management plan:
	  – Scope
	  – Roles and responsibilities
	  – Methodologies
	  – Tools and techniques
	  – Repository processes
	• Information risk profile

APPENDIX B
DETAILED GUIDANCE: PROCESSES ENABLER

The details of all information security-specific processes, according to the process model described in section II, are included in *COBIT 5 for Information Security* (see **figure 24**).

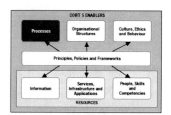

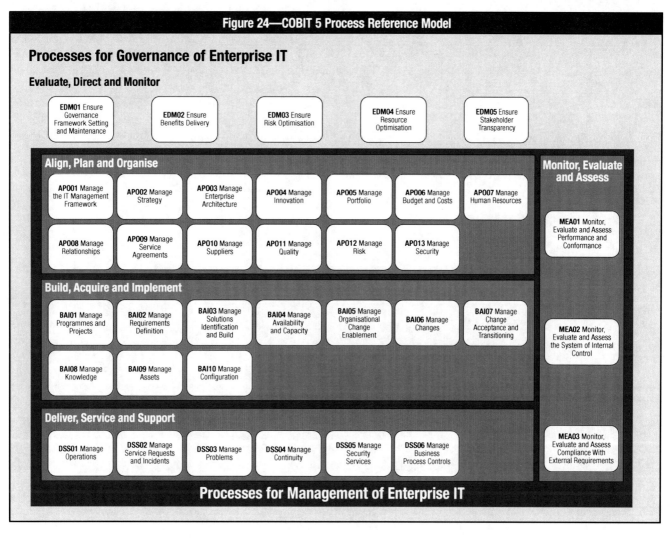

Figure 24—COBIT 5 Process Reference Model

Page intentionally left blank

B.1 EVALUATE, DIRECT AND MONITOR (EDM)

01   Ensure governance framework setting and maintenance.

02   Ensure benefits delivery.

03   Ensure risk optimisation.

04   Ensure resource optimisation.

05   Ensure stakeholder transparency.

Evaluate, Direct and Monitor

Page intentionally left blank

Page intentionally left blank

EDM01 Ensure Governance Framework Setting and Maintenance	Area: Governance Domain: Evaluate, Direct and Monitor

COBIT 5 Process Description
Analyse and articulate the requirements for the governance of enterprise IT, and put in place and maintain effective enabling structures, principles, processes and practices, with clarity of responsibilities and authority to achieve the enterprise's mission, goals and objectives.

COBIT 5 Process Purpose Statement
Provide a consistent approach integrated and aligned with the enterprise governance approach. To ensure that IT-related decisions are made in line with the enterprise's strategies and objectives, ensure that IT-related processes are overseen effectively and transparently, compliance with legal and regulatory requirements is confirmed, and the governance requirements for board members are met.

EDM01 Security-specific Process Goals and Metrics

Security-specific Process Goals	Related Metrics
1. The information security governance system is embedded in the enterprise.	• Number of enterprise and IT processes with which information security is integrated • Percent of processes and practices with clear traceability to principles • Number of information security breaches related to non-compliance with ethical and professional behaviour guidelines
2. Assurance is obtained over the information security governance system.	• Frequency of independent reviews of governance of information security • Frequency of governance of information security reporting to the executive committee and board • Number of external/internal audits and reviews • Number of non-compliance issues

EDM01 Security-specific Process Practices, Inputs/Outputs and Activities

Governance Practice	Security-specific Inputs (in Addition to COBIT 5 Inputs)		Security-specific Outputs (in Addition to COBIT 5 Outputs)	
	From	Description	Description	To
EDM01.01 Evaluate the governance system. Continually identify and engage with the enterprise's stakeholders, document an understanding of the requirements, and make a judgement on the current and future design of governance of enterprise IT.	Outside *COBIT 5 for Information Security*	Internal and external environmental factors (legal, regulatory and contractual obligations) and trends	Information security guiding principles	EDM01.02 APO01.01 APO01.03 APO01.04 APO02.01 APO02.05 APO12.03

Security-specific Activities (in Addition to COBIT 5 Activities)

1. Analyse and identify the internal and external environmental factors (legal, regulatory and contractual obligations) and trends in the business environment that may influence the information security governance design.
2. Evaluate the extent to which information security meets the business and compliance/regulatory needs.
3. Articulate principles that will guide the design of information security enablers and promote a security-positive environment.
4. Understand the enterprise's decision-making culture and determine the optimal decision-making model for information security.

Governance Practice	Security-specific Inputs (in Addition to COBIT 5 Inputs)		Security-specific Outputs (in Addition to COBIT 5 Outputs)	
	From	Description	Description	To
EDM01.02 Direct the governance system. Inform leaders and obtain their support, buy-in and commitment. Guide the structures, processes and practices for the governance of IT in line with agreed-on governance design principles, decision-making models and authority levels. Define the information required for informed decision making.	EDM01.01	Information security guiding principles	Information security-positive culture and environment	Internal
	APO02.05	Information security strategy		

Security-specific Activities (in Addition to COBIT 5 Activities)

1. Obtain senior management commitment to information security and information risk management.
2. Mandate an enterprisewide information security function.
3. Mandate an information security steering committee (ISSC).
4. Implement hierarchical information and decision escalation procedures.
5. Align information security strategy with business strategy.
6. Foster an information security-positive culture and environment.

EDM01 Security-specific Process Practices, Inputs/Outputs and Activities *(cont.)*				
	Security-specific Inputs (in Addition to COBIT 5 Inputs)		Security-specific Outputs (in Addition to COBIT 5 Outputs)	
Governance Practice	From	Description	Description	To
EDM01.03 Monitor the governance system. Monitor the effectiveness and performance of the enterprise's governance of IT. Assess whether the governance system and implemented mechanisms (including structures, principles and processes) are operating effectively and provide appropriate oversight of IT.	Outside *COBIT 5 for Information Security*	Information security-related legislation and regulation	Governance compliance assessment	Internal
Security-specific Activities (in Addition to COBIT 5 Activities)				
1. Monitor regular and routine mechanisms for ensuring that the use of information security measurement systems complies with information security-related legislation and regulation. Analyse overall implications of the changing threat landscape.				

For more information regarding the related enablers, please consult:
• Appendix D. Detailed Guidance: Culture, Ethics and Behaviour Enabler
• Appendix G. Detailed Guidance: People, Skills and Competencies Enabler, G.1. Information Security Governance

Evaluate, Direct and Monitor

EDM02 Ensure Benefits Delivery	Area: Governance Domain: Evaluate, Direct and Monitor

COBIT 5 Process Description
Optimise the value contribution to the business from the business processes, IT services and IT assets resulting from investments made by IT at acceptable costs.

COBIT 5 Process Purpose Statement
Secure optimal value from IT-enabled initiatives, services and assets; cost-efficient delivery of solutions and services; and a reliable and accurate picture of costs and likely benefits so that business needs are supported effectively and efficiently.

EDM02 Security-specific Process Goals and Metrics

Security-specific Process Goals	Related Metrics
1. Benefits, costs and risk of information security investments are balanced and managed and contribute optimal value.	• Percent of risk reduction vs. budget deviation (budgeted vs. projection) • Level of stakeholder satisfaction with the information security measures in place, based on surveys

EDM02 Security-specific Process Practices, Inputs/Outputs and Activities

Governance Practice	Security-specific Inputs (in Addition to COBIT 5 Inputs)		Security-specific Outputs (in Addition to COBIT 5 Outputs)	
	From	Description	Description	To
EDM02.01 Evaluate value optimisation. Continually evaluate the portfolio of IT-enabled investments, services and assets to determine the likelihood of achieving enterprise objectives and delivering value at a reasonable cost. Identify and make judgement on any changes in direction that need to be given to management to optimise value creation.	Outside *COBIT 5 for Information Security*	Evaluation of strategic alignment	Updated portfolio	Internal

Security-specific Activities (in Addition to COBIT 5 Activities)

1. Identify and record the requirements of stakeholders (such as shareholders, regulators, auditors and customers) for protecting their interests and delivering value through information security activity. Set direction accordingly.

Governance Practice	Security-specific Inputs (in Addition to COBIT 5 Inputs)		Security-specific Outputs (in Addition to COBIT 5 Outputs)	
	From	Description	Description	To
EDM02.02 Direct value optimisation. Direct value management principles and practices to enable optimal value realisation from IT-enabled investments throughout their full economic life cycle.	Outside *COBIT 5 for Information Security*	Investment types and criteria	Updated investment types and criteria	Internal

Security-specific Activities (in Addition to COBIT 5 Activities)

1. Establish a method of demonstrating the value of information security (including defining and collecting relevant data) to ensure the efficient use of existing information security-related assets.

2. Ensure the use of financial and non-financial measures to describe the added value of information security initiatives.

3. Use business-focussed methods of reporting on the added value of information security initiatives.

Governance Practice	Security-specific Inputs (in Addition to COBIT 5 Inputs)		Security-specific Outputs (in Addition to COBIT 5 Outputs)	
	From	Description	Description	To
EDM02.03 Monitor value optimisation. Monitor the key goals and metrics to determine the extent to which the business is generating the expected value and benefits to the enterprise from IT-enabled investments and services. Identify significant issues and consider corrective actions.			Feedback on value delivery of information security initiatives	Internal

Security-specific Activities (in Addition to COBIT 5 Activities)

1. Track outcomes of information security initiatives and compare to expectations to ensure value delivery against business goals.

For more information regarding the related enablers, please consult:
• Section II, 6. Enabler: Information, 6.3. Information Stakeholders
• Appendix E. Detailed Guidance: Information Enabler

Evaluate, Direct and Monitor

Page intentionally left blank

EDM03 Ensure Risk Optimisation	Area: Governance Domain: Evaluate, Direct and Monitor

COBIT 5 Process Description
Ensure that the enterprise's risk appetite and tolerance are understood, articulated and communicated, and that risk to enterprise value related to the use of IT is identified and managed.

COBIT 5 Process Purpose Statement
Ensure that IT-related enterprise risk does not exceed risk appetite and risk tolerance, the impact of IT risk to enterprise value is identified and managed, and the potential for compliance failures is minimised.

EDM03 Security-specific Process Goals and Metrics

Security-specific Process Goals	Related Metrics
1. Information risk management is part of overall enterprise risk management (ERM).	• Percent of information security risk that is related to business risk • Percent of business risk that has been effectively mitigated with information security controls

EDM03 Security-specific Process Practices, Inputs/Outputs and Activities

Governance Practice	Security-specific Inputs (in Addition to COBIT 5 Inputs)		Security-specific Outputs (in Addition to COBIT 5 Outputs)	
	From	Description	Description	To
EDM03.01 Evaluate risk management. Continually examine and make judgement on the effect of risk on the current and future use of IT in the enterprise. Consider whether the enterprise's risk appetite is appropriate and that risk to enterprise value related to the use of IT is identified and managed.	Outside *COBIT 5 for Information Security*	• Enterprise key risk indicators (KRIs) • Enterprise risk appetite guidance	Alignment of enterprise KRIs with information security KRIs	EDM03.02
			Information security risk acceptable level	EDM03.02 EDM03.03

Security-specific Activities (in Addition to COBIT 5 Activities)

1. Determine the enterprise risk appetite at the board level.

2. Measure the level of integration of information risk management with the overall ERM model.

Governance Practice	Security-specific Inputs (in Addition to COBIT 5 Inputs)		Security-specific Outputs (in Addition to COBIT 5 Outputs)	
	From	Description	Description	To
EDM03.02 Direct risk management. Direct the establishment of risk management practices to provide reasonable assurance that IT risk management practices are appropriate to ensure that the actual IT risk does not exceed the board's risk appetite.	EDM03.01	• Alignment of enterprise KRIs with information security KRIs • Information security risk acceptable level	Updated risk management policies	Internal

Security-specific Activities (in Addition to COBIT 5 Activities)

1. Integrate information risk management within the overall ERM model.

Governance Practice	Security-specific Inputs (in Addition to COBIT 5 Inputs)		Security-specific Outputs (in Addition to COBIT 5 Outputs)	
	From	Description	Description	To
EDM03.03 Monitor risk management. Monitor the key goals and metrics of the risk management processes and establish how deviations or problems will be identified, tracked and reported for remediation.	EDM03.01	Information security risk acceptable level	Remedial actions to address risk management deviations	Internal
	APO01.03	Information security and related policies		

Security-specific Activities (in Addition to COBIT 5 Activities)

1. Monitor the enterprise information risk profile or risk appetite to achieve optimal balance between business risk and opportunities.

2. Include outcomes of information risk management processes as inputs to the overall business risk dashboard.

For more information regarding the related enablers, please consult:
• Appendix C. Detailed Guidance: Organisational Structures Enabler, C.4. Enterprise Risk Management Committee
• Appendix G. Detailed Guidance: People, Skills and Competencies Enabler, G.3. Information Risk Management

Page intentionally left blank

Evaluate, Direct and Monitor

COBIT⑤ FOR INFORMATION SECURITY

Page intentionally left blank

Evaluate, Direct and Monitor

EDM04 Ensure Resource Optimisation	Area: Governance Domain: Evaluate, Direct and Monitor

COBIT 5 Process Description
Ensure that adequate and sufficient IT-related capabilities (people, process and technology) are available to support enterprise objectives effectively at optimal cost.

COBIT 5 Process Purpose Statement
Ensure that the resource needs of the enterprise are met in the optimal manner, IT costs are optimised, and there is an increased likelihood of benefit realisation and readiness for future change.

EDM04 Security-specific Process Goals and Metrics

Security-specific Process Goals	Related Metrics
1. Information security resources are optimised.	• Benchmarking of information security spending in relation to previous years and/or similar organisations or industry best practices
2. Information security resources are in alignment with business requirements.	• Amount of deviation from information security budget • Percent of reuse of information security solutions

EDM04 Security-specific Process Practices, Inputs/Outputs and Activities

Governance Practice	Security-specific Inputs (in Addition to COBIT 5 Inputs)		Security-specific Outputs (in Addition to COBIT 5 Outputs)	
	From	Description	Description	To
EDM04.01 Evaluate resource management. Continually examine and make judgement on the current and future need for IT-related resources, options for resourcing (including sourcing strategies), and allocation and management principles to meet the needs of the enterprise in the optimal manner.	Outside *COBIT 5 for Information Security*	Approved resources plan	Updated information security resources	Internal

Security-specific Activities (in Addition to COBIT 5 Activities)

1. Evaluate the effectiveness of information security resources in terms of the provision, training, awareness and competencies of necessary resources in comparison with business needs.

Governance Practice	Security-specific Inputs (in Addition to COBIT 5 Inputs)		Security-specific Outputs (in Addition to COBIT 5 Outputs)	
	From	Description	Description	To
EDM04.02 Direct resource management. Ensure the adoption of resource management principles to enable optimal use of IT resources throughout their full economic life cycle.	Outside *COBIT 5 for Information Security*	Assigned responsibilities for resource management	Updated information security resources	Internal

Security-specific Activities (in Addition to COBIT 5 Activities)

1. Ensure that information security resource management is aligned to business needs.

Governance Practice	Security-specific Inputs (in Addition to COBIT 5 Inputs)		Security-specific Outputs (in Addition to COBIT 5 Outputs)	
	From	Description	Description	To
EDM04.03 Monitor resource management. Monitor the key goals and metrics of the resource management processes and establish how deviations or problems will be identified, tracked and reported for remediation.			Remedial actions to address resource management deviations	Internal

Security-specific Activities (in Addition to COBIT 5 Activities)

1. Measure the effectiveness, efficiency and capacity of information security resources against business needs.

For more information regarding the related enablers, please consult:
• Appendix G. Detailed Guidance: People, Skills and Competencies Enabler

Page intentionally left blank

COBIT® 5 FOR INFORMATION SECURITY

Page intentionally left blank

EDM05 Ensure Stakeholder Transparency	Area: Governance Domain: Evaluate, Direct and Monitor

COBIT 5 Process Description
Ensure that enterprise IT performance and conformance measurement and reporting are transparent, with stakeholders approving the goals and metrics and the necessary remedial actions.

COBIT 5 Process Purpose Statement
Make sure that the communication to stakeholders is effective and timely and the basis for reporting is established to increase performance, identify areas for improvement, and confirm that IT-related objectives and strategies are in line with the enterprise's strategy.

EDM05 Security-specific Process Goals and Metrics

Security-specific Process Goals	Related Metrics
1. Information security reporting is established and is complete, timely and accurate.	• Percent of reports that are delivered on time • Percent of reports with validated reporting data
2. Stakeholders are informed of the current status of information security and information risk across the enterprise.	• Stakeholder satisfaction with the information security reporting process (timely, complete, relevant, reliable, accurate, etc.) and frequency, based on surveys

EDM05 Security-specific Process Practices, Inputs/Outputs and Activities

Governance Practice	Security-specific Inputs (in Addition to COBIT 5 Inputs)		Security-specific Outputs (in Addition to COBIT 5 Outputs)	
	From	Description	Description	To
EDM05.01 Evaluate stakeholder reporting requirements. Continually examine and make judgement on the current and future requirements for stakeholder communication and reporting, including both mandatory reporting requirements (e.g., regulatory) and communication to other stakeholders. Establish the principles for communication.	Outside *COBIT 5 for Information Security*	Evaluation of enterprise reporting requirements	Information security reporting requirements and communication channels	Internal

Security-specific Activities (in Addition to COBIT 5 Activities)

1. Determine the audience, including internal and external individuals or groups, for communication and reporting.

2. Identify requirements for reporting on information security to stakeholders (e.g., what information is required, when it is required, how it is presented).

3. Identify the means and channels to communicate information security issues.

Governance Practice	Security-specific Inputs (in Addition to COBIT 5 Inputs)		Security-specific Outputs (in Addition to COBIT 5 Outputs)	
	From	Description	Description	To
EDM05.02 Direct stakeholder communication and reporting. Ensure the establishment of effective stakeholder communication and reporting, including mechanisms for ensuring the quality and completeness of information, oversight of mandatory reporting, and creating a communication strategy for stakeholders.			Information security status reports	Internal

Security-specific Activities (in Addition to COBIT 5 Activities)

1. Prioritise reporting on information security issues to stakeholders.

2. Perform internal and external audits to assess the effectiveness of the information security governance programme.

3. Produce for stakeholders regular information security status reports that include information security activities, performance, achievements, risk profile, business benefits, 'hot topics' (e.g., cloud, consumer products), outstanding risk (including compliance and audit) and capability gaps.

Evaluate, Direct and Monitor

EDM05 Security-specific Process Practices, Inputs/Outputs and Activities *(cont.)*				
	Security-specific Inputs (in Addition to COBIT 5 Inputs)		Security-specific Outputs (in Addition to COBIT 5 Outputs)	
Governance Practice	From	Description	Description	To
EDM05.03 Monitor stakeholder communication. Monitor the effectiveness of stakeholder communication. Assess mechanisms for ensuring accuracy, reliability and effectiveness, and ascertain whether the requirements of different stakeholders are met.			Information security monitoring and reporting	Internal
Security-specific Activities (in Addition to COBIT 5 Activities)				
1. Establish information security monitoring and reporting (e.g., using key performance indicators [KPIs] for information security and information risk management that are based on metrics and measurements in the MEA domain).				

For more information regarding the related enablers, please consult:
• Section II, 6. Enabler: Information, 6.3 Information Stakeholders
• Appendix E. Detailed Guidance: Information Enabler

B.2 ALIGN, PLAN AND ORGANISE (APO)

01   Manage the IT management framework.

02   Manage strategy.

03   Manage enterprise architecture.

04   Manage innovation.

05   Manage portfolio.

06   Manage budget and costs.

07   Manage human resources.

08   Manage relationships.

09   Manage service agreements.

10   Manage suppliers.

11   Manage quality.

12   Manage risk.

13   Manage security.

Page intentionally left blank

Align, Plan and Organise

APO01 Manage the IT Management Framework	Area: Management Domain: Align, Plan and Organise

COBIT 5 Process Description
Clarify and maintain the governance of enterprise IT mission and vision. Implement and maintain mechanisms and authorities to manage information and the use of IT in the enterprise in support of governance objectives in line with guiding principles and policies.

COBIT 5 Process Purpose Statement
Provide a consistent management approach to enable the enterprise governance requirements to be met, covering management processes, organisational structures, roles and responsibilities, reliable and repeatable activities, and skills and competencies.

APO01 Security-specific Process Goals and Metrics

Security-specific Process Goals	Related Metrics
1. Alignment of information security with IT and business frameworks operating in the enterprise is effectively implemented and communicated.	• Percent of information security strategy portfolio activities supporting alignment that are aligned to business strategy

APO01 Security-specific Process Practices, Inputs/Outputs and Activities

Management Practice	Security-specific Inputs (in Addition to COBIT 5 Inputs)		Security-specific Outputs (in Addition to COBIT 5 Outputs)	
	From	Description	Description	To
APO01.01 Define the organisational structure. Establish an internal and extended organisational structure that reflects business needs and IT priorities. Put in place the required management structures (e.g., committees) that enable management decision making to take place in the most effective and efficient manner.	EDM01.01	Information security guiding principles	ISSC mandate and structure	Internal
	Outside *COBIT 5 for Information Security*	• IT strategy • Information security standards and guidelines		

Security-specific Activities (in Addition to COBIT 5 Activities)

1. Align the information security-related organisation with enterprise architecture organisational models.

2. Establish an ISSC (or equivalent).

3. Define the information security function, including internal and external roles, capabilities and decision rights required.

Management Practice	Security-specific Inputs (in Addition to COBIT 5 Inputs)		Security-specific Outputs (in Addition to COBIT 5 Outputs)	
	From	Description	Description	To
APO01.02 Establish roles and responsibilities. Establish, agree on and communicate roles and responsibilities of IT personnel, as well as other stakeholders with responsibilities for enterprise IT, that clearly reflect overall business needs and IT objectives and relevant personnel's authority, responsibilities and accountability.	APO13.01	Information security management system (ISMS) scope statement	Definition of IT-related roles and responsibilities	DSS05.04
	Outside *COBIT 5 for Information Security*	• Applicable regulations • Information security standards and guidelines	Chief information security officer (CISO) and information security manager (ISM) job definitions	Internal
	Principles and policy enabler model	Human resources (HR) and legal policies		

Security-specific Activities (in Addition to COBIT 5 Activities)

1. Establish, agree on and communicate the roles of CISO and ISM (or equivalents).

2. Determine the degree to which other organisational roles have information security obligations, and add these obligations to the relevant job descriptions.

Align, Plan and Organise

Align, Plan and Organise

AP001 Security-specific Process Practices, Inputs/Outputs and Activities *(cont.)*				

Management Practice	Security-specific Inputs (in Addition to COBIT 5 Inputs)		Security-specific Outputs (in Addition to COBIT 5 Outputs)	
	From	Description	Description	To
AP001.03 Maintain the enablers of the management system. Maintain the enablers of the management system and control environment for enterprise IT, and ensure that they are integrated and aligned with the enterprise's governance and management philosophy and operating style. These enablers include the clear communication of expectations/requirements. The management system should encourage cross-divisional co-operation and teamwork, promote compliance and continuous improvement, and handle process deviations (including failure).	EDM01.01	Information security guiding principles	Information security and related policies	EDM03.03 AP007.01 AP007.06 AP012.01 BAI01.01 BAI01.11 BAI02.01 BAI03.08 BAI05.01 BAI06.01 DSS01.02 DSS02.01 MEA01.01 MEA02.01
	Outside *COBIT 5 for Information Security*	• Information security-related rules and regulations • Information security standards and guidelines		

Security-specific Activities (in Addition to COBIT 5 Activities)
1. Consider the enterprise's internal environment, including management culture and philosophy, risk tolerance, ethical values, code of conduct, accountability, and requirements for information security.
2. Align with applicable national and international information security standards and codes of practice, and evaluate available information security good practices.
3. Develop information security and related policies, taking into account business and legal or regulatory requirements and contractual security obligations, high-level organisational policies and the enterprise's internal environment.

Management Practice	Security-specific Inputs (in Addition to COBIT 5 Inputs)		Security-specific Outputs (in Addition to COBIT 5 Outputs)	
	From	Description	Description	To
AP001.04 Communicate management objectives and direction. Communicate awareness and understanding of IT objectives and direction to appropriate stakeholders and users throughout the enterprise.	EDM01.01	Information security guiding principles	Information security training and awareness programme	AP002.06 BAI08.01
	AP002.06	Communication on information security objectives		
	DSS05.01	Malicious software prevention policy		
	DSS05.02	Connectivity security policy		
	DSS05.03	Security policies for endpoint devices		

Security-specific Activities (in Addition to COBIT 5 Activities)
1. Define the expectations with regard to information security, including specific organisational ethics and culture.
2. Develop an information security awareness programme.
3. Establish metrics to measure behaviours regarding information security.

Management Practice	Security-specific Inputs (in Addition to COBIT 5 Inputs)		Security-specific Outputs (in Addition to COBIT 5 Outputs)	
	From	Description	Description	To
AP001.05 Optimise the placement of the IT function. Position the IT capability in the overall organisational structure to reflect an enterprise model relevant to the importance of IT within the enterprise, specifically its criticality to enterprise strategy and the level of operational dependence on IT. The reporting line of the CIO should be commensurate with the importance of IT within the enterprise.			Information security function definition and placement in the enterprise	AP001.06

Security-specific Activities (in Addition to COBIT 5 Activities)
1. Define the information security function and all relevant activities and attributes.
2. Define the placement of the information security function in the enterprise and obtain agreement from all relevant parties.

APO01 Security-specific Process Practices, Inputs/Outputs and Activities *(cont.)*

Management Practice	Security-specific Inputs (in Addition to COBIT 5 Inputs)		Security-specific Outputs (in Addition to COBIT 5 Outputs)	
	From	Description	Description	To
APO01.06 Define information (data) and system ownership. Define and maintain responsibilities for ownership of information (data) and information systems. Ensure that owners make decisions about classifying information and systems and protecting them in line with this classification.	APO01.05	Information security function definition and placement in the enterprise	Information security roles and responsibilities	APO11.01
			Data classification guidelines	DSS05.02

Security-specific Activities (in Addition to COBIT 5 Activities)

1. Define enterprise-level system and data ownership within the information security management processes.

2. Assign data information security custodians within the information security management processes.

Management Practice	Security-specific Inputs (in Addition to COBIT 5 Inputs)		Security-specific Outputs (in Addition to COBIT 5 Outputs)	
	From	Description	Description	To
APO01.07 Manage continual improvement of processes. Assess, plan and execute the continual improvement of processes and their maturity to ensure that they are capable of delivering against enterprise, governance, management and control objectives. Consider COBIT process implementation guidance, emerging standards, compliance requirements, automation opportunities, and the feedback of process users, the process team and other stakeholders. Update the process and consider impacts on process enablers.	MEA01.04	Information security reports and corrective action plans updated	• Documentation of processes, technology and applications, and standardisation • Training of the information security staff	Internal

Security-specific Activities (in Addition to COBIT 5 Activities)

1. Consider ways to improve the efficiency and effectiveness of the information security function, e.g., through training of the information security staff; documentation of processes, technology and applications; and standardisation and automation of the process.

2. Review reports (such as audit reports or risk assessments) detailing information security control and process weaknesses.

Management Practice	Security-specific Inputs (in Addition to COBIT 5 Inputs)		Security-specific Outputs (in Addition to COBIT 5 Outputs)	
	From	Description	Description	To
APO01.08 Maintain compliance with policies and procedures. Put in place procedures to maintain compliance with and performance measurement of policies and other enablers of the control framework, and enforce the consequences of non-compliance or inadequate performance. Track trends and performance and consider these in the future design and improvement of the control framework.	APO02.05	Information security strategy	Information security compliance assessment	APO02.02 APO12.01
	APO02.06	Information security plan		
	Outside *COBIT 5 for Information Security*	• Organisational objectives • Information security-related rules and regulations • Information security standards and guidelines		

Security-specific Activities (in Addition to COBIT 5 Activities)

1. Schedule and perform regular assessments to determine compliance with information security policies and procedures.

For more information regarding the related enablers, please consult:
• Appendix C. Detailed Guidance: Organisational Structures Enabler, C.1. Chief Information Security Officer, C.2. Information Security Steering Committee, C.3. Information Security Manager

Align, Plan and Organise

Page intentionally left blank

Align, Plan and Organise

AP002 Manage Strategy	Area: Management
	Domain: Align, Plan and Organise

COBIT 5 Process Description
Provide a holistic view of the current business and IT environment, the future direction, and the initiatives required to migrate to the desired future environment. Leverage enterprise architecture building blocks and components, including externally provided services and related capabilities to enable nimble, reliable and efficient response to strategic objectives.

COBIT 5 Process Purpose Statement
Align strategic IT plans with business objectives. Clearly communicate the objectives and associated accountabilities so they are understood by all, with the IT strategic options identified, structured and integrated with the business plans.

AP002 Security-specific Process Goals and Metrics

Security-specific Process Goals	Related Metrics
1. An information security policy framework is defined and maintained.	• Number of updates of the information security policy • Management approval of the information security policy
2. A comprehensive information security strategy is in place and is aligned with the overall enterprise and IT strategy.	• Percent of information security initiatives completed vs. planned
3. The information security strategy is cost-effective, appropriate, realistic, achievable, enterprise-focussed and balanced.	• Percent and number of initiatives for which a value metric (e.g., return on investment [ROI]) has been calculated • Enterprise stakeholder satisfaction survey feedback on the effectiveness of the information security strategy
4. The information security strategy is aligned with long-term enterprise strategic goals and objectives.	• Percent of projects in the enterprise and IT project portfolios that involve information security • Percent of IT initiatives/projects that have information security requirements championed by business owners

AP002 Security-specific Process Practices, Inputs/Outputs and Activities

Management Practice	Security-specific Inputs (in Addition to COBIT 5 Inputs)		Security-specific Outputs (in Addition to COBIT 5 Outputs)	
	From	Description	Description	To
AP002.01 Understand enterprise direction. Consider the current enterprise environment and business processes, as well as the enterprise strategy and future objectives. Consider also the external environment of the enterprise (industry drivers, relevant regulations, basis for competition).	EDM01.01	Information security guiding principles	High-level sources and priorities for changes	AP002.02

Security-specific Activities (in Addition to COBIT 5 Activities)
1. Understand how information security should support overall enterprise objectives and protect stakeholder interests by taking into account the need to manage information risk while meeting legal and regulatory compliance requirements and adding value to the enterprise.
2. Understand the current enterprise architecture and identify potential information security gaps.

Management Practice	Security-specific Inputs (in Addition to COBIT 5 Inputs)		Security-specific Outputs (in Addition to COBIT 5 Outputs)	
	From	Description	Description	To
AP002.02 Assess the current environment, capabilities and performance. Assess the performance of current internal business and IT capabilities and external IT services, and develop an understanding of the enterprise architecture in relation to IT. Identify issues currently being experienced and develop recommendations in areas that could benefit from improvement. Consider service provider differentiators and options and the financial impact and potential costs and benefits of using external services.	AP001.08	Information security compliance assessment	Information security capabilities	AP002.03 AP004.04 AP008.05 AP009.05 AP011.01 BAI01.01 BAI02.01 BAI04.01
	AP002.01	High-level sources and priorities for changes		

Security-specific Activities (in Addition to COBIT 5 Activities)
1. Develop an information security capability baseline.
2. Create relevant and clear information security criteria to identify risk and prioritise gaps.

Align, Plan and Organise

Align, Plan and Organise

APO02 Security-specific Process Practices, Inputs/Outputs and Activities *(cont.)*

Management Practice	Security-specific Inputs (in Addition to COBIT 5 Inputs)		Security-specific Outputs (in Addition to COBIT 5 Outputs)	
	From	Description	Description	To
APO02.03 Define the target IT capabilities. Define the target business and IT capabilities and required IT services. This should be based on the understanding of the enterprise environment and requirements; the assessment of the current business process and IT environment and issues; and consideration of reference standards, best practices and validated emerging technologies or innovation proposals.	APO02.02	Information security capabilities	Information security requirements in target IT capabilities	APO02.04
	BAI02.01	Information security requirements		
	Outside *COBIT 5 for Information Security*	Information security standards and regulations		

Security-specific Activities (in Addition to COBIT 5 Activities)

1. Ensure that information security requirements are included in the definition of target IT capabilities.

2. Define the target state for information security.

3. Define and agree on the impact of information security requirements on enterprise architecture, acknowledging the relevant stakeholders.

Management Practice	Security-specific Inputs (in Addition to COBIT 5 Inputs)		Security-specific Outputs (in Addition to COBIT 5 Outputs)	
	From	Description	Description	To
APO02.04 Conduct a gap analysis. Identify the gaps between the current and target environments and consider the alignment of assets (the capabilities that support services) with business outcomes to optimise investment in and utilisation of the internal and external asset base. Consider the critical success factors to support strategy execution.	APO02.03	Information security requirements in target IT capabilities	Information security capability benchmark	APO03.01
			Gaps to be closed and changes required to realise target capability	APO13.02

Security-specific Activities (in Addition to COBIT 5 Activities)

1. Identify all gaps to be closed and changes required to realise the target environment.

2. Benchmark information security against well-understood and reliable industry norms.

3. Examine the current environment with respect to regulations and compliance requirements.

Management Practice	Security-specific Inputs (in Addition to COBIT 5 Inputs)		Security-specific Outputs (in Addition to COBIT 5 Outputs)	
	From	Description	Description	To
APO02.05 Define the strategic plan and road map. Create a strategic plan that defines, in co-operation with relevant stakeholders, how IT-related goals will contribute to the enterprise's strategic goals. Include how IT will support IT-enabled investment programmes, business processes, IT services and IT assets. Direct IT to define the initiatives that will be required to close the gaps, the sourcing strategy and the measurements to be used to monitor achievement of goals, then prioritise the initiatives and combine them in a high-level road map.	EDM01.01	Information security guiding principles	Information security strategy	EDM01.02 APO01.08 APO03.01
	APO13.02	Information security business cases	Information security strategic road map	BAI05.04

Security-specific Activities (in Addition to COBIT 5 Activities)

1. Define the information security strategy and align it with IT and business strategies and the enterprise's overall objectives.

2. Ensure that the current IT strategic plan and road map take into account information security requirements.

3. Create a road map that includes a relative scheduling, interdependencies of the initiatives, metrics (what) and targets (how much) that can be related to enterprise benefits.

APO02 Security-specific Process Practices, Inputs/Outputs and Activities *(cont.)*				
	Security-specific Inputs (in Addition to COBIT 5 Inputs)		Security-specific Outputs (in Addition to COBIT 5 Outputs)	
Management Practice	From	Description	Description	To
APO02.06 Communicate the IT strategy and direction. Create awareness and understanding of the business and IT objectives and direction, as captured in the IT strategy, through communication to appropriate stakeholders and users throughout the enterprise.	APO01.04	Information security training and awareness programme	Communication on information security objectives	APO01.04
			Information security plan	APO01.08 APO04.04 APO04.05 APO07.01 APO07.05 APO07.06 APO09.05 APO11.01 BAI01.01 BAI01.04 BAI01.08 BAI01.11 BAI02.01 BAI05.03 BAI05.04

Security-specific Activities (in Addition to COBIT 5 Activities)
1. Develop the information security plan, outlining the practical consequences of information security for the enterprise.
2. Communicate the information security strategy and information security plan to the enterprise and all relevant stakeholders.
3. Promote the information security function within the enterprise and outside the enterprise, if relevant.

For more information regarding the related enablers, please consult:
- Appendix E. Detailed Guidance: Information Enabler, E.2. Information Security Strategy, E.4. Information Security Plan, E.6. Information Security Requirements
- Appendix G. Detailed Guidance: People, Skills and Competencies Enabler, G.2. Information Security Strategy Formulation, G.4 Information Security Architecture Development

Align, Plan and Organise

Align, Plan and Organise

Page intentionally left blank

APO03 Manage Enterprise Architecture	Area: Management Domain: Align, Plan and Organise

COBIT 5 Process Description
Establish a common architecture consisting of business process, information, data, application and technology architecture layers for effectively and efficiently realising enterprise and IT strategies by creating key models and practices that describe the baseline and target architectures. Define requirements for taxonomy, standards, guidelines, procedures, templates and tools, and provide a linkage for these components. Improve alignment, increase agility, improve quality of information and generate potential cost savings through initiatives such as reuse of building block components.

COBIT 5 Process Purpose Statement
Represent the different building blocks that make up the enterprise and their interrelationships as well as the principles guiding their design and evolution over time, enabling a standard, responsive and efficient delivery of operational and strategic objectives.

APO03 Security-specific Process Goals and Metrics

Process Goals	Related Metrics
1. Information security requirements are embedded within the enterprise architecture and translated into a formal information security architecture.	• Number of exceptions to information security architecture standards
2. Information security architecture is understood as part of the overall enterprise architecture.	• Number of deviations between information security architecture and enterprise architecture
3. Information security architecture is aligned and evolves with changes to the enterprise architecture.	• Date of last review and/or update to information security controls applied to enterprise architecture
4. An information security architecture framework and methodology are used to enable reuse of information security components across the enterprise.	• Percent of projects that use the information security architecture framework and methodology • Number of people trained in the information security framework and methodology

APO03 Security-specific Process Practices, Inputs/Outputs and Activities

Management Practice	Security-specific Inputs (in Addition to COBIT 5 Inputs)		Security-specific Outputs (in Addition to COBIT 5 Outputs)	
	From	Description	Description	To
APO03.01 Develop the enterprise architecture vision. The architecture vision provides a first-cut, high-level description of the baseline and target architectures, covering the business, information, data, application and technology domains. The architecture vision provides the sponsor with a key tool to sell the benefits of the proposed capability to stakeholders within the enterprise. The architecture vision describes how the new capability will meet enterprise goals and strategic objectives and address stakeholder concerns when implemented.	APO02.04	Information security capability benchmark	• Information security architecture vision • Information security value proposition, goals and metrics	Internal
	APO02.05	Information security strategy		

Security-specific Activities (in Addition to COBIT 5 Activities)

1. Define information security objectives and requirements for the enterprise architecture.
2. Define the information security value proposition and related goals and metrics.
3. Consider industry best practices in building the information security architecture vision.

Management Practice	Security-specific Inputs (in Addition to COBIT 5 Inputs)		Security-specific Outputs (in Addition to COBIT 5 Outputs)	
	From	Description	Description	To
APO03.02 Define reference architecture. The reference architecture describes the current and target architectures for the business, information, data, application and technology domains.	Outside *COBIT 5 for Information Security*	Enterprise architecture	Information security target architecture definition	APO03.03
			Baseline domain descriptions and architecture definition	APO13.02
			Information architecture model	DSS05.03 DSS05.04 DSS05.06

Security-specific Activities (in Addition to COBIT 5 Activities)

1. Ensure inclusion of information security artefacts, policies and standards in the architecture repository.
2. Ensure that information security is integrated across all architectural domains (e.g., business, information, data, applications, technology).

Align, Plan and Organise

Align, Plan and Organise

AP003 Security-specific Process Practices, Inputs/Outputs and Activities *(cont.)*				
	Security-specific Inputs (in Addition to COBIT 5 Inputs)		Security-specific Outputs (in Addition to COBIT 5 Outputs)	
Management Practice	**From**	**Description**	**Description**	**To**
AP003.03 Select opportunities and solutions. Rationalise the gaps between baseline and target architectures, taking both business and technical perspectives, and logically group them into project work packages. Integrate the project with any related IT-enabled investment programmes to ensure that the architectural initiatives are aligned with and enable these initiatives as part of overall enterprise change. Make this a collaborative effort with key enterprise stakeholders from business and IT to assess the enterprise's transformation readiness, and identify opportunities, solutions and all implementation constraints.	AP003.02	Information security target architecture definition	Information security architecture implementation and migration strategy	AP003.04
Security-specific Activities (in Addition to COBIT 5 Activities)				
1. Ensure inclusion of information security requirements when analysing gaps and selecting solutions for the enterprise.				

	Security-specific Inputs (in Addition to COBIT 5 Inputs)		Security-specific Outputs (in Addition to COBIT 5 Outputs)	
Management Practice	**From**	**Description**	**Description**	**To**
AP003.04 Define architecture implementation. Create a viable implementation and migration plan in alignment with the programme and project portfolios. Ensure that the plan is closely co-ordinated to ensure that value is delivered and the required resources are available to complete the necessary work.	AP003.03	Information security architecture implementation and migration strategy	Detailed information security architecture and service implementation plan	Internal
Security-specific Activities (in Addition to COBIT 5 Activities)				
1. Align information security and IT architecture.				

	Security-specific Inputs (in Addition to COBIT 5 Inputs)		Security-specific Outputs (in Addition to COBIT 5 Outputs)	
Management Practice	**From**	**Description**	**Description**	**To**
AP003.05 Provide enterprise architecture services. The provision of enterprise architecture services within the enterprise includes guidance to and monitoring of implementation projects, formalising ways of working through architecture contracts, and measuring and communicating architecture's value-add and compliance monitoring.			Information security architecture service implementation guidance	DSS01.01
Security-specific Activities (in Addition to COBIT 5 Activities)				
1. Develop information security standards and design patterns in support of the enterprise architecture.				
2. Ensure that any technology acquisitions and business change activities include information security reviews to confirm that information security requirements are met.				

For more information regarding the related enablers, please consult:
• Appendix E. Detailed Guidance: Information Enabler, E.2. Information Security Strategy
• Appendix G. Detailed Guidance: People, Skills and Competencies Enabler, G.4 Information Security Architecture Development

APO04 Manage Innovation	Area: Management Domain: Align, Plan and Organise

COBIT 5 Process Description
Maintain an awareness of information technology and related service trends, identify innovation opportunities, and plan how to benefit from innovation in relation to business needs. Analyse what opportunities for business innovation or improvement can be created by emerging technologies, services or IT-enabled business innovation, as well as through existing established technologies and by business and IT process innovation. Influence strategic planning and enterprise architecture decisions.

COBIT 5 Process Purpose Statement
Achieve competitive advantage, business innovation, and improved operational effectiveness and efficiency by exploiting information technology developments.

APO04 Security-specific Process Goals and Metrics

Security-specific Process Goals	Related Metrics
1. Innovation is promoted within the information security programme.	• Percent of budget assigned to information security research and development
2. Information security requirements are taken into account when innovation is enabled	• Number of job functions including innovation aspects

APO04 Security-specific Process Practices, Inputs/Outputs and Activities

Management Practice	Security-specific Inputs (in Addition to COBIT 5 Inputs)		Security-specific Outputs (in Addition to COBIT 5 Outputs)	
	From	Description	Description	To
APO04.01 Create an environment conducive to innovation. Create an environment that is conducive to innovation, considering issues such as culture, reward, collaboration, technology forums, and mechanisms to promote and capture employee ideas.			Information security innovation plan	APO04.06

Security-specific Activities (in Addition to COBIT 5 Activities)

1. Maintain information security principles and policies in support of innovation while managing information risk.

2. Establish connections to research and other security advisory services.

Management Practice	Security-specific Inputs (in Addition to COBIT 5 Inputs)		Security-specific Outputs (in Addition to COBIT 5 Outputs)	
	From	Description	Description	To
APO04.02 Maintain an understanding of the enterprise environment. Work with relevant stakeholders to understand their challenges. Maintain an adequate understanding of enterprise strategy and the competitive environment or other constraints so that opportunities enabled by new technologies can be identified.	Outside *COBIT 5 for Information Security*	External research	Information security impact assessments of new initiatives	Internal

Security-specific Activities (in Addition to COBIT 5 Activities)

1. Maintain an understanding of information security drivers to identify opportunities and limitations of technological innovation.

2. Determine the effects and impact of innovations on technology, the environment and information security.

Management Practice	Security-specific Inputs (in Addition to COBIT 5 Inputs)		Security-specific Outputs (in Addition to COBIT 5 Outputs)	
	From	Description	Description	To
APO04.03 Monitor and scan the technology environment. Perform systematic monitoring and scanning of the enterprise's external environment to identify emerging technologies that have the potential to create value (e.g., by realising the enterprise strategy, optimising costs, avoiding obsolescence, and better enabling enterprise and IT processes). Monitor the marketplace, competitive landscape, industry sectors, and legal and regulatory trends to be able to analyse emerging technologies or innovation ideas in the enterprise context.	Outside *COBIT 5 for Information Security*	External research	Identified emerging trends in information security	APO08.02

Security-specific Activities (in Addition to COBIT 5 Activities)

1. Perform research and scan the external environment to identify emerging trends in information security.

2. Encourage stakeholder feedback on information security innovation.

Align, Plan and Organise

Align, Plan and Organise

AP004 Security-specific Process Practices, Inputs/Outputs and Activities *(cont.)*				
	Security-specific Inputs (in Addition to COBIT 5 Inputs)		**Security-specific Outputs (in Addition to COBIT 5 Outputs)**	
Management Practice	**From**	**Description**	**Description**	**To**
APO04.04 Assess the potential of emerging technologies and innovation ideas. Analyse identified emerging technologies and/or other IT innovation suggestions. Work with stakeholders to validate assumptions on the potential of new technologies and innovation.	APO02.02	Information security capabilities	Information security requirements compliance assessment	APO04.05
	APO02.06	Information security plan		
	BAI02.01	Information security requirements		
Security-specific Activities (in Addition to COBIT 5 Activities)				
1. Evaluate identified innovations based on information security drivers.				
2. Assist proof-of-concept activities for innovation initiatives to ensure coverage of information security requirements. Evaluate compliance to these requirements.				
	Security-specific Inputs (in Addition to COBIT 5 Inputs)		**Security-specific Outputs (in Addition to COBIT 5 Outputs)**	
Management Practice	**From**	**Description**	**Description**	**To**
APO04.05 Recommend appropriate further initiatives. Evaluate and monitor the results of proof-of-concept initiatives and, if favourable, generate recommendations for further initiatives and gain stakeholder support.	APO02.06	Information security plan	Information security advice on test results from proof-of-concept	Internal
	APO04.04	Information security requirements compliance assessment		
Security-specific Activities (in Addition to COBIT 5 Activities)				
1. Provide information security advice based on the proof-of-concept results of IT innovation initiatives.				
	Security-specific Inputs (in Addition to COBIT 5 Inputs)		**Security-specific Outputs (in Addition to COBIT 5 Outputs)**	
Management Practice	**From**	**Description**	**Description**	**To**
APO04.06 Monitor the implementation and use of innovation. Monitor the implementation and use of emerging technologies and innovations during integration, adoption and for the full economic life cycle to ensure that the promised benefits are realised and to identify lessons learned.	APO04.01	Information security innovation plan	Adjusted innovation plans	Internal
Security-specific Activities (in Addition to COBIT 5 Activities)				
1. Measure security benefits and risk during proof-of-concept and other innovation activities.				

APO05 Manage Portfolio	Area: Management Domain: Align, Plan and Organise

COBIT 5 Process Description
Execute the strategic direction set for investments in line with the enterprise architecture vision and the desired characteristics of the investment and related services portfolios, and consider the different categories of investments and the resources and funding constraints. Evaluate, prioritise and balance programmes and services, managing demand within resource and funding constraints, based on their alignment with strategic objectives, enterprise worth and risk. Move selected programmes into the active services portfolio for execution. Monitor the performance of the overall portfolio of services and programmes, proposing adjustments as necessary in response to programme and service performance or changing enterprise priorities.

COBIT 5 Process Purpose Statement
Optimise the performance of the overall portfolio of programmes in response to programme and service performance and changing enterprise priorities and demands.

APO05 Security-specific Process Goals and Metrics

Security-specific Process Goals	Related Metrics
1. Information security investments are allocated in accordance to risk appetite.	• Number of information security investment business cases not performing risk assessments
2. Information security programme changes are reflected in relevant IT service, asset and resource portfolios.	• Percent of changes from the information security programme reflected in relevant portfolios

APO05 Security-specific Process Practices, Inputs/Outputs and Activities

Management Practice	Security-specific Inputs (in Addition to COBIT 5 Inputs)		Security-specific Outputs (in Addition to COBIT 5 Outputs)	
	From	Description	Description	To
APO05.01 Establish the target investment mix. Review and ensure clarity of the enterprise and IT strategies and current services. Define an appropriate investment mix based on cost, alignment with strategy, and financial measures such as cost and expected ROI over the full economic life cycle, degree of risk, and type of benefit, for the programmes in the portfolio. Adjust the enterprise and IT strategies where necessary.	Outside *COBIT 5 for Information Security*	Risk assessment	Information security target investment mix	APO05.02

Security-specific Activities (in Addition to COBIT 5 Activities)
1. Develop the information security target investment mix, taking into account enterprise risk, financial and non-financial benefits, and potential return on the initiatives.

Management Practice	Security-specific Inputs (in Addition to COBIT 5 Inputs)		Security-specific Outputs (in Addition to COBIT 5 Outputs)	
	From	Description	Description	To
APO05.02 Determine the availability and sources of funds. Determine potential sources of funds, different funding options and the implications of the funding source on the investment return expectations.	APO05.01	Information security target investment mix	Funding options	APO05.03

Security-specific Activities (in Addition to COBIT 5 Activities)
1. Review internal and external possibilities to cover the required information security resources.

Management Practice	Security-specific Inputs (in Addition to COBIT 5 Inputs)		Security-specific Outputs (in Addition to COBIT 5 Outputs)	
	From	Description	Description	To
APO05.03 Evaluate and select programmes to fund. Based on the overall investment portfolio mix requirements, evaluate and prioritise programme business cases, and decide on investment proposals. Allocate funds and initiate programmes.	APO05.02	Funding options	Information security programme	Internal

Security-specific Activities (in Addition to COBIT 5 Activities)
1. Ensure the existence of an information security programme.

Align, Plan and Organise

AP005 Security-specific Process Practices, Inputs/Outputs and Activities *(cont.)*				
Management Practice	**Security-specific Inputs (in Addition to COBIT 5 Inputs)**		**Security-specific Outputs (in Addition to COBIT 5 Outputs)**	
	From	**Description**	**Description**	**To**
AP005.04 Monitor, optimise and report on investment portfolio performance. On a regular basis, monitor and optimise the performance of the investment portfolio and individual programmes throughout the entire investment life cycle.				

Security-specific Activities (in Addition to COBIT 5 Activities)

0. Information security-specific guidance is not relevant for this practice. The generic COBIT 5 activities can be used as further guidance.

Management Practice	**Security-specific Inputs (in Addition to COBIT 5 Inputs)**		**Security-specific Outputs (in Addition to COBIT 5 Outputs)**	
	From	**Description**	**Description**	**To**
AP005.05 Maintain portfolios. Maintain portfolios of investment programmes and projects, IT services and IT assets.				

Security-specific Activities (in Addition to COBIT 5 Activities)

0. Information security-specific guidance is not relevant for this practice. The generic COBIT 5 activities can be used as further guidance.

Management Practice	**Security-specific Inputs (in Addition to COBIT 5 Inputs)**		**Security-specific Outputs (in Addition to COBIT 5 Outputs)**	
	From	**Description**	**Description**	**To**
AP005.06 Manage benefits achievement. Monitor the benefits of providing and maintaining appropriate IT services and capabilities, based on the agreed-on and current business case.	Outside *COBIT 5 for Information Security*	Programme budget	Updated information security risk profile	Internal

Security-specific Activities (in Addition to COBIT 5 Activities)

1. Provide input on the achievement of confidentiality, integrity and availability of information to perform benefits achievement management.

2. To illustrate benefits achievement, assess the changes in the information security risk profile.

For more information regarding the related enablers, please consult:
• Appendix E. Detailed Guidance: Information Enabler, E.4. Information Security Plan

AP006 Manage Budget and Costs	Area: Management Domain: Align, Plan and Organise

COBIT 5 Process Description
Manage the IT-related financial activities in both the business and IT functions, covering budget, cost and benefit management, and prioritisation of spending through the use of formal budgeting practices and a fair and equitable system of allocating costs to the enterprise. Consult stakeholders to identify and control the total costs and benefits within the context of the IT strategic and tactical plans, and initiate corrective action where needed.

COBIT 5 Process Purpose Statement
Foster partnership between IT and enterprise stakeholders to enable the effective and efficient use of IT-related resources and provide transparency and accountability of the cost and business value of solutions and services. Enable the enterprise to make informed decisions regarding the use of IT solutions and services.

AP006 Security-specific Process Goals and Metrics

Security-specific Process Goals	Related Metrics
1. Allocation of budget and costs for information security is prioritised effectively.	• Percent of alignment between IT resources and high-priority information security and control initiatives • Number of resource allocation issues due to information security incidents • Number of additional budget requests due to information security incidents

AP006 Security-specific Process Practices, Inputs/Outputs and Activities

Management Practice	Security-specific Inputs (in Addition to COBIT 5 Inputs)		Security-specific Outputs (in Addition to COBIT 5 Outputs)	
	From	Description	Description	To
AP006.01 Manage finance and accounting. Establish and maintain a method to account for all IT-related costs, investments and depreciation as an integral part of the enterprise financial systems and chart of accounts to manage the investments and costs of IT. Capture and allocate actual costs, analyse variances between forecasts and actual costs, and report using the enterprise's financial measurement systems.				

Security-specific Activities (in Addition to COBIT 5 Activities)

0. Information security-specific guidance is not relevant for this practice. The generic COBIT 5 activities can be used as further guidance.

Management Practice	Security-specific Inputs (in Addition to COBIT 5 Inputs)		Security-specific Outputs (in Addition to COBIT 5 Outputs)	
	From	Description	Description	To
AP006.02 Prioritise resource allocation. Implement a decision-making process to prioritise the allocation of resources and rules for discretionary investments by individual business units. Include the potential use of external service providers and consider the buy, develop and rent options.			Initiative prioritisation	AP006.03

Security-specific Activities (in Addition to COBIT 5 Activities)

1. Ensure that the criteria for prioritisation in accordance with the information risk profile are taken into account when prioritising resource allocations.

Management Practice	Security-specific Inputs (in Addition to COBIT 5 Inputs)		Security-specific Outputs (in Addition to COBIT 5 Outputs)	
	From	Description	Description	To
AP006.03 Create and maintain budgets. Prepare a budget reflecting the investment priorities supporting strategic objectives based on the portfolio of IT-enabled programmes and IT services.	AP006.02	Initiative prioritisation	Information security budget	Internal

Security-specific Activities (in Addition to COBIT 5 Activities)

1. Develop an information security budget.

Align, Plan and Organise

AP006 Security-specific Process Practices, Inputs/Outputs and Activities *(cont.)*				
	Security-specific Inputs (in Addition to COBIT 5 Inputs)		Security-specific Outputs (in Addition to COBIT 5 Outputs)	
Management Practice	**From**	**Description**	**Description**	**To**
AP006.04 Model and allocate costs. Establish and use an IT costing model based on the service definition, ensuring that allocation of costs for services is identifiable, measurable and predictable, to encourage the responsible use of resources including those provided by service providers. Regularly review and benchmark the appropriateness of the cost/chargeback model to maintain its relevance and appropriateness to the evolving business and IT activities.				
Security-specific Activities (in Addition to COBIT 5 Activities)				
0. Information security-specific guidance is not relevant for this practice. The generic COBIT 5 activities can be used as further guidance.				
	Security-specific Inputs (in Addition to COBIT 5 Inputs)		Security-specific Outputs (in Addition to COBIT 5 Outputs)	
Management Practice	**From**	**Description**	**Description**	**To**
AP006.05 Manage costs. Implement a cost management process comparing actual costs to budgets. Costs should be monitored and reported and, in case of deviations, identified in a timely manner and their impact on enterprise processes and services assessed.				
Security-specific Activities (in Addition to COBIT 5 Activities)				
0. Information security-specific guidance is not relevant for this practice. The generic COBIT 5 activities can be used as further guidance.				

APO07 Manage Human Resources	Area: Management Domain: Align, Plan and Organise

COBIT 5 Process Description
Provide a structured approach to ensure optimal structuring, placement, decision rights and skills of human resources. This includes communicating the defined roles and responsibilities, learning and growth plans, and performance expectations, supported with competent and motivated people.

COBIT 5 Process Purpose Statement
Optimise human resources capabilities to meet enterprise objectives.

APO07 Security-specific Process Goals and Metrics

Security-specific Process Goals	Related Metrics
1. HR capabilities and processes are aligned with information security requirements.	• Percent of employees provided security induction • Rate of turnover in information security • Hiring cycle or on-boarding time • Qualifications of staff in terms of certifications, education and years of experience

APO07 Security-specific Process Practices, Inputs/Outputs and Activities

Management Practice	Security-specific Inputs (in Addition to COBIT 5 Inputs)		Security-specific Outputs (in Addition to COBIT 5 Outputs)	
	From	Description	Description	To
APO07.01 Maintain adequate and appropriate staffing. Evaluate staffing requirements on a regular basis or upon major changes to the enterprise or operational or IT environments to ensure that the enterprise has sufficient human resources to support enterprise goals and objectives. Staffing includes both internal and external resources.	APO01.03	Information security and related policies	Information security requirements for the staffing process	Internal
	APO02.06	Information security plan		
	Outside *COBIT 5 for Information Security*	Local regulations		

Security-specific Activities (in Addition to COBIT 5 Activities)

1. Ensure that information security requirements in the HR staffing process are incorporated in the IT recruitment process for employees, contractors and vendors.

Management Practice	Security-specific Inputs (in Addition to COBIT 5 Inputs)		Security-specific Outputs (in Addition to COBIT 5 Outputs)	
	From	Description	Description	To
APO07.02 Identify key IT personnel. Identify key IT personnel while minimising reliance on a single individual performing a critical job function through knowledge capture (documentation), knowledge sharing, succession planning and staff backup.	Outside *COBIT 5 for Information Security*	• List of internal and external regulations affecting vacation and other personnel rights and obligations • Business impact analysis (BIA) of business processes • List of internal and external regulations affecting segregation of duties, HR or security (personnel) policies • List of business functions and roles and their accountabilities and responsibilities relative to business processes	• Emergency contact lists • Succession plans	Internal

Security-specific Activities (in Addition to COBIT 5 Activities)

1. Ensure the segregation of duties in critical positions.

Align, Plan and Organise

Align, Plan and Organise

AP007 Security-specific Process Practices, Inputs/Outputs and Activities *(cont.)*

Management Practice	Security-specific Inputs (in Addition to COBIT 5 Inputs)		Security-specific Outputs (in Addition to COBIT 5 Outputs)	
	From	Description	Description	To
AP007.03 Maintain the skills and competencies of personnel. Define and manage the skills and competencies required of personnel. Regularly verify that personnel have the competencies to fulfil their roles on the basis of their education, training and/or experience, and verify that these competencies are being maintained, using qualification and certification programmes where appropriate. Provide employees with ongoing learning and opportunities to maintain their knowledge, skills and competencies at a level required to achieve enterprise goals.	Outside *COBIT 5 for Information Security*	• Personnel lists • List of contractors • Personnel skills	Information security training plan	AP007.04
			Information security awareness training	Internal

Security-specific Activities (in Addition to COBIT 5 Activities)

1. Provide professional development training and programmes on information security.

2. Use certification to ensure a quality information security professional skill set.

3. Establish appropriate enterprisewide education, training and awareness programmes for information security.

Management Practice	Security-specific Inputs (in Addition to COBIT 5 Inputs)		Security-specific Outputs (in Addition to COBIT 5 Outputs)	
	From	Description	Description	To
AP007.04 Evaluate employee job performance. Perform timely performance evaluations on a regular basis against individual objectives derived from the enterprise's goals, established standards, specific job responsibilities, and the skills and competency framework. Employees should receive coaching on performance and conduct whenever appropriate.	AP007.03	Information security training plan	Personnel information security evaluations	Internal
	MEA01.02	Agreed-on information security metrics and targets		
	Outside *COBIT 5 for Information Security*	HR policy		

Security-specific Activities (in Addition to COBIT 5 Activities)

1. Incorporate information security criteria in the personnel evaluation process.

Management Practice	Security-specific Inputs (in Addition to COBIT 5 Inputs)		Security-specific Outputs (in Addition to COBIT 5 Outputs)	
	From	Description	Description	To
AP007.05 Plan and track the usage of IT and business human resources. Understand and track the current and future demand for business and IT human resources with responsibilities for enterprise IT. Identify shortfalls and provide input into sourcing plans, enterprise and IT recruitment processes sourcing plans, and business and IT recruitment processes.	AP002.06	Information security plan	• Resource performance tracking plan and indicators • Resource allocation plan	Internal
	Outside *COBIT 5 for Information Security*	• Process resource requirements • Budget allocations • Personnel lists • Personnel skills		

Security-specific Activities (in Addition to COBIT 5 Activities)

1. Manage allocation of information security staff according to the business requirements.

AP007 Security-specific Process Practices, Inputs/Outputs and Activities *(cont.)*				
	Security-specific Inputs (in Addition to COBIT 5 Inputs)		Security-specific Outputs (in Addition to COBIT 5 Outputs)	
Management Practice	**From**	**Description**	**Description**	**To**
APO07.06 Manage contract staff. Ensure that consultants and contract personnel who support the enterprise with IT skills know and comply with the organisation's policies and meet agreed-on contractual requirements.	APO01.03	Information security and related policies	Non-disclosure agreements and other policies signed by other parties	Internal
	APO02.06	Information security plan		
	BAI02.01	Information security requirements		
Security-specific Activities (in Addition to COBIT 5 Activities)				
1. Obtain formal agreement from staff on information security policies and requirements.				

For more information regarding the related enablers, please consult:
• Appendix E. Detailed Guidance: Information Enabler, E.7. Awareness Material • Appendix G. Detailed Guidance: People, Skills and Competencies Enabler

Align, Plan and Organise

Page intentionally left blank

Align, Plan and Organise

APO08 Manage Relationships	Area: Management Domain: Align, Plan and Organise

COBIT 5 Process Description
Manage the relationship between the business and IT in a formalised and transparent way that ensures a focus on achieving a common and shared goal of successful enterprise outcomes in support of strategic goals and within the constraint of budgets and risk tolerance. Base the relationship on mutual trust, using open and understandable terms and common language and a willingness to take ownership and accountability for key decisions.

COBIT 5 Process Purpose Statement
Create improved outcomes, increased confidence, trust in IT and effective use of resources.

APO08 Security-specific Process Goals and Metrics

Security-specific Process Goals	Related Metrics
1. Co-ordination, communication and a liaison structure are established between the information security function and various other stakeholders.	• Percent of information security representation in business committees
2. Stakeholders recognise information security as a business enabler.	• Inclusion rate of information security initiatives in investment proposals

APO08 Security-specific Process Practices, Inputs/Outputs and Activities

Management Practice	Security-specific Inputs (in Addition to COBIT 5 Inputs)		Security-specific Outputs (in Addition to COBIT 5 Outputs)	
	From	Description	Description	To
APO08.01 Understand business expectations. Understand current business issues and objectives and business expectations for IT. Ensure that requirements are understood, managed and communicated, and their status agreed on and approved.	Outside *COBIT 5 for Information Security*	Business goals and objectives	Understanding of business processes of the enterprise	APO08.02 APO08.03

Security-specific Activities (in Addition to COBIT 5 Activities)
1. Understand the business and how information security enables/affects it.

Management Practice	From	Description	Description	To
APO08.02 Identify opportunities, risk and constraints for IT to enhance the business. Identify potential opportunities for IT to be an enabler of enhanced enterprise performance.	APO04.03	Identified emerging trends in information security	Information security innovations	APO08.03
	APO08.01	Understanding of business processes of the enterprise		

Security-specific Activities (in Addition to COBIT 5 Activities)
1. Understand information security trends and new technologies and how they can be applied innovatively to enhance business process performance.

Management Practice	From	Description	Description	To
APO08.03 Manage the business relationship. Manage the relationship with customers (business representatives). Ensure that relationship roles and responsibilities are defined and assigned, and communication is facilitated.	APO08.01	Understanding of business processes of the enterprise	Strategy to obtain stakeholder commitment	Internal
	APO08.02	Information security innovations		
	DSS02.02	Classified and prioritised information security incidents and service requests		

Security-specific Activities (in Addition to COBIT 5 Activities)
1. Establish an approach for influencing key contacts regarding information security.

APO08 Security-specific Process Practices, Inputs/Outputs and Activities *(cont.)*				
	Security-specific Inputs (in Addition to COBIT 5 Inputs)		Security-specific Outputs (in Addition to COBIT 5 Outputs)	
Management Practice	**From**	**Description**	**Description**	**To**
APO08.04 Co-ordinate and communicate. Work with stakeholders and co-ordinate the end-to-end delivery of IT services and solutions provided to the business.	Outside *COBIT 5 for Information Security*	Enterprise communication plan	Information security communication strategy	Internal

Security-specific Activities (in Addition to COBIT 5 Activities)
1. Establish appropriate communication channels between the information security function and the business.
2. Establish the appropriate reporting and metrics regarding information security.

	Security-specific Inputs (in Addition to COBIT 5 Inputs)		Security-specific Outputs (in Addition to COBIT 5 Outputs)	
Management Practice	**From**	**Description**	**Description**	**To**
APO08.05 Provide input to the continual improvement of services. Continually improve and evolve IT-enabled services and service delivery to the enterprise to align with changing enterprise and technology requirements.	APO02.02	Information security capabilities	Integration of information security in continual improvement process	Internal
	BAI02.01	Information security requirements		

Security-specific Activities (in Addition to COBIT 5 Activities)
1. Incorporate information security requirements in the continual improvement process.

For more information regarding the related enablers, please consult:
• Appendix C. Detailed Guidance: Organisational Structures Enabler, C.5. Information Custodians/Business Owners

Align, Plan and Organise

APO09 Manage Service Agreements	Area: Management Domain: Align, Plan and Organise

COBIT 5 Process Description
Align IT-enabled services and service levels with enterprise needs and expectations, including identification, specification, design, publishing, agreement, and monitoring of IT services, service levels and performance indicators.

COBIT 5 Process Purpose Statement
Ensure that IT services and service levels meet current and future enterprise needs.

APO09 Security-specific Process Goals and Metrics

Security-specific Process Goals	Related Metrics
1. Service level agreements (SLAs) take into account information security requirements.	• Percent of service agreements that include information security goals

APO09 Security-specific Process Practices, Inputs/Outputs and Activities

Management Practice	Security-specific Inputs (in Addition to COBIT 5 Inputs)		Security-specific Outputs (in Addition to COBIT 5 Outputs)	
	From	Description	Description	To
APO09.01 Identify IT services. Analyse business requirements and the way in which IT-enabled services and service levels support business processes. Discuss and agree on potential services and service levels with the business, and compare them with the current service portfolio to identify new or changed services or service level options.			Information security requirements of the identified IT services	APO09.02

Security-specific Activities (in Addition to COBIT 5 Activities)
1. Identify the information security requirements of the identified IT services.
2. Develop and verify portfolio information security services.

Management Practice	Security-specific Inputs (in Addition to COBIT 5 Inputs)		Security-specific Outputs (in Addition to COBIT 5 Outputs)	
	From	Description	Description	To
APO09.02 Catalogue IT-enabled services. Define and maintain one or more service catalogues for relevant target groups. Publish and maintain live IT-enabled services in the service catalogues.	APO09.01	Information security requirements of the identified IT services	Information security service catalogue	Internal

Security-specific Activities (in Addition to COBIT 5 Activities)
1. Publish an information security service catalogue.

Management Practice	Security-specific Inputs (in Addition to COBIT 5 Inputs)		Security-specific Outputs (in Addition to COBIT 5 Outputs)	
	From	Description	Description	To
APO09.03 Define and prepare service agreements. Define and prepare service agreements based on the options in the service catalogues. Include internal operational agreements.	BAI03.11	Information security services	SLAs	APO09.04 DSS05.02 DSS05.03
			Operating level agreements (OLAs)	DSS05.03

Security-specific Activities (in Addition to COBIT 5 Activities)
1. Include information security requirements in all SLAs.

Management Practice	Security-specific Inputs (in Addition to COBIT 5 Inputs)		Security-specific Outputs (in Addition to COBIT 5 Outputs)	
	From	Description	Description	To
APO09.4 Monitor and report service levels. Monitor service levels, report on achievements and identify trends. Provide the appropriate management information to aid performance management.	APO09.03	SLAs	Information security service level performance reports	APO09.05
	BAI03.11	Information security services		

Security-specific Activities (in Addition to COBIT 5 Activities)
1. Monitor information security effectiveness within service level monitoring.

Align, Plan and Organise

Align, Plan and Organise

AP009 Security-specific Process Practices, Inputs/Outputs and Activities *(cont.)*				
	Security-specific Inputs (in Addition to COBIT 5 Inputs)		**Security-specific Outputs (in Addition to COBIT 5 Outputs)**	
Management Practice	**From**	**Description**	**Description**	**To**
AP009.05 Review service agreements and contracts. Conduct periodic reviews of the service agreements and revise when needed.	AP002.02	Information security capabilities	Updated SLAs	Internal
	AP002.06	Information security plan		
	AP009.04	Information security service level performance reports		
	BAI02.01	Information security requirements		
Security-specific Activities (in Addition to COBIT 5 Activities)				
1 Periodically review information security requirements based on updated business needs.				

For more information regarding the related enablers, please consult:
• Appendix E. Detailed Guidance: Information Enabler, E.9. Information Security Dashboard
• Appendix F. Detailed Guidance: Services, Infrastructure and Applications Enabler

APO10 Manage Suppliers	Area: Management Domains: Align, Plan and Organise

COBIT 5 Process Description
Manage IT-related services provided by all types of suppliers to meet enterprise requirements, including the selection of suppliers, management of relationships, management of contracts, and reviewing and monitoring of supplier performance for effectiveness and compliance.

COBIT 5 Process Purpose Statement
Minimise the risk associated with non-performing suppliers and ensure competitive pricing.

APO10 Security-specific Process Goals and Metrics

Security-specific Process Goals	Related Metrics
1. Suppliers and contracts are assessed regularly and appropriate risk mitigation plans are provided.	• Percent of suppliers meeting agreed-on information security requirements • Number of system information security breaches caused by suppliers • Number of information security events leading to information security incidents • Frequency of information security incidents with suppliers • Number of independent information security reviews of suppliers
2. Suppliers recognise information security as an important business enabler.	• Percent of supplier contracts that include information security requirements • Number of information security incidents related to suppliers

APO10 Security-specific Process Practices, Inputs/Outputs and Activities

Management Practice	Security-specific Inputs (in Addition to COBIT 5 Inputs)		Security-specific Outputs (in Addition to COBIT 5 Outputs)	
	From	Description	Description	To
APO10.01 Identify and evaluate supplier relationships and contracts. Identify suppliers and associated contracts and categorise them into type, significance and criticality. Establish supplier and contract evaluation criteria and evaluate the overall portfolio of existing and alternative suppliers and contracts.	Outside *COBIT 5 for Information Security*	Vendor risk analysis	Supplier catalogue	APO10.04 APO10.05 BAI03.04

Security-specific Activities (in Addition to COBIT 5 Activities)

1. Conduct information risk assessments and define the information risk profile.

2. Define the supplier relationship and requirements based on the information risk profile.

Management Practice	Security-specific Inputs (in Addition to COBIT 5 Inputs)		Security-specific Outputs (in Addition to COBIT 5 Outputs)	
	From	Description	Description	To
APO10.02 Select suppliers. Select suppliers according to a fair and formal practice to ensure a viable best fit based on specified requirements. Requirements should be optimised with input from potential suppliers.				

Security-specific Activities (in Addition to COBIT 5 Activities)

0. Information security-specific guidance is not relevant for this practice. The generic COBIT 5 activities can be used as further guidance.

Management Practice	Security-specific Inputs (in Addition to COBIT 5 Inputs)		Security-specific Outputs (in Addition to COBIT 5 Outputs)	
	From	Description	Description	To
APO10.03 Manage supplier relationships and contracts. Formalise and manage the supplier relationship for each supplier. Manage, maintain and monitor contracts and service delivery. Ensure that new or changed contracts conform to enterprise standards and legal and regulatory requirements. Deal with contractual disputes.				

Security-specific Activities (in Addition to COBIT 5 Activities)

0. Information security-specific guidance is not relevant for this practice. The generic COBIT 5 activities can be used as further guidance.

Align, Plan and Organise

APO10 Security-specific Process Practices, Inputs/Outputs and Activities *(cont.)*				
	Security-specific Inputs (in Addition to COBIT 5 Inputs)		**Security-specific Outputs (in Addition to COBIT 5 Outputs)**	
Management Practice	**From**	**Description**	**Description**	**To**
APO10.04 Manage supplier risk. Identify and manage risk relating to suppliers' ability to continually provide secure, efficient and effective service delivery.	APO10.01	Supplier catalogue	Updated vendor risk rating	APO10.05
Security-specific Activities (in Addition to COBIT 5 Activities)				
1. Periodically reassess supplier risk profiles based on information security requirements and other requirements.				
	Security-specific Inputs (in Addition to COBIT 5 Inputs)		**Security-specific Outputs (in Addition to COBIT 5 Outputs)**	
Management Practice	**From**	**Description**	**Description**	**To**
APO10.05 Monitor supplier performance and compliance. Periodically review the overall performance of suppliers, compliance to contract requirements, and value for money, and address identified issues.	APO10.01	Supplier catalogue	Supplier compliance monitoring review results	Internal
	APO10.04	Updated vendor risk rating		
Security-specific Activities (in Addition to COBIT 5 Activities)				
1. Monitor whether suppliers guarantee a secure, efficient and effective service delivery.				

For more information regarding the related enablers, please consult:
• Appendix C. Detailed Guidance: Organisational Structures Enabler, C.4. Enterprise Risk Management Committee
• Appendix G. Detailed Guidance: People, Skills and Competencies Enabler, G.3. Information Risk Management

APO11 Manage Quality	Area: Management Domain: Align, Plan and Organise

COBIT 5 Product Description
Define and communicate quality requirements in all processes, procedures and the related enterprise outcomes, including controls, ongoing monitoring, and the use of proven practices and standards in continuous improvement and efficiency efforts.

COBIT 5 Process Purpose Statement
Ensure consistent delivery of solutions and services to meet the quality requirements of the enterprise and satisfy stakeholder needs.

APO11 Security-specific Process Goals and Metrics

Security-specific Process Goals	Related Metrics
1. Operational information security quality requirements for information security services are defined and implemented.	• Percent of stakeholders satisfied with quality of information security services, based on surveys • Number of services with a formal information security plan • Frequency of reporting (weekly, monthly, quarterly, annually) • Timeliness of resolution of information security issues (incidents, vulnerabilities, audit issues, etc.) • Percent of information security staff with professional credentials (CISM, CISSP, etc.) • Number of continuing professional education (CPE) hours or hours of attendance at training or industry events

APO11 Security-specific Process Practices, Inputs/Outputs and Activities

Management Practice	Security-specific Inputs (in Addition to COBIT 5 Inputs)		Security-specific Outputs (in Addition to COBIT 5 Outputs)	
	From	Description	Description	To
APO11.01 Establish a quality management system (QMS). Establish and maintain a QMS that provides a standard, formal and continuous approach to quality management for information, enabling technology and business processes that are aligned with business requirements and enterprise quality management.	APO01.06	Information security roles and responsibilities	Relevant information security best practices and standards	APO11.02
	APO02.02	Information security capabilities		
	APO02.06	Information security plan		

Security-specific Activities (in Addition to COBIT 5 Activities)
1. Determine information security best practices.

Management Practice	Security-specific Inputs (in Addition to COBIT 5 Inputs)		Security-specific Outputs (in Addition to COBIT 5 Outputs)	
	From	Description	Description	To
APO11.02 Define and manage quality standards, practices and procedures. Identify and maintain requirements, standards, procedures and practices for key processes to guide the enterprise in meeting the intent of the agreed-on QMS. This should be in line with the IT control framework requirements. Consider certification for key processes, organisational units, products or services.	APO11.01	Relevant information security best practices and standards	Information security quality standards	APO11.03 BAI03.06

Security-specific Activities (in Addition to COBIT 5 Activities)
1. Align the information security practices with the QMS.

Management Practice	Security-specific Inputs (in Addition to COBIT 5 Inputs)		Security-specific Outputs (in Addition to COBIT 5 Outputs)	
	From	Description	Description	To
APO11.03 Focus quality management on customers. Focus quality management on customers by determining their requirements and ensuring alignment with the quality management practices.	APO11.02	Information security quality standards	Information security quality SLAs agreed on and contractual clauses where appropriate	APO11.04

Security-specific Activities (in Addition to COBIT 5 Activities)
1. Obtain customer agreement on information security SLA requirements.

Align, Plan and Organise

Align, Plan and Organise

APO11 Security-specific Process Practices, Inputs/Outputs and Activities *(cont.)*				
	Security-specific Inputs (in Addition to COBIT 5 Inputs)		Security-specific Outputs (in Addition to COBIT 5 Outputs)	
Management Practice	From	Description	Description	To
APO11.04 Perform quality monitoring, control and reviews. Monitor the quality of processes and services on an ongoing basis as defined by the QMS. Define, plan and implement measurements to monitor customer satisfaction with quality as well as the value the QMS provides. The information gathered should be used by the process owners to improve quality.	APO11.03	Information security quality SLAs agreed on and contractual clauses where appropriate	Information security quality metrics implemented in line with best practices	APO11.05

Security-specific Activities (in Addition to COBIT 5 Activities)
1. Define information security quality metrics to measure the achievement of information security requirements and the efficient functioning of information security controls.
2. Monitor the information security quality metrics.
3. Take corrective action to address quality issues in the information security function.

	Security-specific Inputs (in Addition to COBIT 5 Inputs)		Security-specific Outputs (in Addition to COBIT 5 Outputs)	
Management Practice	From	Description	Description	To
APO11.05 Integrate quality management into solutions for development and service delivery. Incorporate relevant quality management practices into the definition, monitoring, reporting and ongoing management of solutions development and service offerings.	APO11.04	Information security quality metrics implemented in line with best practices	Link to information security incident reporting process	Internal

Security-specific Activities (in Addition to COBIT 5 Activities)
1. Identify, document and communicate root causes for information security issues with quality metrics.
2. Apply corrective practices to remediate quality issues.

	Security-specific Inputs (in Addition to COBIT 5 Inputs)		Security-specific Outputs (in Addition to COBIT 5 Outputs)	
Management Practice	From	Description	Description	To
APO11.06 Maintain continuous improvement. Maintain and regularly communicate an overall quality plan that promotes continuous improvement. This should include the need for, and benefits of, continuous improvement. Collect and analyse data about the QMS, and improve its effectiveness. Correct non-conformities to prevent recurrence. Promote a culture of quality and continual improvement.				

Security-specific Activities (in Addition to COBIT 5 Activities)
0. Information security-specific guidance is not relevant for this practice. The generic COBIT 5 activities can be used as further guidance.

AP012 Manage Risk	Area: Management Domain: Align, Plan and Organise

COBIT 5 Process Description
Continually identify, assess and reduce IT-related risk within levels of tolerance set by enterprise executive management.

COBIT 5 Process Purpose Statement
Integrate the management of IT-related enterprise risk with overall ERM, and balance the costs and benefits of managing IT-related enterprise risk.

AP012 Security-specific Process Goals and Metrics

Security-specific Process Goals	Related Metrics
1. A current and complete information risk profile exists for technology, applications and infrastructure within the enterprise.	• Existence, timeliness and completeness of risk profiles
2. Information security incident response is integrated with the overall risk management process to provide the capability to update the risk management portfolio.	• Number of incidents with appropriately designed risk ratings

AP012 Security-specific Process Practices, Inputs/Outputs and Activities

Management Practice	Security-specific Inputs (in Addition to COBIT 5 Inputs)		Security-specific Outputs (in Addition to COBIT 5 Outputs)	
	From	Description	Description	To
AP012.01 Collect data. Identify and collect relevant data to enable effective IT-related risk identification, analysis and reporting.	APO01.03	Information security and related policies	Data on information security risk	APO12.02 APO12.03
	APO01.08	Information security compliance assessment		
	DSS02.02	Classified and prioritised information security incidents and service requests		

Security-specific Activities (in Addition to COBIT 5 Activities)

1. Identify and collect relevant data to enable effective information security-related risk identification, analysis and reporting.

Management Practice	Security-specific Inputs (in Addition to COBIT 5 Inputs)		Security-specific Outputs (in Addition to COBIT 5 Outputs)	
	From	Description	Description	To
AP012.02 Analyse risk. Develop useful information to support risk decisions that take into account the business relevance of risk factors.	APO12.01	Data on information security risk	Information security risk analysis results	APO12.03
	DSS05.01	Evaluation of potential threats	Information security risk scenarios	APO12.03

Security-specific Activities (in Addition to COBIT 5 Activities)

1. Identify, analyse and evaluate information risk.

Management Practice	Security-specific Inputs (in Addition to COBIT 5 Inputs)		Security-specific Outputs (in Addition to COBIT 5 Outputs)	
	From	Description	Description	To
AP012.03 Maintain a risk profile. Maintain an inventory of known risk and risk attributes (including expected frequency, potential impact and responses) and of related resources, capabilities and current control activities.	EDM01.01	Information security guiding principles	Information security risk profile	APO12.04 APO12.05 BAI01.01 BAI01.11 BAI02.03
	APO12.01	Data on information security risk		
	APO12.02	• Information security risk analysis results • Information security risk scenarios		
	DSS05.01	Evaluation of potential threats		

Security-specific Activities (in Addition to COBIT 5 Activities)

1. Create an information risk profile that includes information security aspects.

Align, Plan and Organise

Align, Plan and Organise

AP012 Security-specific Process Practices, Inputs/Outputs and Activities *(cont.)*				
	Security-specific Inputs (in Addition to COBIT 5 Inputs)		**Security-specific Outputs (in Addition to COBIT 5 Outputs)**	
Management Practice	**From**	**Description**	**Description**	**To**
AP012.04 Articulate risk. Provide information on the current state of IT-related exposures and opportunities in a timely manner to all required stakeholders for appropriate response.	AP012.03	Information security risk profiles	Information security risk response strategies	Internal

Security-specific Activities (in Addition to COBIT 5 Activities)
1. Define and implement risk evaluation and response strategies.

	Security-specific Inputs (in Addition to COBIT 5 Inputs)		**Security-specific Outputs (in Addition to COBIT 5 Outputs)**	
Management Practice	**From**	**Description**	**Description**	**To**
AP012.05 Define a risk management action portfolio. Manage opportunities to reduce risk to an acceptable level as a portfolio.	AP012.03	Information security risk profile	Project proposals for reducing information security risk	AP012.06
			Project proposals for reducing risk	AP013.02

Security-specific Activities (in Addition to COBIT 5 Activities)
1. Continuously monitor IT and information risk levels.

	Security-specific Inputs (in Addition to COBIT 5 Inputs)		**Security-specific Outputs (in Addition to COBIT 5 Outputs)**	
Management Practice	**From**	**Description**	**Description**	**To**
AP012.06 Respond to risk. Respond in a timely manner with effective measures to limit the magnitude of loss from IT-related events.	AP012.05	Project proposals for reducing information security risk	Information security risk mitigation practices	Internal

Security-specific Activities (in Addition to COBIT 5 Activities)
1. Apply selected information security mitigation practices.

For more information regarding the related enablers, please consult:
• Appendix C. Detailed Guidance: Organisational Structures Enabler, C.4. Enterprise Risk Management Committee
• Appendix G. Detailed Guidance: People, Skills and Competencies Enabler, G.3. Information Risk Management

APO13 Manage Security	Area: Management Domain: Align, Plan and Organise

COBIT 5 Process Description
Define, operate and monitor a system for information security management.

COBIT 5 Process Purpose Statement
Keep the impact and occurrence of information security incidents within the enterprise's risk appetite levels.

APO13 Security-specific Process Goals and Metrics

Security-specific Process Goals	Related Metrics
1. A system is in place that considers and effectively addresses enterprise information security requirements.	• Number of key security roles clearly defined • Number of security-related incidents
2. A security plan has been established, accepted and communicated throughout the enterprise.	• Level of stakeholder satisfaction with the security plan throughout the enterprise • Number of security solutions deviating from the plan • Number of security solutions deviating from the enterprise architecture
3. Information security solutions are implemented and operated consistently throughout the enterprise.	• Number of services with confirmed alignment to the security plan • Number of security incidents caused by non-adherence to the security plan • Number of solutions developed with confirmed alignment to the security plan

APO13 Security-specific Process Practices, Inputs/Outputs and Activities

Management Practice	Security-specific Inputs (in Addition to COBIT 5 Inputs)		Security-specific Outputs (in Addition to COBIT 5 Outputs)	
	From	Description	Description	To
APO13.01 Establish and maintain an information security management system (ISMS). Establish and maintain an ISMS that provides a standard, formal and continuous approach to security management for information, enabling secure technology and business processes that are aligned with business requirements and enterprise security management.	Outside *COBIT 5 for Information Security*	Enterprise security approach	ISMS scope statement	APO01.02 DSS06.03
			ISMS policy	Internal

Security-specific Activities (in Addition to COBIT 5 Activities)
1. Define the scope and boundaries of the ISMS in terms of the characteristics of the enterprise, the organisation, its location, assets and technology. Include details of, and justification for, any exclusions from the scope.
2. Define an ISMS in accordance with enterprise policy and aligned with the enterprise, the organisation, its location, assets and technology.
3. Align the ISMS with the overall enterprise approach to the management of security.
4. Obtain management authorisation to implement and operate or change the ISMS.
5. Prepare and maintain a statement of applicability that describes the scope of the ISMS.
6. Define and communicate information security management roles and responsibilities.
7. Communicate the ISMS approach.

Align, Plan and Organise

Align, Plan and Organise

AP013 Security-specific Process Practices, Inputs/Outputs and Activities *(cont.)*				
Management Practice	**Security-specific Inputs (in Addition to COBIT 5 Inputs)**		**Security-specific Outputs (in Addition to COBIT 5 Outputs)**	
	From	**Description**	**Description**	**To**
AP013.02 Define and manage an information security risk treatment plan. Maintain an information security plan that describes how information security risk is to be managed and aligned with the enterprise strategy and enterprise architecture. Ensure that recommendations for implementing security improvements are based on approved business cases and implemented as an integral part of services and solutions development, then operated as an integral part of business operation.	APO02.04	Gaps to be closed and changes required to realise target capability	Information security business cases	APO02.05
	APO03.02	Baseline domain descriptions and architecture definition		
	APO12.05	Project proposals for reducing risk		

Security-specific Activities (in Addition to COBIT 5 Activities)
1. Formulate and maintain an information security risk treatment plan aligned with strategic objectives and the enterprise architecture. Ensure that the plan identifies the appropriate and optimal management practices and security solutions, with associated resources, responsibilities and priorities for managing identified information security risk.
2. Maintain, as part of the enterprise architecture, an inventory of solution components that are in place to manage security-related risk.
3. Develop proposals to implement the information security risk treatment plan, supported by suitable business cases, which include consideration of funding and allocation of roles and responsibilities.
4. Provide input to the design and development of management practices and solutions selected from the information security risk treatment plan.
5. Define how to measure the effectiveness of the selected management practices and specify how these measurements are to be used to assess effectiveness to produce comparable and reproducible results.
6. Recommend information security training and awareness programmes.
7. Integrate the planning, design, implementation and monitoring of information security procedures and other controls capable of enabling prevention, and prompt detection of security events, and response to security incidents.

Management Practice	**Security-specific Inputs (in Addition to COBIT 5 Inputs)**		**Security-specific Outputs (in Addition to COBIT 5 Outputs)**	
	From	**Description**	**Description**	**To**
AP013.03 Monitor and review the ISMS. Maintain and regularly communicate the need for, and benefits of, continuous information security improvement. Collect and analyse data about the ISMS, and improve the effectiveness of the ISMS. Correct non-conformities to prevent recurrence. Promote a culture of security and continual improvement.	DSS02.02	Classified and prioritised incidents and service requests	Recommendations for improving the ISMS	Internal
			ISMS audit reports	MEA02.01

Security-specific Activities (in Addition to COBIT 5 Activities)
1. Undertake regular reviews of the effectiveness of the ISMS, including meeting ISMS policy and objectives, and review of security practices. Take into account results of security audits, incidents, results from effectiveness measurements, suggestions and feedback from all interested parties.
2. Conduct internal ISMS audits at planned intervals.
3. Undertake a management review of the ISMS on a regular basis to ensure that the scope remains adequate and improvements in the ISMS process are identified.
4. Provide input to the maintenance of the security plans to take into account the findings of monitoring and review activities.
5. Record actions and events that could have an impact on the effectiveness or performance of the ISMS.

B.3 BUILD, ACQUIRE AND IMPLEMENT (BAI)

01   Manage programmes and projects.

02   Manage requirements definition.

03   Manage solutions identification and build.

04   Manage availability and capacity.

05   Manage organisational change enablement.

06   Manage changes.

07   Manage change acceptance and transitioning.

08   Manage knowledge.

09   Manage assets.

10   Manage configuration.

Build, Acquire and Implement

Page intentionally left blank

Build, Acquire and Implement

BAI01 Manage Programmes and Projects	Area: Management Domain: Build, Acquire and Implement

COBIT 5 Process Description
Manage all programmes and projects from the investment portfolio in alignment with enterprise strategy and in a co-ordinated way. Initiate, plan, control, and execute programmes and projects, and close with a post-implementation review.

COBIT 5 Process Purpose Statement
Realise business benefits and reduce the risk of unexpected delays, costs and value erosion by improving communications to and involvement of business and end users, ensuring the value and quality of project deliverables and maximising their contribution to the investment and services portfolio.

BAI01 Security-specific Process Goals and Metrics

Security-specific Process Goals	Related Metrics
1. Information security requirements are considered and incorporated in all programmes and projects.	• Percent of programme and project stakeholders effectively engaged in managing information security • Percent of programmes and projects that have a security risk assessment and an information security plan to address the risk • Percent of information security subject matter experts involved in projects • Percent of stakeholder sign-offs for information security stage reviews and remediation plans • Frequency of information security status reviews • Level of stakeholder satisfaction with project information security aspects at project closure review

BAI01 Security-specific Process Practices, Inputs/Outputs and Activities

Management Practice	Security-specific Inputs (in Addition to COBIT 5 Inputs)		Security-specific Outputs (in Addition to COBIT 5 Outputs)	
	From	Description	Description	To
BAI01.01 Maintain a standard approach for programme and project management. Maintain a standard approach for programme and project management that enables governance and management review and decision making and delivery management activities focussed on achieving value and goals (requirements, risk, costs, schedule, quality) for the business in a consistent manner.	AP001.03	Information security and related policies	Information security requirements in the feasibility study	BAI01.02 BAI02.02 BAI03.01
	AP002.02	Information security capabilities		
	AP002.06	Information security plan		
	AP012.03	Information security risk profile		
	BAI02.01	Information security requirements		

Security-specific Activities (in Addition to COBIT 5 Activities)

1. Incorporate information security requirements in the feasibility study for each project within programmes.

2. Establish a process to ensure that all project-related information that is gathered or produced as part of the project is secured.

Management Practice	Security-specific Inputs (in Addition to COBIT 5 Inputs)		Security-specific Outputs (in Addition to COBIT 5 Outputs)	
	From	Description	Description	To
BAI01.02 Initiate a programme. Initiate a programme to confirm the expected benefits and obtain authorisation to proceed. This includes agreeing on programme sponsorship, confirming the programme mandate through approval of the conceptual business case, appointing programme board or committee members, producing the programme brief, reviewing and updating the business case, developing a benefits realisation plan, and obtaining approval from sponsors to proceed.	BAI01.01	Information security requirements in the feasibility study	Programme concept business case including mandatory information security activities	BAI01.04 BAI01.08

Security-specific Activities (in Addition to COBIT 5 Activities)

1. Plan information security activities for each project within the overall programme.

Build, Acquire and Implement

Build, Acquire and Implement

BAI01 Security-specific Process Practices, Inputs/Outputs and Activities *(cont.)*				
Management Practice	**Security-specific Inputs (in Addition to COBIT 5 Inputs)**		**Security-specific Outputs (in Addition to COBIT 5 Outputs)**	
	From	**Description**	**Description**	**To**
BAI01.03 Manage stakeholder engagement. Manage stakeholder engagement to ensure an active exchange of accurate, consistent and timely information that reaches all relevant stakeholders. This includes planning, identifying and engaging stakeholders and managing their expectations.				

Security-specific Activities (in Addition to COBIT 5 Activities)
0. Information security-specific guidance is not relevant for this practice. The generic COBIT 5 activities can be used as further guidance.

Management Practice	**Security-specific Inputs (in Addition to COBIT 5 Inputs)**		**Security-specific Outputs (in Addition to COBIT 5 Outputs)**	
	From	**Description**	**Description**	**To**
BAI01.04 Develop and maintain the programme plan. Formulate a programme to lay the initial groundwork and to position it for successful execution by formalising the scope of the work to be accomplished and identifying the deliverables that will satisfy its goals and deliver value. Maintain and update the programme plan and business case throughout the full economic life cycle of the programme, ensuring alignment with strategic objectives and reflecting the current status and updated insights gained to date.	APO02.06 BAI01.02	Information security plan Programme concept business case including mandatory information security activities	Programme concept plan including mandatory information security activities	BAI01.08

Security-specific Activities (in Addition to COBIT 5 Activities)
1. Develop an information security plan that identifies the information security environment and controls to be implemented by the project team to protect organisational assets.
2. Include the necessary resource(s) on projects to effectively identify and implement information security requirements.

Management Practice	**Security-specific Inputs (in Addition to COBIT 5 Inputs)**		**Security-specific Outputs (in Addition to COBIT 5 Outputs)**	
	From	**Description**	**Description**	**To**
BAI01.05 Launch and execute the programme. Launch and execute the programme to acquire and direct the resources needed to accomplish the goals and benefits of the programme as defined in the programme plan. In accordance with stage-gate or release review criteria, prepare for stage-gate, iteration or release reviews to report on the progress of the programme and to be able to make the case for funding up to the following stage-gate or release review.				

Security-specific Activities (in Addition to COBIT 5 Activities)
0. Information security-specific guidance is not relevant for this practice. The generic COBIT 5 activities can be used as further guidance.

Management Practice	**Security-specific Inputs (in Addition to COBIT 5 Inputs)**		**Security-specific Outputs (in Addition to COBIT 5 Outputs)**	
	From	**Description**	**Description**	**To**
BAI01.06 Monitor, control and report on the programme outcomes. Monitor and control programme (solution delivery) and enterprise (value/outcome) performance against plan throughout the full economic life cycle of the investment. Report this performance to the programme steering committee and the sponsors.				

Security-specific Activities (in Addition to COBIT 5 Activities)
0. Information security-specific guidance is not relevant for this practice. The generic COBIT 5 activities can be used as further guidance.

BAI01 Security-specific Process Practices, Inputs/Outputs and Activities *(cont.)*				
	Security-specific Inputs (in Addition to COBIT 5 Inputs)		**Security-specific Outputs (in Addition to COBIT 5 Outputs)**	
Management Practice	**From**	**Description**	**Description**	**To**
BAI01.07 Start up and initiate projects within a programme. Define and document the nature and scope of the project to confirm and develop amongst stakeholders a common understanding of project scope and how it relates to other projects within the overall IT-enabled investment programme. The definition should be formally approved by the programme and project sponsors.				
Security-specific Activities (in Addition to COBIT 5 Activities)				
0. Information security-specific guidance is not relevant for this practice. The generic COBIT 5 activities can be used as further guidance.				
	Security-specific Inputs (in Addition to COBIT 5 Inputs)		**Security-specific Outputs (in Addition to COBIT 5 Outputs)**	
Management Practice	**From**	**Description**	**Description**	**To**
BAI01.08 Plan projects. Establish and maintain a formal, approved integrated project plan (covering business and IT resources) to guide project execution and control throughout the life of the project. The scope of projects should be clearly defined and tied to building or enhancing business capability.	APO02.06	Information security plan	Project plan including the information security goals, objectives and requirements	BAI01.10
	BAI01.02	Programme concept business case including mandatory information security activities		
	BAI01.04	Programme concept plan including mandatory information security activities		
Security-specific Activities (in Addition to COBIT 5 Activities)				
1. Integrate information security in IT and business project management.				
	Security-specific Inputs (in Addition to COBIT 5 Inputs)		**Security-specific Outputs (in Addition to COBIT 5 Outputs)**	
Management Practice	**From**	**Description**	**Description**	**To**
BAI01.09 Manage programme and project quality. Prepare and execute a quality management plan, processes and practices, aligned with the QMS that describes the programme and project quality approach and how it will be implemented. The plan should be formally reviewed and agreed on by all parties concerned and then incorporated into the integrated programme and project plans.				
Security-specific Activities (in Addition to COBIT 5 Activities)				
0. Information security-specific guidance is not relevant for this practice. The generic COBIT 5 activities can be used as further guidance.				
	Security-specific Inputs (in Addition to COBIT 5 Inputs)		**Security-specific Outputs (in Addition to COBIT 5 Outputs)**	
Management Practice	**From**	**Description**	**Description**	**To**
BAI01.10 Manage programme and project risk. Eliminate or minimise specific risk associated with programmes and projects through a systematic process of planning, identifying, analysing, responding to and monitoring and controlling the areas or events that have the potential to cause unwanted change. Risk faced by programme and project management should be established and centrally recorded.	BAI01.08	Project plan including the information security goals, objectives and requirements	Information security risk log included as part of the overall project risk log	Internal
Security-specific Activities (in Addition to COBIT 5 Activities)				
1. Establish an information risk log and remediation actions to identified risk. Periodically review and update the risk log.				
2. Integrate information security projects in the enterprise's programme and project management process.				

Build, Acquire and Implement

119

Build, Acquire and Implement

BAI01 Security-specific Process Practices, Inputs/Outputs and Activities *(cont.)*				
	Security-specific Inputs (in Addition to COBIT 5 Inputs)		Security-specific Outputs (in Addition to COBIT 5 Outputs)	
Management Practice	From	Description	Description	To
BAI01.11 Monitor and control projects. Measure project performance against key project performance criteria such as schedule, quality, cost and risk. Identify any deviations from the expected. Assess the impact of deviations on the project and overall programme, and report results to key stakeholders.	APO01.03	Information security and related policies	Information security project assessment report identifying control weaknesses and recommended corrective action plans	Internal
	APO02.06	Information security plan		
	APO12.03	Information security risk profile		

Security-specific Activities (in Addition to COBIT 5 Activities)
1. Perform periodic independent assessments of projects to ensure that information security requirements are implemented effectively.

	Security-specific Inputs (in Addition to COBIT 5 Inputs)		Security-specific Outputs (in Addition to COBIT 5 Outputs)	
Management Practice	From	Description	Description	To
BAI01.12 Manage project resources and work packages. Manage project work packages by placing formal requirements on authorising and accepting work packages, and assigning and co-ordinating appropriate business and IT resources.				

Security-specific Activities (in Addition to COBIT 5 Activities)
0. Information security-specific guidance is not relevant for this practice. The generic COBIT 5 activities can be used as further guidance.

	Security-specific Inputs (in Addition to COBIT 5 Inputs)		Security-specific Outputs (in Addition to COBIT 5 Outputs)	
Management Practice	From	Description	Description	To
BAI01.13 Close a project or iteration. At the end of each project, release or iteration, require the project stakeholders to ascertain whether the project, release or iteration delivered the planned results and value. Identify and communicate any outstanding activities required to achieve the planned results of the project and the benefits of the programme, and identify and document lessons learned for use on future projects, releases, iterations and programmes.				

Security-specific Activities (in Addition to COBIT 5 Activities)
0. Information security-specific guidance is not relevant for this practice. The generic COBIT 5 activities can be used as further guidance.

	Security-specific Inputs (in Addition to COBIT 5 Inputs)		Security-specific Outputs (in Addition to COBIT 5 Outputs)	
Management Practice	From	Description	Description	To
BAI01.14 Close a programme. Remove the programme from the active investment portfolio when there is agreement that the desired value has been achieved or when it is clear it will not be achieved within the value criteria set for the programme.				

Security-specific Activities (in Addition to COBIT 5 Activities)
0. Information security-specific guidance is not relevant for this practice. The generic COBIT 5 activities can be used as further guidance.

For more information regarding the related enablers, please consult:
• Appendix E. Detailed Guidance: Information Enabler, E.4. Information Security Plan, E.6. Information Security Requirements • Appendix G. Detailed Guidance: People, Skills and Competencies Enabler, G.3. Information Risk Management

BAI02 Manage Requirements Definition	Area: Management Domain: Build, Acquire and Implement

COBIT 5 Process Description
Identify solutions and analyse requirements before acquisition or creation to ensure that they are in line with enterprise strategic requirements covering business processes, applications, information/data, infrastructure and services. Co-ordinate with affected stakeholders the review of feasible options including relative costs and benefits, risk analysis, and approval of requirements and proposed solutions.

COBIT 5 Process Purpose Statement
Create feasible optimal solutions that meet enterprise needs while minimising risk.

BAI02 Security-specific Process Goals and Metrics

Security-specific Process Goals	Related Metrics
1. All relevant information security aspects for business functional and technical requirements are identified and implemented.	• Percent of new information security requirements added due to business requirements • Percent of requirements reworked due to information security requirements
2. Information risk associated with business functional and technical requirements is captured and addressed.	• New information security risk identified • Number of information security incidents indicating/pointing to new or unknown risk • Number of information security incidents based on known risk

BAI02 Security-specific Process Practices, Inputs/Outputs and Activities

Management Practice	Security-specific Inputs (in Addition to COBIT 5 Inputs)		Security-specific Outputs (in Addition to COBIT 5 Outputs)	
	From	Description	Description	To
BAI02.01 Define and maintain business functional and technical requirements. Based on the business case, identify, prioritise, specify and agree on business information, functional, technical and control requirements covering the scope/understanding of all initiatives required to achieve the expected outcomes of the proposed IT-enabled business solution.	AP001.03	Information security and related policies	Information security requirements	AP002.03 AP004.04 AP007.06 AP008.05 AP009.05 BAI01.01 BAI02.04 BAI03.01 BAI03.04 BAI03.07 BAI03.09 BAI04.03 BAI05.01 MEA01.01 MEA03.01
	AP002.02	Information security capabilities		
	AP002.06	Information security plan		
	MEA03.01	External information security compliance requirements		

Security-specific Activities (in Addition to COBIT 5 Activities)

1. Research, define and document information security requirements, i.e., confidentiality requirements, integrity requirements and availability requirements.

2. Research and analyse information security requirements with stakeholders, business sponsors and technical implementation personnel.

3. Ensure that the business requirements take into account the need to protect the security of information.

Management Practice	Security-specific Inputs (in Addition to COBIT 5 Inputs)		Security-specific Outputs (in Addition to COBIT 5 Outputs)	
	From	Description	Description	To
BAI02.02 Perform a feasibility study and formulate alternative solutions. Perform a feasibility study of potential alternative solutions, assess their viability and select the preferred option. If appropriate, implement the selected option as a pilot to determine possible improvements.	BAI01.01	Information security requirements in the feasibility study	Feasibility study report	Internal

Security-specific Activities (in Addition to COBIT 5 Activities)

1. Ensure that information security requirements are included in the feasibility study.

Build, Acquire and Implement

BAI02 Security-specific Process Practices, Inputs/Outputs and Activities *(cont.)*

Management Practice	Security-specific Inputs (in Addition to COBIT 5 Inputs)		Security-specific Outputs (in Addition to COBIT 5 Outputs)	
	From	Description	Description	To
BAI02.03 Manage requirements risk. Identify, document, prioritise and mitigate functional, technical and information processing-related risk associated with the enterprise requirements and proposed solution.	APO12.03	Information security risk profile	Risk mitigation actions	Internal

Security-specific Activities (in Addition to COBIT 5 Activities)
1. Perform an information risk assessment to identify the information security controls for the relevant business activities (programme and project management included).
2. Co-operate with the risk office to manage the information risk.

Management Practice	Security-specific Inputs (in Addition to COBIT 5 Inputs)		Security-specific Outputs (in Addition to COBIT 5 Outputs)	
	From	Description	Description	To
BAI02.04 Obtain approval of requirements and solutions. Co-ordinate feedback from affected stakeholders and, at predetermined key stages, obtain business sponsor or product owner approval and sign-off on functional and technical requirements, feasibility studies, risk analyses and recommended solutions.	BAI02.01	Information security requirements	Approval over information security requirements	Internal

Security-specific Activities (in Addition to COBIT 5 Activities)
1. Validate information security requirements with stakeholders, business sponsors and technical implementation personnel.

For more information regarding the related enablers, please consult:
- Appendix E. Detailed Guidance: Information Enabler, E.6. Information Security Requirements
- Appendix G. Detailed Guidance: People, Skills and Competencies Enabler, G.3. Information Risk Management

Build, Acquire and Implement

BAI03 Manage Solutions Identification and Build	Area: Management Domain: Build, Acquire and Implement

COBIT 5 Process Description
Establish and maintain identified solutions in line with enterprise requirements covering design, development, procurement/sourcing and partnering with suppliers/vendors. Manage configuration, test preparation, testing, requirements management and maintenance of business processes, applications, information/data, infrastructure and services.

COBIT 5 Process Purpose Statement
Establish timely and cost-effective solutions capable of supporting enterprise strategic and operational objectives.

BAI03 Security-specific Process Goals and Metrics

Security-specific Process Goals	Related Metrics
1. Information security measures are embedded in the solution and effectively support business strategic and operational objectives.	• Number of solution designs added due to information security requirements • Number of information security exceptions in the design and implementation
2. Information security solutions are accepted and have been successfully tested.	• Number of additional tests for information security
3. Changes to information security requirements are correctly incorporated in the solution.	• Number of approved changes to information security requirements

BAI03 Security-specific Process Practices, Inputs/Outputs and Activities

Management Practice	Security-specific Inputs (in Addition to COBIT 5 Inputs)		Security-specific Outputs (in Addition to COBIT 5 Outputs)	
	From	Description	Description	To
BAI03.01 Design high-level solutions. Develop and document high-level designs using agreed-on and appropriate phased or rapid agile development techniques. Ensure alignment with the IT strategy and enterprise architecture. Reassess and update the designs when significant issues occur during detailed design or building phases or as the solution evolves. Ensure that stakeholders actively participate in the design and approve each version.	BAI01.01	Information security requirements in the feasibility study	Information security specifications in line with high-level design	BAI03.02
	BAI02.01	Information security requirements		

Security-specific Activities (in Addition to COBIT 5 Activities)
1. Define the information security specifications in line with high-level design.

Management Practice	Security-specific Inputs (in Addition to COBIT 5 Inputs)		Security-specific Outputs (in Addition to COBIT 5 Outputs)	
	From	Description	Description	To
BAI03.02 Design detailed solution components. Develop, document and elaborate detailed designs progressively using agreed-on and appropriate phased or rapid agile development techniques, addressing all components (business processes and related automated and manual controls, supporting IT applications, infrastructure services and technology products, and partners/suppliers). Ensure that the detailed design includes internal and external SLAs and OLAs.	BAI03.01	Information security specifications in line with high-level design	Information security design in the solution components	BAI03.03

Security-specific Activities (in Addition to COBIT 5 Activities)
1. Integrate information security design in the solution components.

Build, Acquire and Implement

123

BAI03 Security-specific Process Practices, Inputs/Outputs and Activities *(cont.)*				
Management Practice	**Security-specific Inputs** (in Addition to COBIT 5 Inputs)		**Security-specific Outputs** (in Addition to COBIT 5 Outputs)	
	From	**Description**	**Description**	**To**
BAI03.03 Develop solution components. Develop solution components progressively in accordance with detailed designs following development methods and documentation standards, quality assurance (QA) requirements, and approval standards. Ensure that all control requirements in the business processes, supporting IT applications and infrastructure services, services and technology products, and partners/suppliers are addressed.	BAI03.02	Information security design in the solution components	Secure coding practices and secure infrastructure libraries	Internal
Security-specific Activities (in Addition to COBIT 5 Activities)				
1. Ensure that solution components integrate secure coding practices and secure infrastructure libraries.				
Management Practice	**Security-specific Inputs** (in Addition to COBIT 5 Inputs)		**Security-specific Outputs** (in Addition to COBIT 5 Outputs)	
	From	**Description**	**Description**	**To**
BAI03.04 Procure solution components. Procure solution components based on the acquisition plan in accordance with requirements and detailed designs, architecture principles and standards, and the enterprise's overall procurement and contract procedures, QA requirements, and approval standards. Ensure that all legal and contractual requirements are identified and addressed by the supplier.	APO10.01	Supplier catalogue	Information security requirements within the procurement planning	Internal
	BAI02.01	Information security requirements		
Security-specific Activities (in Addition to COBIT 5 Activities)				
1. Ensure that information security requirements are part of the procurement planning and appropriate information security assessments have been performed.				
Management Practice	**Security-specific Inputs** (in Addition to COBIT 5 Inputs)		**Security-specific Outputs** (in Addition to COBIT 5 Outputs)	
	From	**Description**	**Description**	**To**
BAI03.05 Build solutions. Install and configure solutions and integrate with business process activities. Implement control, security and auditability measures during configuration, and during integration of hardware and infrastructural software, to protect resources and ensure availability and data integrity. Update the services catalogue to reflect the new solutions.			Secure solutions	Internal
Security-specific Activities (in Addition to COBIT 5 Activities)				
1. Verify that information security aspects are included in building the solution.				
Management Practice	**Security-specific Inputs** (in Addition to COBIT 5 Inputs)		**Security-specific Outputs** (in Addition to COBIT 5 Outputs)	
	From	**Description**	**Description**	**To**
BAI03.06 Perform quality assurance (QA). Develop, resource and execute a QA plan aligned with the QMS to obtain the quality specified in the requirements definition and the enterprise's quality policies and procedures.	APO11.02	Information security quality standards	Information security quality review results, exceptions and corrections	Internal
Security-specific Activities (in Addition to COBIT 5 Activities)				
1. Verify that information security aspects are included in quality assurance.				

BAI03 Security-specific Process Practices, Inputs/Outputs and Activities *(cont.)*				
	Security-specific Inputs (in Addition to COBIT 5 Inputs)		Security-specific Outputs (in Addition to COBIT 5 Outputs)	
Management Practice	From	Description	Description	To
BAI03.07 Prepare for solution testing. Establish a test plan and required environments to test the individual and integrated solution components, including the business processes and supporting services, applications and infrastructure.	BAI02.01	Information security requirements	Information security test cases	Internal

Security-specific Activities (in Addition to COBIT 5 Activities)
1. Include information security test cases in test plans.

	Security-specific Inputs (in Addition to COBIT 5 Inputs)		Security-specific Outputs (in Addition to COBIT 5 Outputs)	
Management Practice	From	Description	Description	To
BAI03.08 Execute solution testing. Execute testing continually during development, including control testing, in accordance with the defined test plan and development practices in the appropriate environment. Engage business process owners and end users in the test team. Identify, log and prioritise errors and issues identified during testing.	APO01.03	Information security and related policies	Security acceptance report	Internal

Security-specific Activities (in Addition to COBIT 5 Activities)
1. Ensure information security of any production data used in test cases, including the use of a secure process to privatise sensitive data before use.

	Security-specific Inputs (in Addition to COBIT 5 Inputs)		Security-specific Outputs (in Addition to COBIT 5 Outputs)	
Management Practice	From	Description	Description	To
BAI03.09 Manage changes to requirements. Track the status of individual requirements (including all rejected requirements) throughout the project life cycle and manage the approval of changes to requirements.	BAI02.01	Information security requirements	Record of all approved and applied change requests	Internal

Security-specific Activities (in Addition to COBIT 5 Activities)
1. Manage changes to information security aspects and requirements.

	Security-specific Inputs (in Addition to COBIT 5 Inputs)		Security-specific Outputs (in Addition to COBIT 5 Outputs)	
Management Practice	From	Description	Description	To
BAI03.10 Maintain solutions. Develop and execute a plan for the maintenance of solution and infrastructure components. Include periodic reviews against business needs and operational requirements.			Updated secure solutions	Internal

Security-specific Activities (in Addition to COBIT 5 Activities)
1. Ensure that updates to information security requirements are reflected in the maintenance updates of solutions.

	Security-specific Inputs (in Addition to COBIT 5 Inputs)		Security-specific Outputs (in Addition to COBIT 5 Outputs)	
Management Practice	From	Description	Description	To
BAI03.11 Define IT services and maintain the service portfolio. Define and agree on new or changed IT services and service level options. Document new or changed service definitions and service level options to be updated in the services portfolio.	Organisational structures enabler model	Roles and responsibilities	Information security services	APO09.03 APO09.04
	Outside *COBIT 5 for Information Security*	• Business mission/vision • Business goals and objectives		

Security-specific Activities (in Addition to COBIT 5 Activities)
1. Define information security services in accordance with business needs and compliance/regulatory needs.
2. Define information security processes within IT services.

For more information regarding the related enablers, please consult: • Appendix F. Detailed Guidance: Services, Infrastructure and Applications Enabler

Build, Acquire and Implement

Page intentionally left blank

Build, Acquire and Implement

BAI04 Manage Availability and Capacity	Area: Management Domain: Build, Acquire and Implement

COBIT 5 Process Description
Balance current and future needs for availability, performance and capacity with cost-effective service provision. Include assessment of current capabilities, forecasting of future needs based on business requirements, analysis of business impacts, and assessment of risk to plan and implement actions to meet the identified requirements.

COBIT 5 Process Purpose Statement
Maintain service availability, efficient management of resources, and optimisation of system performance through prediction of future performance and capacity requirements.

BAI04 Security-specific Process Goals and Metrics

Security-specific Process Goals	Related Metrics
1. Information security requirements are included in the availability, performance and capacity management plans.	• Percent of information security commitments met
2. Information security impact on availability, performance and capacity is monitored and optimised.	• Percent of availability, performance and capacity incidents per year caused by information security controls

BAI04 Security-specific Process Practices, Inputs/Outputs and Activities

Management Practice	Security-specific Inputs (in Addition to COBIT 5 Inputs)		Security-specific Outputs (in Addition to COBIT 5 Outputs)	
	From	Description	Description	To
BAI04.01 Assess current availability, performance and capacity and create a baseline. Assess availability, performance and capacity of services and resources to ensure that cost-justifiable capacity and performance are available to support business needs and deliver against SLAs. Create availability, performance and capacity baselines for future comparison.	APO02.02	Information security capabilities	List of technical and procedural information security issues related to availability, performance and capacity	BAI04.02

Security-specific Activities (in Addition to COBIT 5 Activities)

1. Identify the technical and procedural information security issues related to availability, performance and capacity.

Management Practice	Security-specific Inputs (in Addition to COBIT 5 Inputs)		Security-specific Outputs (in Addition to COBIT 5 Outputs)	
	From	Description	Description	To
BAI04.02 Assess business impact. Identify important services to the enterprise, map services and resources to business processes, and identify business dependencies. Ensure that the impact of unavailable resources is fully agreed-on and accepted by the customer. Ensure that, for vital business functions, the SLA availability requirements can be satisfied.	BAI04.01	List of technical and procedural information security issues related to availability, performance and capacity	Availability, performance and capacity information security impact assessments	BAI04.03

Security-specific Activities (in Addition to COBIT 5 Activities)

1. Assess the information security impact of potential unavailability, underperformance and lack of capacity.

Management Practice	Security-specific Inputs (in Addition to COBIT 5 Inputs)		Security-specific Outputs (in Addition to COBIT 5 Outputs)	
	From	Description	Description	To
BAI04.03 Plan for new or changed service requirements. Plan and prioritise availability, performance and capacity implications of changing business needs and service requirements.	BAI02.01	Information security requirements	Updates to information security requirements	Internal
	BAI04.02	Availability, performance and capacity information security impact assessments		

Security-specific Activities (in Addition to COBIT 5 Activities)

1. Assess the impact of new or changed service requirements on information security.

Build, Acquire and Implement

BAI04 Security-specific Process Practices, Inputs/Outputs and Activities *(cont.)*				
	Security-specific Inputs (in Addition to COBIT 5 Inputs)		Security-specific Outputs (in Addition to COBIT 5 Outputs)	
Management Practice	From	Description	Description	To
BAI04.04 Monitor and review availability and capacity. Monitor, measure, analyse, report and review availability, performance and capacity. Identify deviations from established baselines. Review trend analysis reports identifying any significant issues and variances, initiating actions where necessary, and ensuring that all outstanding issues are followed up.				
Security-specific Activities (in Addition to COBIT 5 Activities)				
0. Information security-specific guidance is not relevant for this practice. The generic COBIT 5 activities can be used as further guidance.				
	Security-specific Inputs (in Addition to COBIT 5 Inputs)		Security-specific Outputs (in Addition to COBIT 5 Outputs)	
Management Practice	From	Description	Description	To
BAI04.05 Investigate and address availability, performance and capacity issues. Address deviations by investigating and resolving identified availability, performance and capacity issues.			Updates to corrective actions to close capacity issues	Internal
Security-specific Activities (in Addition to COBIT 5 Activities)				
1. Assess and investigate any information security issue that impacts availability, performance and capacity.				

Build, Acquire and Implement

BAI05 Manage Organisational Change Enablement	Area: Management Domain: Build, Acquire and Implement

COBIT 5 Process Description
Maximise the likelihood of successfully implementing sustainable enterprisewide organisational change quickly and with reduced risk, covering the complete life cycle of the change and all affected stakeholders in the business and IT.

COBIT 5 Process Purpose Statement
Prepare and commit stakeholders for business change and reduce the risk of failure.

BAI05 Security-specific Process Goals and Metrics

Security-specific Process Goals	Related Metrics
1. Information security alerts and trends are used effectively to enable change in the enterprise and influence the enterprise's culture on information security culture.	• Level of senior management involvement with information security programmes and strategies • Level of satisfaction of role players operating, using and maintaining the change • Percent of users appropriately trained for information security changes and as part of organisational change
2. Information security protocols are revised and refined as the enterprise changes through information security awareness.	• Level of satisfaction of users with the adoption of the change

BAI05 Security-specific Process Practices, Inputs/Outputs and Activities

Management Practice	Security-specific Inputs (in Addition to COBIT 5 Inputs)		Security-specific Outputs (in Addition to COBIT 5 Outputs)	
	From	Description	Description	To
BAI05.01 Establish the desire to change. Understand the scope and impact of the envisioned change and stakeholder readiness/willingness to change. Identify actions to motivate stakeholders to accept and want to make the change work successfully.	APO01.03	Information security and related policies	• Communication plan with senior management • Agreed-on change control process aligned with best practice guidance	Internal
	BAI02.01	Information security requirements		

Security-specific Activities (in Addition to COBIT 5 Activities)

1. Establish a proactive information security culture.

2. Identify and communicate information security watch or pain points and desirable behaviours, and include changes needed to address these points.

3. Provide visible leadership through executive (C-level, highest level) commitment to information security for facilitating change.

Management Practice	Security-specific Inputs (in Addition to COBIT 5 Inputs)		Security-specific Outputs (in Addition to COBIT 5 Outputs)	
	From	Description	Description	To
BAI05.02 Form an effective implementation team. Establish an effective implementation team by assembling appropriate members, creating trust, and establishing common goals and effectiveness measures.	Outside *COBIT 5* for Information Security	Personnel skills	Information security implementation teams	Internal

Security-specific Activities (in Addition to COBIT 5 Activities)

1. Designate qualified information security professionals to serve on implementation teams.

2. Develop a common vision for the information security team.

Management Practice	Security-specific Inputs (in Addition to COBIT 5 Inputs)		Security-specific Outputs (in Addition to COBIT 5 Outputs)	
	From	Description	Description	To
BAI05.03 Communicate desired vision. Communicate the desired vision for the change in the language of those affected by it. The communication should be made by senior management and include the rationale for, and benefits of, the change; the impacts of not making the change; and the vision, the road map and the involvement required of the various stakeholders.	APO02.06	Information security plan	Information security vision communication plan	BAI05.04
	Outside *COBIT 5* for Information Security	Corporate vision/mission statements		

Security-specific Activities (in Addition to COBIT 5 Activities)

1. Communicate the information security vision in support of the corporate vision statement.

Build, Acquire and Implement

Build, Acquire and Implement

BAI05 Security-specific Process Practices, Inputs/Outputs and Activities *(cont.)*				
Management Practice	**Security-specific Inputs** **(in Addition to COBIT 5 Inputs)**		**Security-specific Outputs** **(in Addition to COBIT 5 Outputs)**	
	From	**Description**	**Description**	**To**
BAI05.04 Empower role players and identify short-term wins. Empower those with implementation roles by ensuring that accountabilities are assigned, providing training, and aligning organisational structures and HR processes. Identify and communicate short-term wins that can be realised and are important from a change enablement perspective.	APO02.05	Information security strategic road map	List of potential short-term wins	BAI05.05
	APO02.06	Information security plan		
	BAI05.03	Information security vision communication plan		

Security-specific Activities (in Addition to COBIT 5 Activities)
1. Align information security practices to support the vision.
2. Assign clear responsibility for each person on the team and include performance criteria to establish accountability.

Management Practice	**Security-specific Inputs** **(in Addition to COBIT 5 Inputs)**		**Security-specific Outputs** **(in Addition to COBIT 5 Outputs)**	
	From	**Description**	**Description**	**To**
BAI05.05 Enable operation and use. Plan and implement all technical, operational and usage aspects such that all those who are involved in the future state environment can exercise their responsibility.	BAI05.04	List of potential short-term wins	Practical information security measures	BAI05.06

Security-specific Activities (in Addition to COBIT 5 Activities)
1. Develop practical information security measures.

Management Practice	**Security-specific Inputs** **(in Addition to COBIT 5 Inputs)**		**Security-specific Outputs** **(in Addition to COBIT 5 Outputs)**	
	From	**Description**	**Description**	**To**
BAI05.06 Embed new approaches. Embed the new approaches by tracking implemented changes, assessing the effectiveness of the operation and use plan, and sustaining ongoing awareness through regular communication. Take corrective measures as appropriate, which may include enforcing compliance.	BAI05.05	Practical information security measures	Information security operational practices	Internal

Security-specific Activities (in Addition to COBIT 5 Activities)
1. Follow up on day-to-day information security awareness and adapt the measures accordingly.

Management Practice	**Security-specific Inputs** **(in Addition to COBIT 5 Inputs)**		**Security-specific Outputs** **(in Addition to COBIT 5 Outputs)**	
	From	**Description**	**Description**	**To**
BAI05.07 Sustain Changes. Sustain changes through effective training of new staff, ongoing communication campaigns, continued top management commitment, adoption monitoring and sharing of lessons learned across the enterprise.			Reviews of operational use	Internal

Security-specific Activities (in Addition to COBIT 5 Activities)
1. Inform and train new staff and provide refresh sessions regarding information security awareness.

For more information regarding the related enablers, please consult: • Appendix D. Detailed Guidance: Culture, Ethics and Behaviour Enabler

BAI06 Manage Changes	Area: Management Domain: Build, Acquire and Implement

COBIT 5 Process Description
Manage all changes in a controlled manner, including standard changes and emergency maintenance relating to business processes, applications and infrastructure. This includes change standards and procedures, impact assessment, prioritisation and authorisation, emergency changes, tracking, reporting, closure and documentation.

COBIT 5 Process Purpose Statement
Enable fast and reliable delivery of change to the business and mitigation of the risk of negatively impacting the stability or integrity of the changed environment.

BAI06 Security-specific Process Goals and Metrics

Security-specific Process Goals	Related Metrics
1. Information security requirements are incorporated during impact assessments of processes, applications and infrastructure changes.	• Number of information security-relevant changes and number of changes that had an information security impact • Number of information security requirements that have not been met after the change
2. Emergency changes take into account the necessary information security requirements.	• Number of information security incidents related to changes in the environment • Number of information security incidents related to changes made in hardware and software

BAI06 Security-specific Process Practices, Inputs/Outputs and Activities

Management Practice	Security-specific Inputs (in Addition to COBIT 5 Inputs)		Security-specific Outputs (in Addition to COBIT 5 Outputs)	
	From	Description	Description	To
BAI06.01 Evaluate, prioritise and authorise change requests. Evaluate all requests for change to determine the impact on business processes and IT services, and to assess whether change will adversely affect the operational environment and introduce unacceptable risk. Ensure that changes are logged, prioritised, categorised, assessed, authorised, planned and scheduled.	APO01.03	Information security and related policies	Impact assessments	Internal

Security-specific Activities (in Addition to COBIT 5 Activities)

1. Ensure that assessment of the potential impact of changes on information security is undertaken.

2. Ensure that the information security policy is adaptive to the business goals within an enterprise.

3. Ensure that changes conform with the information security policy.

4. Develop practices to consider the information security impact of emerging trends and technologies.

Management Practice	Security-specific Inputs (in Addition to COBIT 5 Inputs)		Security-specific Outputs (in Addition to COBIT 5 Outputs)	
	From	Description	Description	To
BAI06.02 Manage emergency changes. Carefully manage emergency changes to minimise further incidents and make sure the change is controlled and takes place securely. Verify that emergency changes are appropriately assessed and authorised after the change.			Post-implementation information security review of emergency changes	Internal

Security-specific Activities (in Addition to COBIT 5 Activities)

1. Develop measures that will address emergency changes and maintenance without compromising information security.

2. To assure proper follow-up, maintain an information risk register when new risk is introduced in an emergency change.

Build, Acquire and Implement

BAI06 Security-specific Process Practices, Inputs/Outputs and Activities *(cont.)*				
Management Practice	**Security-specific Inputs (in Addition to COBIT 5 Inputs)**		**Security-specific Outputs (in Addition to COBIT 5 Outputs)**	
	From	**Description**	**Description**	**To**
BAI06.03 Track and report change status. Maintain a tracking and reporting system to document rejected changes, communicate the status of approved and in-process changes, and complete changes. Make certain that approved changes are implemented as planned.			Updated change request status reports	Internal
Security-specific Activities (in Addition to COBIT 5 Activities)				
1. Address potential performance and capacity issues resulting from the proposed information security changes.				
Management Practice	**Security-specific Inputs (in Addition to COBIT 5 Inputs)**		**Security-specific Outputs (in Addition to COBIT 5 Outputs)**	
	From	**Description**	**Description**	**To**
BAI06.04 Close and document the changes. Whenever changes are implemented, update accordingly the solution and user documentation and the procedures affected by the change.				
Security-specific Activities (in Addition to COBIT 5 Activities)				
0. Information security-specific guidance is not relevant for this practice. The generic COBIT 5 activities can be used as further guidance.				

For more information regarding the related enablers, please consult:
• Appendix A. Detailed Guidance: Principles, Policies and Frameworks Enabler
• Appendix F. Detailed Guidance: Services, Infrastructure and Applications Enabler

Build, Acquire and Implement

BAI07 Manage Change Acceptance and Transitioning	Area: Management Domain: Build, Acquire and Implement

COBIT 5 Process Description
Formally accept and make operational new solutions, including implementation planning, system and data conversion, acceptance testing, communication, release preparation, promotion to production of new or changed business processes and IT services, early production support, and a post-implementation review.

COBIT 5 Process Purpose Statement
Implement solutions safely and in line with the agreed-on expectations and outcomes.

BAI07 Security-specific Process Goals and Metrics

Security-specific Process Goals	Related Metrics
1. Information security testing is an integral part of acceptance testing.	• Number of information security-related changes rejected or not implemented • Percent of information security-related changes accepted
2. Information security improvements identified are incorporated in future releases.	• Number of open information security issues per release • Change in number of unresolved information security issues per release • Percent of information security testing completed on changes

BAI07 Security-specific Process Practices, Inputs/Outputs and Activities

Management Practice	Security-specific Inputs (in Addition to COBIT 5 Inputs)		Security-specific Outputs (in Addition to COBIT 5 Outputs)	
	From	Description	Description	To
BAI07.01 Establish an implementation plan. Establish an implementation plan that covers system and data conversion, acceptance testing criteria, communication, training, release preparation, promotion to production, early production support, a fallback/backout plan, and a post-implementation review. Obtain approval from relevant parties.	Outside *COBIT 5 for Information Security*	IT implementation plan	Updated IT implementation plan	Internal

Security-specific Activities (in Addition to COBIT 5 Activities)

1. Include information security aspects in the acceptance and transition implementation plan.

Management Practice	Security-specific Inputs (in Addition to COBIT 5 Inputs)		Security-specific Outputs (in Addition to COBIT 5 Outputs)	
	From	Description	Description	To
BAI07.02 Plan business process, system and data conversion. Prepare for business process, IT service data and infrastructure migration as part of the enterprise's development methods, including audit trails and a recovery plan should the migration fail.				

Security-specific Activities (in Addition to COBIT 5 Activities)

0. Information security-specific guidance is not relevant for this practice. The generic COBIT 5 activities can be used as further guidance.

Management Practice	Security-specific Inputs (in Addition to COBIT 5 Inputs)		Security-specific Outputs (in Addition to COBIT 5 Outputs)	
	From	Description	Description	To
BAI07.03 Plan acceptance tests. Establish a test plan based on enterprisewide standards that define roles, responsibilities, and entry and exit criteria. Ensure that the plan is approved by relevant parties.	Outside *COBIT 5 for Information Security*	Test plans	Information security measures within the test environment	Internal

Security-specific Activities (in Addition to COBIT 5 Activities)

1. Ensure that information security acceptance tests are part of the test plan.

Build, Acquire and Implement

133

Build, Acquire and Implement

BAI07 Security-specific Process Practices, Inputs/Outputs and Activities *(cont.)*

Management Practice	Security-specific Inputs (in Addition to COBIT 5 Inputs)		Security-specific Outputs (in Addition to COBIT 5 Outputs)	
	From	Description	Description	To
BAI07.04 Establish a test environment. Define and establish a secure test environment representative of the planned business process and IT operations environment, performance and capacity, security, internal controls, operational practices, data quality and privacy requirements, and workloads.	Outside *COBIT 5 for Information Security*	Test data and environment architecture	Secure test environments	Internal

Security-specific Activities (in Addition to COBIT 5 Activities)

1. Ensure that appropriate information security is in place for the test environment (e.g., anonymise sensitive data).

Management Practice	Security-specific Inputs (in Addition to COBIT 5 Inputs)		Security-specific Outputs (in Addition to COBIT 5 Outputs)	
	From	Description	Description	To
BAI07.05 Perform acceptance tests. Test changes independently in accordance with the defined test plan prior to migration to the live operational environment.	Outside *COBIT 5 for Information Security*	Acceptance tests	Updated acceptance tests	Internal

Security-specific Activities (in Addition to COBIT 5 Activities)

1. Develop and perform information security acceptance tests.

Management Practice	Security-specific Inputs (in Addition to COBIT 5 Inputs)		Security-specific Outputs (in Addition to COBIT 5 Outputs)	
	From	Description	Description	To
BAI07.06 Promote to production and manage releases. Promote the accepted solution to the business and operations. Where appropriate, run the solution as a pilot implementation or in parallel with the old solution for a defined period and compare behaviour and results. If significant problems occur, revert back to the original environment based on the fallback/backout plan. Manage releases of solution components.	Outside *COBIT 5 for Information Security*	Release plans	Updated release plans	Internal

Security-specific Activities (in Addition to COBIT 5 Activities)

1. Ensure that information security is managed during promotion to production and release management.

Management Practice	Security-specific Inputs (in Addition to COBIT 5 Inputs)		Security-specific Outputs (in Addition to COBIT 5 Outputs)	
	From	Description	Description	To
BAI07.07 Provide early production support. Provide early support to the users and IT operations for an agreed-on period of time to deal with issues and help stabilise the new solution.				

Security-specific Activities (in Addition to COBIT 5 Activities)

0. Information security-specific guidance is not relevant for this practice. The generic COBIT 5 activities can be used as further guidance.

Management Practice	Security-specific Inputs (in Addition to COBIT 5 Inputs)		Security-specific Outputs (in Addition to COBIT 5 Outputs)	
	From	Description	Description	To
BAI07.08 Perform a post-implementation review. Conduct a post-implementation review to confirm outcome and results, identify lessons learned, and develop an action plan. Evaluate and check the actual performance and outcomes of the new or changed service against the predicted performance and outcomes (i.e., the service expected by the user or customer).	Outside *COBIT 5 for Information Security*	Post-implementation review reports	Updated post-implementation review reports	Internal

Security-specific Activities (in Addition to COBIT 5 Activities)

1. Ensure that information security is included in a post-implementation review.

For more information regarding the related enablers, please consult:
- Appendix F. Detailed Guidance: Services, Infrastructure and Applications Enabler
- Appendix G. Detailed Guidance: People, Skills and Competencies Enabler, G.5. Information Security Operations

BAI08 Manage Knowledge	Area: Management Domain: Build, Acquire and Implement

COBIT 5 Process Description
Maintain the availability of relevant, current, validated and reliable knowledge to support all process activities and to facilitate decision making. Plan for the identification, gathering, organising, maintaining, use and retirement of knowledge.

COBIT 5 Process Purpose Statement
Provide the knowledge required to support all staff in their work activities and for informed decision making and enhanced productivity.

BAI08 Security-specific Process Goals and Metrics

Security-specific Process Goals	Related Metrics
1. Knowledge sharing is supported with the proper safeguards.	• Number of information leakage events • Number of employees trained in information security • Percent of information security categories covered

BAI08 Security-specific Process Practices, Inputs/Outputs and Activities

Management Practice	Security-specific Inputs (in Addition to COBIT 5 Inputs)		Security-specific Outputs (in Addition to COBIT 5 Outputs)	
	From	Description	Description	To
BAI08.01 Nurture and facilitate a knowledge-sharing culture. Devise and implement a scheme to nurture and facilitate a knowledge-sharing culture.	APO01.04	Information security training and awareness programme	Data loss prevention measures	Internal

Security-specific Activities (in Addition to COBIT 5 Activities)
1. Ensure that the proper measures for data loss prevention are in place.
2. Provide awareness training on information security relative to the sharing of information.
3. Incorporate information security considerations into the enterprise information life cycle.

Management Practice	Security-specific Inputs (in Addition to COBIT 5 Inputs)		Security-specific Outputs (in Addition to COBIT 5 Outputs)	
	From	Description	Description	To
BAI08.02 Identify and classify sources of information. Identify, validate and classify diverse sources of internal and external information required to enable effective use and operation of business processes and IT services.			Updated classification of information sources	Internal

Security-specific Activities (in Addition to COBIT 5 Activities)
1. Support the use and sharing of information relative to its classification and sensitivity.
2. Develop a structure for how to categorise systems.
3. Develop a structure for how to classify information.

Management Practice	Security-specific Inputs (in Addition to COBIT 5 Inputs)		Security-specific Outputs (in Addition to COBIT 5 Outputs)	
	From	Description	Description	To
BAI08.03 Organise and contextualise information into knowledge. Organise information based upon classification criteria. Identify and create meaningful relationships between information elements and enable use of information. Identify owners and define and implement levels of access to knowledge resources.			Published knowledge repositories	Internal

Security-specific Activities (in Addition to COBIT 5 Activities)
1. Map roles to knowledge areas and ensure that proper access control is in place for relevant information.

Build, Acquire and Implement

BAI08 Security-specific Process Practices, Inputs/Outputs and Activities *(cont.)*				
Management Practice	**Security-specific Inputs (in Addition to COBIT 5 Inputs)**		**Security-specific Outputs (in Addition to COBIT 5 Outputs)**	
	From	**Description**	**Description**	**To**
BAI08.04 Use and share knowledge. Propagate available knowledge resources to relevant stakeholders and communicate how these resources can be used to address different needs (e.g., problem solving, learning, strategic planning and decision making).			Updated access control	Internal

Security-specific Activities (in Addition to COBIT 5 Activities)
1. Ensure the proper measures for data loss prevention.
2. Implement access controls through the use of policies and processes to restrict unauthorised use and sharing of information.

Management Practice	**Security-specific Inputs (in Addition to COBIT 5 Inputs)**		**Security-specific Outputs (in Addition to COBIT 5 Outputs)**	
	From	**Description**	**Description**	**To**
BAI08.05 Evaluate and retire information. Measure the use and evaluate the currency and relevance of information. Retire obsolete information.			Updated rules for knowledge retirement	Internal

Security-specific Activities (in Addition to COBIT 5 Activities)
1. Securely dispose of information. Include deletion of traceability (personal data/privacy issues).
2. Maintain and document a solid/accepted audit trail for information.
3. Align information security measures relevant to classification.
4. Develop secure information destruction policies and processes.

For more information regarding the related enablers, please consult: • Appendix E. Detailed Guidance: Information Enabler

Build, Acquire and Implement

BAI09 Manage Assets	Area: Management Domain: Build, Acquire and Implement

COBIT 5 Process Description

Manage IT assets through their life cycle to make sure that their use delivers value at optimal cost, they remain operational (fit for purpose), they are accounted for and physically protected, and those assets that are critical to support service capability are reliable and available. Manage software licences to ensure that the optimal number are acquired, retained and deployed in relation to required business usage, and the software installed is in compliance with licence agreements.

COBIT 5 Process Purpose Statement

Account for all IT assets and optimise the value provided by these assets.

BAI09 Security-specific Process Goals and Metrics

Security-specific Process Goals	Related Metrics
1. All assets acquired meet information security requirements.	• Frequency of review of information security requirements
2. All assets are assigned roles and responsibilities.	• Percent of assets with assigned owners
3. Information security mechanisms are in place to prevent the use of unauthorised assets.	• Number of identified unauthorised assets

BAI09 Security-specific Process Practices, Inputs/Outputs and Activities

Management Practice	Security-specific Inputs (in Addition to COBIT 5 Inputs)		Security-specific Outputs (in Addition to COBIT 5 Outputs)	
	From	Description	Description	To
BAI09.01 Identify and record current assets. Maintain an up-to-date and accurate record of all IT assets required to deliver services and ensure alignment with configuration management and financial management.	Outside *COBIT 5* for Information Security	Asset inventory	Information security requirements for IT assets	BAI09.02
			Results of physical inventory checks	DSS05.03

Security-specific Activities (in Addition to COBIT 5 Activities)
1. Identify dependencies between assets.
2. Identify information security requirements for current assets and take into account the dependencies.
3. Address information security for IT assets, data and forms, etc.

Management Practice	Security-specific Inputs (in Addition to COBIT 5 Inputs)		Security-specific Outputs (in Addition to COBIT 5 Outputs)	
	From	Description	Description	To
BAI09.02 Manage critical assets. Identify assets that are critical in providing service capability and take steps to maximise their reliability and availability to support business needs.	BAI09.01	Information security requirements for IT assets	Criticality levels for IT assets	BAI09.03

Security-specific Activities (in Addition to COBIT 5 Activities)
1. Define criticality levels and identify asset criticality in an asset register.
2. Enforce information security requirements on assets.

Management Practice	Security-specific Inputs (in Addition to COBIT 5 Inputs)		Security-specific Outputs (in Addition to COBIT 5 Outputs)	
	From	Description	Description	To
BAI09.03 Manage the asset life cycle. Manage assets from procurement to disposal to ensure that assets are utilised as effectively and efficiently as possible and are accounted for and physically protected.	BAI09.02	Criticality levels for IT assets	Updated asset management procedures	Internal

Security-specific Activities (in Addition to COBIT 5 Activities)
1. Identify and communicate the risk for information security non-compliance related to the asset life cycle.
2. Ensure that information security measures and requirements are met throughout the life cycle.

Build, Acquire and Implement

BAI09 Security-specific Process Practices, Inputs/Outputs and Activities *(cont.)*				
Management Practice	Security-specific Inputs (in Addition to COBIT 5 Inputs)		Security-specific Outputs (in Addition to COBIT 5 Outputs)	
	From	Description	Description	To
BAI09.04 Optimise asset costs. Regularly review the overall asset base to identify ways to optimise costs and maintain alignment with business needs.				
Security-specific Activities (in Addition to COBIT 5 Activities)				
0. Information security-specific guidance is not relevant for this practice. The generic COBIT 5 activities can be used as further guidance.				
Management Practice	Security-specific Inputs (in Addition to COBIT 5 Inputs)		Security-specific Outputs (in Addition to COBIT 5 Outputs)	
	From	Description	Description	To
BAI09.05 Manage licences. Manage software licences so that the optimal number of licences is maintained to support business requirements and the number of licences owned is sufficient to cover the installed software in use.			Updated register of software licences	Internal
Security-specific Activities (in Addition to COBIT 5 Activities)				
1. Establish a procedure for control of software installations and other IT assets.				
2. Perform regular network checks for unauthorised software.				

For more information regarding the related enablers, please consult:
• Appendix E. Detailed Guidance: Information Enabler
• Appendix F. Detailed Guidance: Services, Infrastructure and Applications Enabler
• Appendix G. Detailed Guidance: People, Skills and Competencies Enabler, G.5. Information Security Operations

BAI10 Manage Configuration	Area: Management Domain: Build, Acquire and Implement

COBIT 5 Process Description
Define and maintain descriptions and relationships between key resources and capabilities required to deliver IT-enabled services, including collecting configuration information, establishing baselines, verifying and auditing configuration information, and updating the configuration repository.

COBIT 5 Process Purpose Statement
Provide sufficient information about service assets to enable the service to be effectively managed, assess the impact of changes and deal with service incidents.

BAI10 Security-specific Process Goals and Metrics

Security-specific Process Goals	Related Metrics
1. Information security configuration baselines are approved, implemented and maintained across the enterprise.	• Number of times and time since baselines have been reviewed and validated based on a predetermined time period or major changes • Number of discrepancies between standard information security baselines and actual configurations

BAI10 Security-specific Process Practices, Inputs/Outputs and Activities

Management Practice	Security-specific Inputs (in Addition to COBIT 5 Inputs)		Security-specific Outputs (in Addition to COBIT 5 Outputs)	
	From	Description	Description	To
BAI10.01 Establish and maintain a configuration model. Establish and maintain a logical model of the services, assets and infrastructure and how to record configuration items (CIs) and the relationships amongst them. Include the CIs considered necessary to manage services effectively and to provide a single reliable description of the assets in a service.			Information security alerts	Internal

Security-specific Activities (in Addition to COBIT 5 Activities)

0. Information security-specific guidance is not relevant for this practice. The generic COBIT 5 activities can be used as further guidance.

Management Practice	Security-specific Inputs (in Addition to COBIT 5 Inputs)		Security-specific Outputs (in Addition to COBIT 5 Outputs)	
	From	Description	Description	To
BAI10.02 Establish and maintain a configuration repository and baseline. Establish and maintain a configuration management repository and create controlled configuration baselines.			Vulnerability assessment report	Internal

Security-specific Activities (in Addition to COBIT 5 Activities)

1. Include an information security configuration for configurable items such as servers/hardware, network devices and endpoint devices.

2. Identify information security requirements for current assets and take into account the dependencies.

3. Monitor compliance with established and approved secure configuration baselines and updates.

Management Practice	Security-specific Inputs (in Addition to COBIT 5 Inputs)		Security-specific Outputs (in Addition to COBIT 5 Outputs)	
	From	Description	Description	To
BAI10.03 Maintain and control configuration items. Maintain an up-to-date repository of configuration items by populating with changes.			Configuration management plan	Internal

Security-specific Activities (in Addition to COBIT 5 Activities)

0. Information security-specific guidance is not relevant for this practice. The generic COBIT 5 activities can be used as further guidance.

Build, Acquire and Implement

BAI10 Security-specific Process Practices, Inputs/Outputs and Activities *(cont.)*				
Management Practice	**Security-specific Inputs (in Addition to COBIT 5 Inputs)**		**Security-specific Outputs (in Addition to COBIT 5 Outputs)**	
	From	**Description**	**Description**	**To**
BAI10.04 Produce status and configuration reports. Define and produce configuration reports on status changes of configuration items.				
Security-specific Activities (in Addition to COBIT 5 Activities)				
0. Information security-specific guidance is not relevant for this practice. The generic COBIT 5 activities can be used as further guidance.				
Management Practice	**Security-specific Inputs (in Addition to COBIT 5 Inputs)**		**Security-specific Outputs (in Addition to COBIT 5 Outputs)**	
	From	**Description**	**Description**	**To**
BAI10.05 Verify and review integrity of the configuration repository. Periodically review the configuration repository and verify completeness and correctness against the desired target.				
Security-specific Activities (in Addition to COBIT 5 Activities)				
0. Information security-specific guidance is not relevant for this practice. The generic COBIT 5 activities can be used as further guidance.				

For more information regarding the related enablers, please consult:
• Appendix F. Detailed Guidance: Services, Infrastructure and Applications Enabler
• Appendix G. Detailed Guidance: People, Skills and Competencies Enabler, G.5. Information Security Operations

B.4 DELIVER, SERVICE AND SUPPORT (DSS)

01 Manage operations.

02 Manage service requests and incidents.

03 Manage problems.

04 Manage continuity.

05 Manage security services.

06 Manage business process controls.

Deliver, Service and Support

Page intentionally left blank

Deliver, Service and Support

COBIT® FOR INFORMATION SECURITY

DSS01 Manage Operations	Area: Management Domain: Deliver, Service and Support

COBIT 5 Process Description
Co-ordinate and execute the activities and operational procedures required to deliver internal and outsourced IT services, including the execution of pre-defined standard operating procedures and the required monitoring activities.

COBIT 5 Process Purpose Statement
Deliver IT operational service outcomes as planned.

DSS01 Security-specific Process Goals and Metrics

Security-specific Process Goals	Related Metrics
1. Information security operations are performed according to an information security operational plan in line with the information security strategy.	• Number of information security incidents caused by operational problems
2. Applicable information security standards are identified and met.	• Number of information security issues not addressed by information security standards • Number of information security standards not addressed and met by the information security operational plan

DSS01 Security-specific Process Practices, Inputs/Outputs and Activities

Management Practice	Security-specific Inputs (in Addition to COBIT 5 Inputs)		Security-specific Outputs (in Addition to COBIT 5 Outputs)	
	From	Description	Description	To
DSS01.01 Perform operational procedures. Maintain and perform operational procedures and operational tasks reliably and consistently.	APO03.05	Information security architecture service implementation guidance	Information security operational procedures	Internal

Security-specific Activities (in Addition to COBIT 5 Activities)

1. Verify that relevant information security operational procedures are included in the regular operational procedures.

2. Ensure that the information processing life cycle (receipt, processing, storage and output) incorporates the information security policy and regulatory requirements.

3. Ensure that information security operations are planned, performed and controlled in line with the operational plan.

4. Apply information security and access rights to all data.

Management Practice	Security-specific Inputs (in Addition to COBIT 5 Inputs)		Security-specific Outputs (in Addition to COBIT 5 Outputs)	
	From	Description	Description	To
DSS01.02 Manage outsourced IT services. Manage the operation of outsourced IT services to maintain the protection of enterprise information and reliability of service delivery.	APO01.03	Information security and related policies	Third-party assurance plans	Internal

Security-specific Activities (in Addition to COBIT 5 Activities)

1. Ensure and actively monitor third-party compliance with the enterprise information security policies, standards and information security requirements.

Management Practice	Security-specific Inputs (in Addition to COBIT 5 Inputs)		Security-specific Outputs (in Addition to COBIT 5 Outputs)	
	From	Description	Description	To
DSS01.03 Monitor IT infrastructure. Monitor the IT infrastructure and related events. Store sufficient chronological information in operations logs to enable the reconstruction, review and examination of the time sequences of operations and the other activities surrounding or supporting operations.	Outside *COBIT 5 for Information Security*	Asset monitoring rules and event conditions	Updated asset monitoring rules	Internal

Security-specific Activities (in Addition to COBIT 5 Activities)

1. Ensure that IT actively monitors information security aspects of IT infrastructure, such as configuration, operations, access and use.

DSS01 Security-specific Process Practices, Inputs/Outputs and Activities *(cont.)*				
	Security-specific Inputs (in Addition to COBIT 5 Inputs)		Security-specific Outputs (in Addition to COBIT 5 Outputs)	
Management Practice	**From**	**Description**	**Description**	**To**
DSS01.04 Manage the environment. Maintain measures for protection against environmental factors. Install specialised equipment and devices to monitor and control the environment.	Outside *COBIT 5 for Information Security*	Environmental policies	Updated environmental policies	Internal
Security-specific Activities (in Addition to COBIT 5 Activities)				
1. Ensure that environmental management adheres to information security requirements.				
	Security-specific Inputs (in Addition to COBIT 5 Inputs)		Security-specific Outputs (in Addition to COBIT 5 Outputs)	
Management Practice	**From**	**Description**	**Description**	**To**
DSS01.05 Manage facilities. Manage facilities, including power and communications equipment, in line with laws and regulations, technical and business requirements, vendor specifications, and health and safety guidelines.	Outside *COBIT 5 for Information Security*	Facilities assessment reports	Updated facilities assessment reports	Internal
Security-specific Activities (in Addition to COBIT 5 Activities)				
1. Ensure that facilities management adheres to information security requirements.				

For more information regarding the related enablers, please consult: • Appendix F. Detailed Guidance: Services, Infrastructure and Applications Enabler • Appendix G. Detailed Guidance: People, Skills and Competencies Enabler, G.5. Information Security Operations

Deliver, Service and Support

DSS02 Manage Service Requests and Incidents	Area: Management Domain: Deliver, Service and Support

COBIT 5 Process Description
Provide timely and effective response to user requests and resolution of all types of incidents. Restore normal service; record and fulfil user requests; and record, investigate, diagnose, escalate and resolve incidents.

COBIT 5 Process Purpose Statement
Achieve increased productivity and minimise disruptions through quick resolution of user queries and incidents.

DSS02 Security-specific Process Goals and Metrics

Security-specific Process Goals	Related Metrics
1. An effective information security incident response programme is established and maintained.	• Mean time to resolve information security incidents • Number and percent of information security-related incidents causing disruption to business-critical processes • Number of information security incidents open/closed and their risk rankings • Frequency of information security incident response plan testing

DSS02 Security-specific Process Practices, Inputs/Outputs and Activities

Management Practice	Security-specific Inputs (in Addition to COBIT 5 Inputs)		Security-specific Outputs (in Addition to COBIT 5 Outputs)	
	From	Description	Description	To
DSS02.01 Define incident and service request classification schemes. Define incident and service request classification schemes and models.	APO01.03	Information security and related policies	Information security incident classification scheme	DSS02.02

Security-specific Activities (in Addition to COBIT 5 Activities)
1. Define and communicate the nature and characteristics of potential security-related incidents so they can be easily recognised and their impact understood to enable a commensurate response.

Management Practice	Security-specific Inputs (in Addition to COBIT 5 Inputs)		Security-specific Outputs (in Addition to COBIT 5 Outputs)	
	From	Description	Description	To
DSS02.02 Record, classify and prioritise requests and incidents. Identify, record and classify service requests and incidents, and assign a priority according to business criticality and service agreements.	DSS02.01	Information security incident classification scheme	Classified and prioritised information security incidents and service requests	APO08.03 APO12.01 APO13.03 DSS02.07
	DSS05.07	Security incident tickets		

Security-specific Activities (in Addition to COBIT 5 Activities)
1. Maintain a security incident investigation and response procedure. Ensure that measures are in place to protect the confidentiality of information related to security incidents and that all staff are made aware of the procedure.

Management Practice	Security-specific Inputs (in Addition to COBIT 5 Inputs)		Security-specific Outputs (in Addition to COBIT 5 Outputs)	
	From	Description	Description	To
DSS02.03 Verify, approve and fulfil service requests. Select the appropriate request procedures and verify that the service requests fulfil defined request criteria. Obtain approval, if required, and fulfil the requests.				

Security-specific Activities (in Addition to COBIT 5 Activities)
0. Information security-specific guidance is not relevant for this practice. The generic COBIT 5 activities can be used as further guidance.

Deliver, Service and Support

DSS02 Security-specific Process Practices, Inputs/Outputs and Activities *(cont.)*

Management Practice	Security-specific Inputs (in Addition to COBIT 5 Inputs)		Security-specific Outputs (in Addition to COBIT 5 Outputs)	
	From	Description	Description	To
DSS02.04 Investigate, diagnose and allocate incidents. Identify and record incident symptoms, determine possible causes, and allocate for resolution.			Evidence collection procedure	Internal

Security-specific activities (in addition to COBIT 5 activities)

1. Maintain a procedure for evidence collection in line with local forensic evidence rules and ensure that all staff are made aware of the requirements.

Management Practice	Security-specific Inputs (in Addition to COBIT 5 Inputs)		Security-specific Outputs (in Addition to COBIT 5 Outputs)	
	From	Description	Description	To
DSS02.05 Resolve and recover from incidents. Document, apply and test the identified solutions or workarounds and perform recovery actions to restore the IT-related service.	Outside *COBIT 5 for Information Security*	Business impact assessment, organisational risk management policy, incident classification scheme	Incident response plan	DSS02.07

Security-specific Activities (in Addition to COBIT 5 Activities)

1. Define an information security incident response plan.

Management Practice	Security-specific Inputs (in Addition to COBIT 5 Inputs)		Security-specific Outputs (in Addition to COBIT 5 Outputs)	
	From	Description	Description	To
DSS02.06 Close service requests and incidents. Verify satisfactory incident resolution and/or request fulfilment, and close.				

Security-specific Activities (in Addition to COBIT 5 Activities)

0. Information security-specific guidance is not relevant for this practice. The generic COBIT 5 activities can be used as further guidance.

Management Practice	Security-specific Inputs (in Addition to COBIT 5 Inputs)		Security-specific Outputs (in Addition to COBIT 5 Outputs)	
	From	Description	Description	To
DSS02.07 Track status and produce reports. Regularly track, analyse and report incident and request fulfilment trends to provide information for continual improvement.	DSS02.02	Classified and prioritised information security incidents and service requests	Lessons learned	Internal
	DSS02.05	Incident response plan		

Security-specific Activities (in Addition to COBIT 5 Activities)

1. Report the outcome of security incident investigations to appropriate stakeholders, including periodic reports to executive management.

2. Ensure that security incidents and appropriate follow-up actions, including root cause analysis, follow the existing incident and problem management processes.

For more information regarding the related enablers, please consult:
- Appendix E. Detailed Guidance: Information Enabler, E.9 Information Security Dashboard
- Appendix F. Detailed Guidance: Services, Infrastructure and Applications Enabler
- Appendix G. Detailed Guidance: People, Skills and Competencies Enabler, G.5 Information Security Operations

Deliver, Service and Support

DSS03 Manage Problems	Area: Management Domain: Deliver, Service and Support

COBIT 5 Process Description

Identify and classify problems and their root causes and provide timely resolution to prevent recurring incidents. Provide recommendations for improvements.

COBIT 5 Process Purpose Statement

Increase availability, improve service levels, reduce costs, and improve customer convenience and satisfaction by reducing the number of operational problems.

DSS03 Security-specific Process Goals and Metrics

Security-specific Process Goals	Related Metrics
1. Information security problems are solved in a sustainable way.	• Number of recurring information security problems that remain unresolved • Number of information security-related problems for which a satisfactory resolution that addressed critical information security issues was found

DSS03 Security-specific Process Practices, Inputs/Outputs and Activities

Management Practice	Security-specific Inputs (in Addition to COBIT 5 Inputs)		Security-specific Outputs (in Addition to COBIT 5 Outputs)	
	From	Description	Description	To
DSS03.01 Identify and classify problems. Define and implement criteria and procedures to report problems identified, including problem classification, categorisation and prioritisation.	Outside *COBIT 5 for Information Security*	Vulnerability assessments	Information security problems classification scheme	DSS03.04

Security-specific Activities (in Addition to COBIT 5 Activities)

1. Classify, categorise and prioritise information security problems.

Management Practice	Security-specific Inputs (in Addition to COBIT 5 Inputs)		Security-specific Outputs (in Addition to COBIT 5 Outputs)	
	From	Description	Description	To
DSS03.02 Investigate and diagnose problems. Investigate and diagnose problems using relevant subject matter experts to assess and analyse root causes.			Updated root cause of problems	Internal

Security-specific Activities (in Addition to COBIT 5 Activities)

1. Investigate information security problems.

Management Practice	Security-specific Inputs (in Addition to COBIT 5 Inputs)		Security-specific Outputs (in Addition to COBIT 5 Outputs)	
	From	Description	Description	To
DSS03.03 Raise known errors. As soon as the root causes of problems are identified, create known-error records and an appropriate workaround, and identify potential solutions.			Updated known errors records	Internal

Security-specific Activities (in Addition to COBIT 5 Activities)

1. Escalate information security problems as necessary.

Management Practice	Security-specific Inputs (in Addition to COBIT 5 Inputs)		Security-specific Outputs (in Addition to COBIT 5 Outputs)	
	From	Description	Description	To
DSS03.04 Resolve and close problems. Identify and initiate sustainable solutions addressing the root cause, raising change requests via the established change management process if required to resolve errors. Ensure that the personnel affected are aware of the actions taken and the plans developed to prevent future incidents from occurring.	DSS03.01	Information security problems classification scheme	Root causes of problems	DSS03.05

Security-specific Activities (in Addition to COBIT 5 Activities)

1. Conduct root cause analysis, resolve information security problems and update the incident response plan. Track or log information security problems.

Deliver, Service and Support

DSS03 Security-specific Process Practices, Inputs/Outputs and Activities *(cont.)*				
	Security-specific Inputs (in Addition to COBIT 5 Inputs)		Security-specific Outputs (in Addition to COBIT 5 Outputs)	
Management Practice	From	Description	Description	To
DSS03.05 Perform proactive problem management. Collect and analyse operational data (especially incident and change records) to identify emerging trends that may indicate problems. Log problem records to enable assessment.	DSS03.04	Root causes of problems	Implementation of information security policies and procedures and action plans to address root causes	Internal
Security-specific Activities (in Addition to COBIT 5 Activities)				
1. Conduct and leverage lessons learned.				

For more information regarding the related enablers, please consult:
- Appendix E. Detailed Guidance: Information Enabler, E.9. Information Security Dashboard
- Appendix F. Detailed Guidance: Services, Infrastructure and Applications Enabler
- Appendix G. Detailed Guidance: People, Skills and Competencies Enabler, G.5. Information Security Operations

Deliver, Service and Support

DSS04 Manage Continuity	Area: Management Domain: Deliver, Service and Support

COBIT 5 Process Description
Establish and maintain a plan to enable the business and IT to respond to incidents and disruptions in order to continue operation of critical business processes and required IT services and maintain availability of information at a level acceptable to the enterprise.

COBIT 5 Process Purpose Statement
Continue critical business operations and maintain availability of information at a level acceptable to the enterprise in the event of a significant disruption.

DSS04 Security-specific Process Goals and Metrics

Security-specific Process Goals	Related Metrics
1. Information risk is properly identified and addressed in the information and communications technology (ICT) continuity plan.	• Number of invoked declarations based on information security incidents • Number of information security incidents escalated to ICT continuity activation • Number of critical information security systems covered by the ICT continuity plan

DSS04 Security-specific Process Practices, Inputs/Outputs and Activities

Management Practice	Security-specific Inputs (in Addition to COBIT 5 Inputs)		Security-specific Outputs (in Addition to COBIT 5 Outputs)	
	From	Description	Description	To
DSS04.01 Define the business continuity policy, objectives and scope. Define business continuity policy and scope aligned with enterprise and stakeholder objectives.	Outside *COBIT 5 for Information Security*	Policy for business continuity	Updated policy for business continuity	Internal

Security-specific Activities (in Addition to COBIT 5 Activities)
1. Ensure that information security is part of the business continuity life cycle.

Management Practice	Security-specific Inputs (in Addition to COBIT 5 Inputs)		Security-specific Outputs (in Addition to COBIT 5 Outputs)	
	From	Description	Description	To
DSS04.02 Maintain a continuity strategy. Evaluate business continuity management options and choose a cost-effective and viable continuity strategy that will ensure enterprise recovery and continuity in the face of a disaster or other major incident or disruption.	Outside *COBIT 5 for Information Security*	BIA	Updated BIA	Internal

Security-specific Activities (in Addition to COBIT 5 Activities)
1. Include scenarios that take information security into account.

Management Practice	Security-specific Inputs (in Addition to COBIT 5 Inputs)		Security-specific Outputs (in Addition to COBIT 5 Outputs)	
	From	Description	Description	To
DSS04.03 Develop and implement a business continuity response. Develop a business continuity plan (BCP) based on the strategy that documents the procedures and information in readiness for use in an incident to enable the enterprise to continue its critical activities.	Outside *COBIT 5 for Information Security*	BCP	Updated BCP	Internal

Security-specific Activities (in Addition to COBIT 5 Activities)
1. Include information security requirements in the BCP.

Management Practice	Security-specific Inputs (in Addition to COBIT 5 Inputs)		Security-specific Outputs (in Addition to COBIT 5 Outputs)	
	From	Description	Description	To
DSS04.04 Exercise, test and review the BCP. Test the continuity arrangements on a regular basis to exercise the recovery plans against predetermined outcomes and to allow innovative solutions to be developed and help to verify over time that the plan will work as anticipated.				

Security-specific Activities (in Addition to COBIT 5 Activities)
0. Information security-specific guidance is not relevant for this practice. The generic COBIT 5 activities can be used as further guidance.

Deliver, Service and Support

DSS04 Security-specific Process Practices, Inputs/Outputs and Activities *(cont.)*				
	Security-specific Inputs (in Addition to COBIT 5 Inputs)		Security-specific Outputs (in Addition to COBIT 5 Outputs)	
Management Practice	**From**	**Description**	**Description**	**To**
DSS04.05 Review, maintain and improve the continuity plan. Conduct a management review of the continuity capability at regular intervals to ensure its continued suitability, adequacy and effectiveness. Manage changes to the plan in accordance with the change control process to ensure that the continuity plan is kept up to date and continually reflects actual business requirements.	Outside *COBIT 5 for Information Security*	BCP	Updated BCP	Internal

Security-specific Activities (in Addition to COBIT 5 Activities)
1. Consider information security incidents as important triggers to improve the BCP.

	Security-specific Inputs (in Addition to COBIT 5 Inputs)		Security-specific Outputs (in Addition to COBIT 5 Outputs)	
Management Practice	**From**	**Description**	**Description**	**To**
DSS04.06 Conduct continuity plan training. Provide all concerned internal and external parties with regular training sessions regarding the procedures and their roles and responsibilities in case of disruption.				

Security-specific Activities (in Addition to COBIT 5 Activities)
0. Information security-specific guidance is not relevant for this practice. The generic COBIT 5 activities can be used as further guidance.

	Security-specific Inputs (in Addition to COBIT 5 Inputs)		Security-specific Outputs (in Addition to COBIT 5 Outputs)	
Management Practice	**From**	**Description**	**Description**	**To**
DSS04.07 Manage backup arrangements. Maintain availability of business-critical information.	Outside *COBIT 5 for Information Security*	Test results of backup data	Updated test results of backup data	Internal

Security-specific Activities (in Addition to COBIT 5 Activities)
1. Ensure that information security requirements are included in the backup and restore arrangements.

	Security-specific Inputs (in Addition to COBIT 5 Inputs)		Security-specific Outputs (in Addition to COBIT 5 Outputs)	
Management Practice	**From**	**Description**	**Description**	**To**
DSS04.08 Conduct post-resumption review. Assess the adequacy of the BCP following the successful resumption of business processes and services after a disruption.	Outside *COBIT 5 for Information Security*	Post-resumption review reports	Updated post-resumption review reports	Internal

Security-specific Activities (in Addition to COBIT 5 Activities)
1. Ensure that information security is included in a post-resumption review.

For more information regarding the related enablers, please consult:
• Appendix A. Detailed Guidance: Principles, Policies and Frameworks Enabler

Deliver, Service and Support

DSS05 Manage Security Services	Area: Management Domain: Deliver, Service and Support

COBIT 5 Process Description
Protect enterprise information to maintain the level of information security risk acceptable to the enterprise in accordance with the security policy. Establish and maintain information security roles and access privileges and perform security monitoring.

COBIT 5 Process Purpose Statement
Minimise the business impact of operational information security vulnerabilities and incidents.

DSS05 Security-specific Process Goals and Metrics

Security-specific Process Goals	Related Metrics
1. Network and communication security meet business needs.	• Number of vulnerabilities discovered • Number of firewall breaches
2. Information processed on, stored on and transmitted by endpoint devices is protected.	• Percent of individuals receiving awareness training relating to use of endpoint devices • Number of incidents involving endpoint devices • Number of unauthorised devices detected on the network or in the end-user environment
3. All users are uniquely identifiable and have access rights in accordance with their business roles.	• Average time between change and update of accounts • Number of accounts (vs. number of authorised users/staff)
4. Physical measures have been implemented to protect information from unauthorised access, damage and interference when being processed, stored or transmitted.	• Percent of periodic tests of environmental security devices • Average rating for physical security assessments • Number of physical security-related incidents
5. Electronic information is properly secured when stored, transmitted or destroyed.	• Number of incidents relating to unauthorised access to information

DSS05 Security-specific Process Practices, Inputs/Outputs and Activities

Management Practice	Security-specific Inputs (in Addition to COBIT 5 Inputs)		Security-specific Outputs (in Addition to COBIT 5 Outputs)	
	From	Description	Description	To
DSS05.01 Protect against malware. Implement and maintain preventive, detective and corrective measures in place (especially up-to-date security patches and virus control) across the enterprise to protect information systems and technology from malware (e.g., viruses, worms, spyware, spam).			Malicious software prevention policy	APO01.04
			Evaluation of potential threats	APO12.02 APO12.03

Security-specific Activities (in Addition to COBIT 5 Activities)
1. Communicate malicious software awareness and enforce prevention procedures and responsibilities.
2. Install and activate malicious software protection tools on all processing facilities, with malicious software definition files that are updated as required (automatically or semi-automatically).
3. Distribute all protection software centrally (version and patch-level) using centralised configuration and change management.
4. Regularly review and evaluate information on new potential threats (e.g., reviewing vendor products and services security advisories).
5. Filter incoming traffic, such as email and downloads, to protect against unsolicited information (e.g., spyware, phishing emails).
6. Conduct periodic training about malware in email and Internet usage. Train users not to install shared or unapproved software.

Deliver, Service and Support

DSS05 Security-specific Process Practices, Inputs/Outputs and Activities *(cont.)*				
	Security-specific Inputs (in Addition to COBIT 5 Inputs)		Security-specific Outputs (in Addition to COBIT 5 Outputs)	
Management Practice	From	Description	Description	To
DSS05.02 Manage network and connectivity security. Use security measures and related management procedures to protect information over all methods of connectivity.	AP001.06	Data classification guidelines	Connectivity security policy	AP001.04
	AP009.03	SLAs	Results of penetration tests	MEA02.08

Security-specific Activities (in Addition to COBIT 5 Activities)
1. Establish and maintain a policy for security of connectivity based on risk assessments and business requirements.
2. Allow only authorised devices to have access to corporate information and the enterprise network. Configure these devices to force password entry.
3. Implement network filtering mechanisms, such as firewalls and intrusion detection software, with appropriate policies to control inbound and outbound traffic.
4. Encrypt information in transit according to its classification.
5. Apply approved security protocols to network connectivity.
6. Configure network equipment in a secure manner.
7. Establish trusted mechanisms to support the secure transmission and receipt of information.
8. Carry out periodic penetration testing to determine adequacy of network protection.
9. Carry out periodic testing of system security to determine adequacy of system protection.

	Security-specific Inputs (in Addition to COBIT 5 Inputs)		Security-specific Outputs (in Addition to COBIT 5 Outputs)	
Management Practice	From	Description	Description	To
DSS05.03 Manage endpoint security. Ensure that endpoints (e.g., laptop, desktop, server, and other mobile and network devices or software) are secured at a level that is equal to or greater than the defined security requirements of the information processed, stored or transmitted.	AP003.02	Information architecture model	Security policies for endpoint devices	AP001.04
	AP009.03	• OLAs • SLAs		
	BAI09.01	Results of physical inventory checks		
	DSS06.06	Reports of violations		

Security-specific Activities (in Addition to COBIT 5 Activities)
1. Configure operating systems in a secure manner.
2. Implement device lockdown mechanisms.
3. Encrypt information in storage according to its classification.
4. Manage remote access and control.
5. Manage network configuration in a secure manner.
6. Implement network traffic filtering on endpoint devices.
7. Protect system integrity.
8. Provide physical protection of endpoint devices.
9. Dispose of endpoint devices securely.

Deliver, Service and Support

DSS05 Security-specific Process Practices, Inputs/Outputs and Activities *(cont.)*				
Management Practice	**Security-specific Inputs (in Addition to COBIT 5 Inputs)**		**Security-specific Outputs (in Addition to COBIT 5 Outputs)**	
	From	**Description**	**Description**	**To**
DSS05.04 Manage user identity and logical access. Ensure that all users have information access rights in accordance with their business requirements and co-ordinate with business units that manage their own access rights within business processes.	APO01.02	Definition of IT-related roles and responsibilities	• Results of reviews of user accounts and privileges • Approved user access rights	Internal
	APO03.02	Information architecture model		

Security-specific Activities (in Addition to COBIT 5 Activities)
1. Maintain user access rights in accordance with business function and process requirements. Align the management of identities and access rights to the defined roles and responsibilities, based on least-privilege, need-to-have and need-to-know principles.
2. Uniquely identify all information processing activities by functional roles, co-ordinating with business units to ensure that all roles are consistently defined, including roles that are defined by the business itself within business process applications.
3. Authenticate all access to information assets based on their security classification, co-ordinating with business units that manage authentication within applications used in business processes to ensure that authentication controls have been properly administered.
4. Administer all changes to access rights (creation, modifications and deletions) to take effect at the appropriate time, based only on approved and documented transactions authorised by designated management individuals.
5. Segregate and manage privileged user accounts.
6. Perform regular management review of all accounts and related privileges.
7. Ensure that all users (internal, external and temporary) and their activity on IT systems (business application, IT infrastructure, system operations, development and maintenance) are uniquely identifiable. Uniquely identify all information processing activities by user.
8. Maintain an audit trail of access to information classified as highly sensitive.

Management Practice	**Security-specific Inputs (in Addition to COBIT 5 Inputs)**		**Security-specific Outputs (in Addition to COBIT 5 Outputs)**	
	From	**Description**	**Description**	**To**
DSS05.05 Manage physical access to IT assets. Define and implement procedures to grant, limit and revoke access to premises, buildings and areas according to business needs, including emergencies. Access to premises, buildings and areas should be justified, authorised, logged and monitored. This should apply to all persons entering the premises, including staff, temporary staff, clients, vendors, visitors or any other third party.			Access logs	DSS06.03
			Approved access requests	Internal

Security-specific Activities (in Addition to COBIT 5 Activities)
1. Manage the requesting and granting of access to the computing facilities. Formal access requests are to be completed and authorised by management of the IT site, and the request records retained. The forms should specifically identify the areas to which the individual is granted access.
2. Ensure that access profiles remain current. Base access to IT sites (server rooms, buildings, areas or zones) on job function and responsibilities.
3. Log and monitor all entry points to IT sites. Register all visitors, including contractors and vendors, to the site.
4. Instruct all personnel to display visible identification at all times. Prevent the issuance of identity cards or badges without proper authorisation.
5. Require visitors to be escorted at all times while on-site. If an unaccompanied, unfamiliar individual who is not wearing staff identification is identified, alert security personnel.
6. Restrict access to sensitive IT sites by establishing perimeter restrictions, such as fences, walls and security devices on interior and exterior doors. Ensure that the devices record entry and trigger an alarm in the event of unauthorised access. Examples of such devices include badges or key cards, keypads, closed-circuit television and biometric scanners.
7. Conduct regular physical security awareness training.

Deliver, Service and Support

DSS05 Security-specific Process Practices, Inputs/Outputs and Activities *(cont.)*				
Management Practice	**Security-specific Inputs (in Addition to COBIT 5 Inputs)**		**Security-specific Outputs (in Addition to COBIT 5 Outputs)**	
	From	**Description**	**Description**	**To**
DSS05.06 Manage sensitive documents and output devices. Establish appropriate physical safeguards, accounting practices and inventory management over sensitive IT assets, such as special forms, negotiable instruments, special-purpose printers or security tokens.	AP003.02	Information architecture model	• Access privileges • Inventory of sensitive documents and devices	Internal

Security-specific Activities (in Addition to COBIT 5 Activities)
1. Establish procedures to govern the receipt, use, removal and disposal of special forms and output devices into, within and outside of the enterprise.
2. Assign access privileges to sensitive documents and output devices based on the least-privilege principle, balancing risk and business requirements.
3. Establish an inventory of sensitive documents and output devices, and conduct regular reconciliations.
4. Establish appropriate physical safeguards over special forms and sensitive devices.
5. Destroy sensitive information and protect output devices (e.g., degaussing of electronic media, physical destruction of memory devices, making shredders or locked paper baskets available to destroy special forms and other confidential papers).

Management Practice	**Security-specific Inputs (in Addition to COBIT 5 Inputs)**		**Security-specific Outputs (in Addition to COBIT 5 Outputs)**	
	From	**Description**	**Description**	**To**
DSS05.07 Monitor the infrastructure for security-related events. Using intrusion detection tools, monitor the infrastructure for unauthorised access and ensure any events are integrated with general event monitoring and incident management.			Security incident tickets	DSS02.02
			• Security incident characteristics • Security event logs	Internal

Security-specific Activities (in Addition to COBIT 5 Activities)
1. Log security-related events reported by infrastructure security monitoring tools, identifying the level of information to be recorded based on a consideration of risk and retain them for an appropriate period to assist in future investigations.
2. Define and communicate the nature and characteristics of potential security-related incidents so they can be easily recognised and their impacts understood to enable a commensurate response.
3. Regularly review the event logs for potential incidents.
4. Maintain a procedure for evidence collection in line with local forensic evidence rules and ensure that all staff are made aware of the requirements.
5. Ensure that security incident tickets are created in a timely manner when monitoring identifies potential security incidents.

Deliver, Service and Support

DSS06 Manage Business Process Controls	Area: Management Domain: Deliver, Service and Support

COBIT 5 Process Description
Define and maintain appropriate business process controls to ensure that information related to and processed by in-house or outsourced business processes satisfies all relevant information control requirements. Identify the relevant information control requirements and manage and operate adequate controls to ensure that information and information processing satisfy these requirements.

COBIT 5 Process Purpose Statement
Maintain information integrity and the security of information assets handled within business processes in the enterprise or outsourced.

DSS06 Security-specific Process Goals and Metrics

Security-specific Process Goals	Related Metrics
1. Appropriate controls over information security processes are in place, reviewed and updated.	• Percent of information security measures that are appropriately implemented or still valid
2. Proper controls are in place that protect the confidentiality, integrity and availability of business processes.	• Number of information security related incidents due to inadequate information security controls in place

DSS06 Security-specific Process Practices, Inputs/Outputs and Activities

Management Practice	Security-specific Inputs (in Addition to COBIT 5 Inputs)		Security-specific Outputs (in Addition to COBIT 5 Outputs)	
	From	Description	Description	To
DSS06.01 Align control activities embedded in business processes with enterprise objectives. Continually assess and monitor the execution of the business process activities and related controls, based on enterprise risk, to ensure that the processing controls are aligned with business needs.			Secure application controls	Internal

Security-specific Activities (in Addition to COBIT 5 Activities)

1. Identify and prioritise information security processes in line with business risk, compliance, etc.

2. Identify specific operational information security requirements (e.g., compliance).

3. Identify and implement needed application controls.

Management Practice	Security-specific Inputs (in Addition to COBIT 5 Inputs)		Security-specific Outputs (in Addition to COBIT 5 Outputs)	
	From	Description	Description	To
DSS06.02 Control the processing of information. Operate the execution of the business process activities and related controls, based on enterprise risk, to ensure that information processing is valid, complete, accurate, timely, and secure (i.e., reflects legitimate and authorised business use).				

Security-specific Activities (in Addition to COBIT 5 Activities)

0. Information security-specific guidance is not relevant for this practice. The generic COBIT 5 activities can be used as further guidance.

Deliver, Service and Support

DSS06 Security-specific Process Practices, Inputs/Outputs and Activities *(cont.)*				
	Security-specific Inputs (in Addition to COBIT 5 Inputs)		Security-specific Outputs (in Addition to COBIT 5 Outputs)	
Management Practice	**From**	**Description**	**Description**	**To**
DSS06.03 Manage roles, responsibilities, access privileges and levels of authority. Manage the business roles, responsibilities, levels of authority and segregation of duties needed to support the business process objectives. Authorise access to any information assets related to business information processes, including those under the custody of the business, IT and third parties. This ensures that the business knows where the data are and who is handling data on its behalf.	AP013.01	ISMS scope statement	Updated roles, responsibilities, access privileges and levels of authority	Internal
	DSS05.05	Access logs		
	Outside *COBIT 5 for Information Security*	Allocated roles and responsibilities		

Security-specific Activities (in Addition to COBIT 5 Activities)
1. Manage roles, responsibilities, access privileges and levels of authority for information.
2. Allocate access rights on need-to-know and least-privilege principles and job requirements.
3. Delete/remove access rights when users leave positions/units.
4. Implement segregation of duties according to business processes to avoid fraud and unauthorised access.
5. Follow up on authorisations.

	Security-specific Inputs (in Addition to COBIT 5 Inputs)		Security-specific Outputs (in Addition to COBIT 5 Outputs)	
Management Practice	**From**	**Description**	**Description**	**To**
DSS06.04 Manage errors and exceptions. Manage business process exceptions and errors and facilitate their correction. Include escalation of business process errors and exceptions and the execution of defined corrective actions. This provides assurance of the accuracy and integrity of the business information process.			Updated access privileges	Internal

Security-specific Activities (in Addition to COBIT 5 Activities)
1. Grant/remove access in emergency situations.

	Security-specific Inputs (in Addition to COBIT 5 Inputs)		Security-specific Outputs (in Addition to COBIT 5 Outputs)	
Management Practice	**From**	**Description**	**Description**	**To**
DSS06.05 Ensure traceability of Information events and accountabilities. Ensure that business information can be traced to the originating business event and accountable parties. This enables traceability of the information through its life cycle and related processes. This provides assurance that information that drives the business is reliable and has been processed in accordance with defined objectives.				

Security-specific Activities (in Addition to COBIT 5 Activities)
0. Information security-specific guidance is not relevant for this practice. The generic COBIT 5 activities can be used as further guidance.

Deliver, Service and Support

DSS06 Security-specific Process Practices, Inputs/Outputs and Activities *(cont.)*				
	Security-specific Inputs (in Addition to COBIT 5 Inputs)		Security-specific Outputs (in Addition to COBIT 5 Outputs)	
Management Practice	From	Description	Description	To
DSS06.06 Secure information assets. Secure information assets accessible by the business through approved methods, including information in electronic form (such as methods that create new assets in any form, portable media devices, user applications and storage devices), information in physical form (such as source documents or output reports) and information during transit. This benefits the business by providing end-to-end safeguarding of information.	Outside *COBIT 5 for Information Security*	Asset inventory	Reports of violations	DSS05.03
Security-specific Activities (in Addition to COBIT 5 Activities)				
1. Enforce data classification, acceptable use, and security policies and procedures to support information asset protection.				

For more information regarding the related enablers, please consult:
• Appendix C. Detailed Guidance: Organisational Structures Enabler, C.5. Information Custodians/Business Owners
• Appendix E. Detailed Guidance: Information Enabler

Deliver, Service and Support

Page intentionally left blank

B.5 MONITOR, EVALUATE AND ASSESS (MEA)

01 Monitor, evaluate and assess performance and conformance.

02 Monitor, evaluate and assess the system of internal control.

03 Monitor, evaluate and assess compliance with external requirements.

Monitor, Evaluate and Assess

Page intentionally left blank

MEA01 Monitor, Evaluate and Assess Performance and Conformance	Area: Management Domain: Monitor, Evaluate and Assess

COBIT 5 Process Description
Collect, validate and evaluate business, IT and process goals and metrics. Monitor that processes are performing against agreed-on performance and conformance goals and metrics and provide reporting that is systematic and timely.

COBIT 5 Process Purpose Statement
Provide transparency of performance and conformance and drive achievement of goals.

MEA01 Security-specific Process Goals and Metrics

Security-specific Process Goals	Related Metrics
1. Information security performance is monitored on an ongoing basis.	• Percent of business processes that meet defined information security requirements
2. Information security and information risk practices conform to internal compliance requirements.	• Percent of information security practices that satisfy internal compliance requirements

MEA01 Security-specific Process Practices, Inputs/Outputs and Activities

Management Practice	Security-specific Inputs (in Addition to COBIT 5 Inputs)		Security-specific Outputs (in Addition to COBIT 5 Outputs)	
	From	Description	Description	To
MEA01.01 Establish a monitoring approach. Engage with stakeholders to establish and maintain a monitoring approach to define the objectives, scope and method for measuring business solution and service delivery and contribution to enterprise objectives. Integrate this approach with the corporate performance management system.	APO01.03	Information security and related policies	Information security monitoring process and procedure	MEA01.02
	BAI02.01	Information security requirements		
	Outside *COBIT 5 for Information Security*	Information security standards and regulations		

Security-specific Activities (in Addition to COBIT 5 Activities)

1. Identify and confirm information security stakeholders.

2. Engage with stakeholders and communicate the information security requirements and objectives for monitoring and reporting.

3. Align and continually maintain the information security monitoring and evaluation approach with the IT and enterprise approaches.

4. Establish the information security monitoring process and procedure.

5. Agree on a life cycle management and change control process for information security monitoring and reporting.

6. Request, prioritise and allocate resources for monitoring information security.

Management Practice	Security-specific Inputs (in Addition to COBIT 5 Inputs)		Security-specific Outputs (in Addition to COBIT 5 Outputs)	
	From	Description	Description	To
MEA01.02 Set performance and conformance targets. Work with the stakeholders to define, periodically review, update and approve performance and conformance targets within the performance measurement system.	MEA01.01	Information security monitoring process and procedure	Agreed-on information security metrics and targets	APO07.04 MEA01.04

Security-specific Activities (in Addition to COBIT 5 Activities)

1. Define information security performance targets consistent with overall IT performance standards.

2. Communicate information security performance and conformance targets with key due diligence stakeholders.

3. Evaluate whether the information security goals and metrics are adequate, i.e., specific, measurable, achievable, relevant and time-bound.

MEA01 Security-specific Process Practices, Inputs/Outputs and Activities *(cont.)*				
	Security-specific Inputs (in Addition to COBIT 5 Inputs)		Security-specific Outputs (in Addition to COBIT 5 Outputs)	
Management Practice	**From**	**Description**	**Description**	**To**
MEA01.03 Collect and process performance and conformance data. Collect and process timely and accurate data aligned with enterprise approaches.	Outside *COBIT 5 for Information Security*	Applicable regulations	Processed monitoring data	Internal
Security-specific Activities (in Addition to COBIT 5 Activities)				
1. Collect and analyse performance and conformance data relating to information security and information risk management (e.g., information security metrics, information security reports).				
2. Assess the efficiency, appropriateness and integrity of collected data.				
	Security-specific Inputs (in Addition to COBIT 5 Inputs)		Security-specific Outputs (in Addition to COBIT 5 Outputs)	
Management Practice	**From**	**Description**	**Description**	**To**
MEA01.04 Analyse and report performance. Periodically review and report performance against targets, using a method that provides a succinct all-around view of IT performance and fits within the enterprise monitoring system.	MEA01.02	Agreed-on information security metrics and targets	Information security reports and corrective action plans updated	APO01.07
Security-specific Activities (in Addition to COBIT 5 Activities)				
1. Design, implement and agree on a range of information security performance reports.				
2. Compare the performance values to internal targets and benchmarks and, where possible, to external benchmarks (industry and key competitors).				
	Security-specific Inputs (in Addition to COBIT 5 Inputs)		Security-specific Outputs (in Addition to COBIT 5 Outputs)	
Management Practice	**From**	**Description**	**Description**	**To**
MEA01.05 Ensure the implementation of corrective actions. Assist stakeholders in identifying, initiating and tracking corrective actions to address anomalies.	Outside *COBIT 5 for Information Security*	Escalation guidelines	Tracking process for corrective actions on information security issues	Internal
Security-specific Activities (in Addition to COBIT 5 Activities)				
1. Develop a tracking process for corrective actions on information security issues.				

For more information regarding the related enablers, please consult:
- Appendix F. Detailed Guidance: Services, Infrastructure and Applications Enabler, F.10 Provide Monitoring and Alert Services for Security-related Events
- Appendix G. Detailed Guidance: People, Skills and Competencies Enabler, G.6. Information Assessment and Testing and Compliance

Monitor, Evaluate and Assess

MEA02 Monitor, Evaluate and Assess the System of Internal Control	Area: Management Domain: Monitor, Evaluate and Assess

COBIT 5 Process Description
Continuously monitor and evaluate the control environment, including self-assessments and independent assurance reviews. Enable management to identify control deficiencies and inefficiencies and to initiate improvement actions. Plan, organise and maintain standards for internal control assessment and assurance activities.

COBIT 5 Process Purpose Statement
Obtain transparency for key stakeholders on the adequacy of the system of internal controls and thus provide trust in operations, confidence in the achievement of enterprise objectives and an adequate understanding of residual risk.

MEA02 Security-specific Process Goals and Metrics

Security-specific Process Goals	Related Metrics
1. Information security controls are deployed and operating effectively.	• Percent of processes that satisfy information security control requirements • Percent of controls in which information security control requirements are met
2. Monitoring processes for information security controls are in place and results are reported.	• Percent of information security controls appropriately monitored and results reported and reviewed

MEA02 Security-specific Process Practices, Inputs/Outputs and Activities

Management Practice	Security-specific Inputs (in Addition to COBIT 5 Inputs)		Security-specific Outputs (in Addition to COBIT 5 Outputs)	
	From	Description	Description	To
MEA02.01 Monitor internal controls. Continuously monitor, benchmark and improve the IT control environment and control framework to meet organisational objectives.	AP001.03	Information security and related policies	Defined information security assurance scope and approach to assess internal controls	MEA02.03
	AP013.03	ISMS audit report		
	Outside *COBIT 5 for Information Security*	Independent external audits		

Security-specific Activities (in Addition to COBIT 5 Activities)
1. Perform a periodic review of information security policies and procedures.
2. Determine the assurance scope, i.e., information security controls to be assessed.
3. Establish a formal approach to information security assurance.

Management Practice	Security-specific Inputs (in Addition to COBIT 5 Inputs)		Security-specific Outputs (in Addition to COBIT 5 Outputs)	
	From	Description	Description	To
MEA02.02 Review business process controls effectiveness. Review the operation of controls, including a review of monitoring and test evidence, to ensure that controls within business processes operate effectively. Include activities to maintain evidence of the effective operation of controls through mechanisms such as periodic testing of controls, continuous controls monitoring, independent assessments, command and control centres, and network operations centres. This provides the business with the assurance of control effectiveness to meet requirements related to business, regulatory and social responsibilities.			Evidence of effectiveness of information security controls	Internal

Security-specific Activities (in Addition to COBIT 5 Activities)
1. Measure the effectiveness of information security controls.
2. Perform regular reviews of applications, systems and networks.

Monitor, Evaluate and Assess

MEA02 Security-specific Process Practices, Inputs/Outputs and Activities *(cont.)*

Management Practice	Security-specific Inputs (in Addition to COBIT 5 Inputs)		Security-specific Outputs (in Addition to COBIT 5 Outputs)	
	From	Description	Description	To
MEA02.03 Perform control self-assessments. Encourage management and process owners to take positive ownership of control improvement through a continuing programme of self-assessment to evaluate the completeness and effectiveness of management's control over processes, policies and contracts.	MEA02.01	Defined information security assurance scope and approach to assess internal controls	Information security assurance assessments	MEA02.04

Security-specific Activities (in Addition to COBIT 5 Activities)
1. Perform information security assurance assessments (independent and self-assessment) to identify control weaknesses.

Management Practice	Security-specific Inputs (in Addition to COBIT 5 Inputs)		Security-specific Outputs (in Addition to COBIT 5 Outputs)	
	From	Description	Description	To
MEA02.04 Identify and report control deficiencies. Identify control deficiencies and analyse and identify their underlying root causes. Escalate control deficiencies and report to stakeholders.	MEA02.03	Information security assurance assessments	Assessment results and remedial actions	MEA02.08

Security-specific Activities (in Addition to COBIT 5 Activities)
1. Review information security incident reports for control deficiencies. Report and address noted deficiencies.

Management Practice	Security-specific Inputs (in Addition to COBIT 5 Inputs)		Security-specific Outputs (in Addition to COBIT 5 Outputs)	
	From	Description	Description	To
MEA02.05 Ensure that assurance providers are independent and qualified. Ensure that the entities performing assurance are independent from the function, groups or organisations in scope. The entities performing assurance should demonstrate an appropriate attitude and appearance, competence in the skills and knowledge necessary to perform assurance, and adherence to codes of ethics and professional standards.			Competence in skills and knowledge	Internal

Security-specific Activities (in Addition to COBIT 5 Activities)
1. Establish competencies and qualifications for the assurance provider.

Management Practice	Security-specific Inputs (in Addition to COBIT 5 Inputs)		Security-specific Outputs (in Addition to COBIT 5 Outputs)	
	From	Description	Description	To
MEA02.06 Plan assurance initiatives. Plan assurance initiatives based on enterprise objectives and strategic priorities, inherent risk, resource constraints, and sufficient knowledge of the enterprise.	Outside *COBIT 5 for Information Security*	Engagement plan	Updated engagement plan	Internal

Security-specific Activities (in Addition to COBIT 5 Activities)
1. Agree to the objectives of the information security assurance review.

Management Practice	Security-specific Inputs (in Addition to COBIT 5 Inputs)		Security-specific Outputs (in Addition to COBIT 5 Outputs)	
	From	Description	Description	To
MEA02.07 Scope assurance initiatives. Define and agree with management on the scope of the assurance initiative, based on the assurance objectives.	Outside *COBIT 5 for Information Security*	Engagement plan	Updated engagement plan	Internal

Security-specific Activities (in Addition to COBIT 5 Activities)
1. Document the details of the engagement with the organisation completing the review.

MEA02 Security-specific Process Practices, Inputs/Outputs and Activities *(cont.)*				
	Security-specific Inputs (in Addition to COBIT 5 Inputs)		Security-specific Outputs (in Addition to COBIT 5 Outputs)	
Management Practice	From	Description	Description	To
MEA02.08 Execute assurance initiatives. Execute the planned assurance initiative. Report on identified findings. Provide positive assurance opinions, where appropriate, and recommendations for improvement relating to identified operational performance, external compliance and internal control system residual risk.	DSS05.02	Results of penetration tests	External audit information security report and recommendations	Internal
	MEA02.04	Assessment results and remedial actions		
Security-specific Activities (in Addition to COBIT 5 Activities)				
1. Produce and issue signed-off information security assurance report.				

For more information regarding the related enablers, please consult:
• Appendix A. Detailed Guidance: Principles, Policies and Frameworks Enabler
• Appendix F. Detailed Guidance: Services, Infrastructure and Applications Enabler, F.10 Provide Monitoring and Alert Services for Security-related Events
• Appendix G. Detailed Guidance: People, Skills and Competencies Enabler, G.6. Information Assessment and Testing and Compliance

Monitor, Evaluate and Assess

Page intentionally left blank

MEA03 Monitor, Evaluate and Assess Compliance with External Requirements	Area: Management Domain: Monitor, Evaluate and Assess

COBIT 5 Process Description
Evaluate that IT processes and IT-supported business processes are compliant with laws, regulations and contractual requirements. Obtain assurance that the requirements have been identified and complied with, and integrate IT compliance with overall enterprise compliance.

COBIT 5 Process Purpose Statement
Ensure that the enterprise is compliant with all applicable external requirements.

MEA03 Security-specific Process Goals and Metrics

Security-specific Process Goals	Related Metrics
1. Information security and information risk practices conform to external compliance requirements.	• Percent of information security practices that satisfy external compliance requirements
2. Monitoring is conducted for new or revised external requirements with an impact on information security.	• Number or percent of projects initiated by information security to implement new external requirements

MEA03 Security-specific Process Practices, Inputs/Outputs and Activities

Management Practice	Security-specific Inputs (in Addition to COBIT 5 Inputs)		Security-specific Outputs (in Addition to COBIT 5 Outputs)	
	From	Description	Description	To
MEA03.01 Identify external compliance requirements. On a continuous basis, identify and monitor for changes in local and international laws, regulations and other external requirements that must be complied with from an IT perspective.	BAI02.01	Information security requirements	External information security compliance requirements	BAI02.01
	Outside *COBIT 5 for Information Security*	Information security standards and regulations		

Security-specific Activities (in Addition to COBIT 5 Activities)
1. Establish arrangements for monitoring information security compliance to external requirements.
2. Identify information security compliance targets for external requirements.
3. Determine external compliance requirements to be met (including legal, regulatory, privacy and contractual).
4. Identify and communicate sources of information security material to help meet external compliance requirements.

Management Practice	Security-specific Inputs (in Addition to COBIT 5 Inputs)		Security-specific Outputs (in Addition to COBIT 5 Outputs)	
	From	Description	Description	To
MEA03.02 Optimise response to external requirements. Review and adjust policies, principles, standards, procedures and methodologies to ensure that legal, regulatory and contractual requirements are addressed and communicated. Consider industry standards, codes of good practice, and best practice guidance for adoption and adaptation.	Outside *COBIT 5 for Information Security*	Applicable regulations	Updated external requirements	Internal

Security-specific Activities (in Addition to COBIT 5 Activities)
1. Review and communicate external requirements to all relevant stakeholders.

Management Practice	Security-specific Inputs (in Addition to COBIT 5 Inputs)		Security-specific Outputs (in Addition to COBIT 5 Outputs)	
	From	Description	Description	To
MEA03.03 Confirm external compliance. Confirm compliance of policies, principles, standards, procedures and methodologies with legal, regulatory and contractual requirements.			Information security compliance report	Internal

Security-specific Activities (in Addition to COBIT 5 Activities)
1. Collect and analyse compliance data relating to information security and information risk management.

Monitor, Evaluate and Assess

MEA03 Security-specific Process Practices, Inputs/Outputs and Activities *(cont.)*

Management Practice	Security-specific Inputs (in Addition to COBIT 5 Inputs)		Security-specific Outputs (in Addition to COBIT 5 Outputs)	
	From	Description	Description	To
MEA03.04 Obtain assurance of external compliance. Obtain and report assurance of compliance and adherence with policies, principles, standards, procedures and methodologies. Confirm that corrective actions to address compliance gaps are closed in a timely manner.			Compliance assurance reports	Internal

Security-specific Activities (in Addition to COBIT 5 Activities)

1. Gain evidence from the third parties.

For more information regarding the related enablers, please consult:
- Appendix A. Detailed Guidance: Principles, Policies and Frameworks Enabler
- Appendix F. Detailed Guidance: Services, Infrastructure and Applications Enabler, F.10 Provide Monitoring and Alert Services for Security-related Events
- Appendix G. Detailed Guidance: People, Skills and Competencies Enabler, G.6. Information Assessment and Testing and Compliance

Monitor, Evaluate and Assess

APPENDIX C
DETAILED GUIDANCE: ORGANISATIONAL STRUCTURES ENABLER

This appendix discusses the use and optimisation of the key information security decision-making entities in an enterprise, based on the introduction of the organisational structures enabler in section II:
• CISO (as defined in the COBIT 5 framework)
• ISSC
• ISM (as defined in the COBIT 5 framework)
• ERM committee
• Information custodians/business owners

Detailed descriptions of these groups and roles are provided, including:
• **Composition**—An appropriate skill set should be required of all members of the organisational group.
• **Mandate, operating principles, span of control and authority level**—These elements describe the practical arrangements of how the structure will operate, the boundaries of the organisational structure's decision rights, the responsibilities and accountabilities, and the escalation path or required actions in case of problems.
• **High-level RACI chart**—RACI charts link process activities to organisational structures and/or individual roles in the enterprise. They describe the level of involvement of each role for each process practice: accountable, responsible, consulted or informed.
• **Inputs/Outputs**—A structure requires inputs (typically information) before it can take informed decisions, and it produces outputs such as decisions, other information or requests for additional inputs.

C.1 Chief Information Security Officer

Mandate, Operating Principles, Span of Control and Authority Level
Figure 25 lists the characteristics of the CISO.

Figure 25—CISO: Mandate, Operating Principles, Span of Control and Authority Level	
Area	**Characteristic**
Mandate	The overall responsibility of the enterprise information security programme
Operating principles	Depending on a variety factors within the enterprise, the CISO may report to the CEO, COO, CIO, CRO or other senior executive management. The CISO is the liaison between executive management and the information security programme. The CISO should also communicate and co-ordinate closely with key business stakeholders to address information protection needs. The CISO must: • Have an accurate understanding of the business strategic vision • Be an effective communicator • Be adept at building effective relationships with business leaders • Be able to translate business objectives into information security requirements
Span of control	The CISO is responsible for: • Establishing and maintaining an information security management system (ISMS) • Defining and managing an information security risk treatment plan • Monitoring and reviewing the ISMS
Authority level/decision rights	The CISO is responsible for implementing and maintaining the information security strategy. Accountability (and sign-off of important decisions) resides in the function to which the CISO reports, for example, senior executive management team member or the ISSC.
Delegation rights	The CISO should delegate tasks to information security managers and business people.
Escalation path	The CISO should escalate key information risk-related issues to his/her direct supervisor and/or the ISSC.

High-level RACI Chart

The RACI chart in **figure 26** is limited to important examples of key practices for which the CISO could be held accountable or responsible.

Figure 26—CISO: High-level RACI Chart With Key Practices	
Process Practice	**Level of Involvement (RACI)**
Identify and communicate information security threats, desirable behaviours and changes needed to address these points.	Accountable
Ensure that environmental and facilities management adheres to information security requirements.	Accountable
Protect against malware.	Accountable
Manage network and connectivity security.	Accountable
Manage endpoint security.	Accountable
Manage user identity and logical access.	Accountable
Manage physical access to IT assets.	Accountable
Monitor the infrastructure for security-related events.	Accountable
Provide ways to improve efficiency and effectiveness of the information security function (e.g., through training of information security staff; documentation of processes, technology and applications; and standardisation and automation of the process).	Accountable
Monitor IT risk management.	Responsible
Define and communicate an information security strategy that is in line with the business strategy.	Responsible
Research, define and document information security requirements.	Responsible
Validate information security requirements with stakeholders, business sponsors and technical implementation personnel.	Responsible
Develop information security policies and procedures.	Responsible
Define and implement risk evaluation and response strategies and co-operate with the risk office to manage the information risk.	Responsible
Ensure that potential impact of changes is assessed.	Responsible
Collect and analyse performance and compliance data relating to information security and information risk management.	Responsible

Inputs/Outputs

A structure requires inputs (typically information) before it can take informed decisions, and it produces outputs such as decisions, other information, or requests for additional inputs. **Figure 27** contains a non-exhaustive list of such inputs and outputs.[5]

Figure 27—CISO: Inputs and Outputs			
Input	**From**	**Output**	**To**
Risk tolerance	ERM	Information security strategy	ERM committee
Regulatory/compliance mandates	External	Policies, standards, procedures	Enterprise
Business and IT strategy	Organisation/IT	Remediation plan to audit recommendations	Audit
Audit reports	Audit		

---

[5] These inputs and outputs should not be confused with the process inputs and outputs as described in section II. However, in some instances, the organisational structure inputs and outputs are information delivered by a process, in which case they are process outputs.

C.2 Information Security Steering Committee

Composition
Figure 28 describes the roles of ISSC members.

Figure 28—ISSC: Composition	
Role	**Description**
CISO	• ISSC chair and liaison to ERM committee • Responsible for overall enterprise information security
ISM	Communication of design, implementation and monitoring of practices When applicable, the ISM discusses design solutions beforehand with the information security architects to mitigate identified information risk.
Information custodians/ business owners	• In charge of certain processes or business applications • Responsible for communicating business initiatives that may impact information security and information security practices that may impact the user community • May have an understanding of business/operational risk, costs and benefits, and specific information security requirements for his/her business area
IT manager	Reports on the status of IT-related information security initiatives
Representatives of specialist functions	Bring specialist input to the table when relevant, for example, from representatives of internal audit, HR, legal, risk, project management office (PMO). These functions can be asked to join the ISSC on occasion or as permanent members. It may be worthwhile to have representatives of internal audit as permanent members to advise the committee on compliance risk.

Mandate, Operating Principles, Span of Control and Authority Level
Figure 29 describes the characteristics of the ISSC.

Figure 29—ISSC: Mandate, Operating Principles, Span of Control and Authority Level	
Area	**Characteristic**
Mandate	To ensure good practice, information security is applied effectively and consistently throughout the enterprise.
Operating principles	• The ISSC meets on a regular basis, as needed by the enterprise. More frequent meetings may be scheduled during specific initiatives or when issues need to be dealt with on an urgent basis. • Substitutes or proxies are allowed, but should be limited. • The committee membership should be limited to a relatively small group of strategic and tactical leaders to ensure appropriate bidirectional communication and decision making. Other business leaders can be invited on an as-needed basis. • Minutes of all meetings should be approved within a certain period and retained. • The CISO chairs the ISSC meetings.
Span of control	The ISSC is responsible for enterprisewide information security decision making.
Authority level/decision rights	The ISSC is responsible for enterprise information security decisions in support of strategic decisions of the ERM committee.
Delegation rights	The ISSC is ultimately responsible for the design and implementation strategy of the information security programme and cannot delegate this responsibility to other member roles.
Escalation path	All issues should be escalated to the involved senior executive management team member accountable for information security. Enterprise information risk strategies should be escalated to the ERM committee for approval.

High-level RACI Chart

Figure 30 describes ISSC level of involvement.

Figure 30—ISSC: High-level RACI Chart	
Process Practice	**Level of Involvement (RACI)**
Define and communicate an information security strategy that is in line with the business strategy.	Accountable
Research, define and document information security requirements.	Accountable
Validate information security requirements with stakeholders, business sponsors and technical implementation personnel.	Accountable
Develop information security policies and procedures.	Accountable
Develop an information security plan that identifies the information security environment and activities to be implemented by the project team to protect organisational assets.	Accountable
Ensure that the potential impact of changes is assessed.	Accountable
Collect and analyse performance and compliance data relating to information security and information risk management.	Accountable
Establish, agree on and communicate the role of the CISO and the ISM.	Responsible
Raise the profile of the information security function within the enterprise and potentially outside the enterprise.	Responsible
Provide input to the overall enterprise business continuity management endeavour.	Responsible

Inputs/Outputs

A structure requires inputs (typically, information) before it can take informed decisions, and it produces outputs such as decisions, other information, or requests for additional inputs. **Figure 31** contains a non-exhaustive list of such inputs and outputs.[6]

Figure 31—ISSC: Inputs and Outputs			
Input	**From**	**Output**	**To**
Business strategy	Board of directors	Information security strategy and programme	ERM committee, ISMs, information custodians/business owners
Risk acceptance levels	ERM committee	Information risk profile	ERM committee
IT strategy	IT		
Enterprise projects listing	Information custodians/business owners, PMO		
Internal audit reports	Internal audit		

C.3 Information Security Manager

Mandate, Operating Principles, Span of Control and Authority Level

Figure 32 presents the characteristics of the ISM.

Figure 32—ISM: Mandate, Operating Principles, Span of Control and Authority Level	
Area	**Characteristic**
Mandate	Overall responsibility for the management of information security efforts
Operating principles	Reports to the CISO (or, in some enterprises, to business unit leads)
Span of control	Application information security, infrastructure information security, access management, threat and incident management, risk management, awareness programme, metrics, vendor assessments
Authority level/decision rights	Overall decision-making authority over information security domain practices
Delegation rights	Should not delegate decisions related to information security domain practices
Escalation path	Escalate issues to the CISO

---

[6] These inputs and outputs should not be confused with the process inputs and outputs as described in section II. However, in some instances, the organisational structure inputs and outputs are information delivered by a process, in which case they are process outputs.

High-level RACI Chart

Figure 33 lists the level of involvement of the ISM.

Figure 33—ISM: High-level RACI Chart	
Process Practice	**Level of Involvement (RACI)**
Develop and communicate a common vision for the information security team that is in line with the corporate vision statement.	Responsible
Manage allocation of information security staff according to business requirements.	Responsible
Conduct information risk assessments and define the information risk profile.	Responsible
Manage roles, responsibilities, access privileges and levels of authority.	Responsible
Develop an information security plan that identifies the information security environment and controls to be implemented by the project team to protect organisational assets. Monitor these internal controls and adjust/improve when required.	Responsible
Identify and communicate information security pain points, desirable behaviours and changes needed to address these points.	Responsible
Provide ways to improve efficiency and effectiveness of the information security function (e.g., through training of information security staff; documentation of processes, technology and applications; and standardisation and automation of the process).	Responsible
Collect and analyse performance and compliance data relating to information security and information risk management.	Responsible
Ensure that environmental and facilities management adheres to information security requirements.	Responsible

Inputs/Outputs

A structure requires inputs (typically, information) before it can take informed decisions, and it produces outputs such as decisions, other information, or requests for additional inputs **Figure 34** contains a non-exhaustive list of such inputs and outputs.[7]

Figure 34—ISM: Inputs and Outputs			
Input	**From**	**Output**	**To**
Information security strategy	ISSC	Design, implementation and improvement plans for information security practices	Enterprise
IT infrastructure plans/architecture/configurations	IT	Periodic information risk assessments and testing of information security practices and countermeasures	CISO, Lines of business
Information security policies/standards/procedures	CISO/ISM	Information security implementation status reports	CISO
Risk tolerance	ERM		
Regulatory/compliance mandates	External		
Business and IT strategy	Organisation/IT		
Audit reports	Audit		

---

[7] These inputs and outputs should not be confused with the process inputs and outputs as described in section II. However, in some instances, the organisational structure inputs and outputs are information delivered by a process, in which case they are process outputs.

C.4 Enterprise Risk Management Committee

The ERM committee is responsible for the enteprise's decision making relative to assessing, controlling, optimising, financing and monitoring risk from all sources for the purpose of increasing the enterprise's short- and long-term value to its stakeholders.

Composition
Figure 35 lists the roles of the ERM committee members.

Figure 35—ERM Committee: Composition	
Role	**Description**
CISO	In the optimal scenario, the CISO is a member of the ERM committee, to provide the committee with advice on specific information risk.
CEO, COO, CFO, etc.	Representative of senior executive management
Core process business owners	• In charge of certain processes or business applications • Responsible for communicating business initiatives that may impact information security along with the impact that information security practices may have on the user community • May have an understanding of business/operational risk, costs and benefits, and specific information security requirements for their business area
Audit/compliance	Provide specialist input when relevant. Can be asked to join the ERM committee on occasion or as permanent members. For example, it might be worthwhile to have representatives of internal audit as permanent members to advise the committee on compliance risk.
Legal representative	Provide legal input. Can be asked to join the ERM committee on occasion or as a permanent member.
CRO	Provide specialist input when relevant. Can be asked to join the ERM committee on occasion or as a permanent member.

High-level RACI Chart
Figure 36 lists the level of involvement of the ERM committee members.

Figure 36—ERM Committee: High-level RACI Chart	
Process Practice	**Level of Involvement (RACI)**
Advise on the information security strategy defined by the ISSC.	Responsible
Establish enterprise risk tolerance levels.	Accountable
Define and implement risk evaluation and response strategies.	Accountable
Review information risk assessments and risk profiles.	Accountable

C.5 Information Custodians/Business Owners

Composition
Information custodians or business owners act as the liaison between the business and information security functions. They can be associated with types of information, specific applications, or business units in an enterprise. The person in this role should possess a good understanding of the business and the types of information processed and requiring protection. They serve as trusted advisors and monitoring agents regarding information within the business.

This role should balance business and information risk so that the business does not always trump information security decisions.

High-level RACI Chart
Figure 37 lists the level of involvement of information custodians and business owners.

Figure 37—Information Custodians/Business Owners: High-level RACI Chart	
Process Practice	**Level of Involvement (RACI)**
Communicate, co-ordinate and advise on information risk management efforts with line managers.	Responsible
Report changes in business processes and/or strategies (i.e., new products or services) to the ISSC.	Responsible
Raise the profile of the information security function and information security policies and procedures within the enterprise.	Responsible

APPENDIX D
DETAILED GUIDANCE: CULTURE, ETHICS AND BEHAVIOUR ENABLER

This appendix provides details on information security behaviours as presented in section II. Eight desirable information security behaviours (discussed in the remainder of the appendix) can be identified that will positively influence culture towards information security and its actual implementation in the enterprise's day-to-day life.

For each of the behaviours defined, the following attributes are described in this appendix:
- **Organisational ethics**—Determined by the values by which the enterprise wants to live
- **Individual ethics**—Determined by the personal values of each individual in the enterprise, and to an important extent are dependent on external factors such as beliefs, ethnicity, socio-economic background, geographic location and personal experiences
- **Leadership**—Ways leadership can influence appropriate behaviour:
  - How communication, enforcement, and rules and norms can be used to influence behaviour
  - The incentives and rewards that can be used to influence behaviour
  - Raising awareness

D.1 Behaviours

Each of the following behaviours occurs in an enterprise at two levels: the **organisational level** where behaviours are determined by the values (ethics, culture or attitude) by which the enterprise wants to live, and the **individual level** where behaviours are defined by the personal values (ethics, culture or attitude) of the individual.

Behaviour 1: Information security is practiced in daily operations.
Information security is part of the enterprise's daily functioning. At the organisational level, the behaviour indicates that information security is accepted as a business imperative in organisational goal setting. At the individual level, it means that the individual cares about the well-being of the enterprise and applies a prudent approach and information security techniques to his/her daily operations.

Behaviour 2: People respect the importance of information security policies and principles.
The importance of information security policies and principles is acknowledged by the people in the enterprise. At the organisational level, policies and principles are endorsed by senior management, and approval, review and communication of policies occurs on a regular basis. At the individual level, people have read and understood the policies, and they feel empowered to follow enterprise guidance.

Behaviour 3: People are provided with sufficient and detailed information security guidance and are encouraged to participate in and challenge the current information security situation.
People are provided with sufficient information security guidance and are encouraged to challenge the current information security situation at two levels. The organisational culture indicates a two-way communication process for guidance and feedback and provides stakeholders an opportunity to comment on changes; the individual culture demonstrates stakeholder participation by questioning and providing comments when requested.

Behaviour 4: Everyone is accountable for the protection of information within the enterprise.
This accountability is reflected at two levels in the enterprise. At the organisational level, issues requiring accountability (discipline) are acted upon and the roles of stakeholders are confirmed for enforcement. The individual level requires each individual to understand the responsibilities regarding information security.

Behaviour 5: Stakeholders are aware of how to identify and respond to threats to the enterprise.
Appropriate processes for identifying and reacting to threats can be implemented at the organisational level by installing a reporting process and an incident response process to minimise losses. At the individual level, people must be educated on what an information security incident is and how to report and react to it.

Behaviour 6: Management proactively supports and anticipates new information security innovations and communicates this to the enterprise. The enterprise is receptive to account for and deal with new information security challenges.

Information security innovations and challenges are tackled at the organisational level through an information security research and development team. The individual culture contributes when stakeholders bring new ideas forward.

Behaviour 7: Business management engages in continuous cross-functional collaboration to allow for efficient and effective information security programmes.

Cross-functional collaboration is leveraged in the enterprise by organisational acceptance of a holistic information security strategy and improved integration with the business. The individual contributes by reaching out to other business functions and by identifying potential synergies.

Behaviour 8: Executive management recognises the business value of information security.

The business value of information security is recognised at the organisational level when information security is viewed as a means to improve business value (revenue, expense, reputation and competitive advantage), transparency in response to incidents is key, and an understanding of consumer expectations is essential. At the individual level, the behaviour is evidenced by the generation of creative ideas to improve value (various layers of information security).

D.2 Leadership

The behaviours just described can be influenced by leadership at different levels of the enterprise, as outlined in section II, subsection 5.3. Three levels of leadership can be distinguished: information security management (CISO/ISM) at the information security level, business management at the business unit level, and executive management at the top level. These layers of leadership influence behaviour through the use of communication, enforcement and rules, incentives and rewards, and awareness.

Influencing Behaviour Through Communication, Enforcement, and Rules and Norms

Leadership uses communication, enforcement, and rules and norms to influence behaviours in an enterprise. Communication is always essential to influence any kind of behaviour. Enforcement of an information security culture is dependent on the degree of importance of that aspect of a culture. Rules can be used to force internal action where information security is legally mandated.

Information security management (CISO/ISM) makes sure that information security is embedded in enterprise policies and procedures and regular guidance and updates are performed. Furthermore, the CISO/ISM ensures a yearly recertification of policies and principles. Together with **executive management**, the CISO/ISM ensures a formal sign-off of these policies. Business unit managers follow up on corrective actions and executive management performs an annual review of information security performance.

The **CISO/ISM** works together with **business unit management** to ensure stakeholder acknowledgement. The business unit managers also set an example by leading. The CISO/ISM implements an incident management process, supported by a reporting mechanism, which includes trigger points for stakeholders (clients, vendors, etc.). Market trends are tracked by the CISO/ISM as well, for both information security and the business.

While **executive management** ensures that information security is represented in the correct structures (committees, task forces, implementation teams), the **CISO/ISM** communicates the information security processes to the entire enterprise.

Influencing Behaviour Through Incentives and Rewards

Management influences behaviour through measures designed to provide positive reinforcement for desired conduct and negative reinforcement for conduct it wishes to discourage. An absence of rewards inhibits adoption of an information security culture. Business management needs to know that secure behaviour will be rewarded; this, in turn, means that executive management must make its intentions clear by encouraging the implementation of security safeguards and promoting attitudes that constitute a culture of security. These rewards do not involve money that goes directly to the individual; instead, they may constitute organisational advancement in the form of budget, influence, management attention, etc. Some people are motivated solely by remuneration, others also appreciate other types of recognition.

The following incentives and rewards may be used by the various management levels to influence behaviour.

Information security management (CISO/ISM) may organise sessions regarding information security in personal life (e.g., covering children and social media, wireless network set up) to embed information security in daily operations, give positive recognition for the information security achievement, and distribute bonuses for innovation within the information security function. The CISO/ISM is not the only level of management to give bonuses; **executive management** may also give rewards for alerting of threats or for any profitable idea.

Business management focusses on information security as a component of performance evaluation and ensures that it is embedded in all job descriptions, while **executive management** tailors incentives and rewards to the responsibility of the stakeholders. **Business management** is responsible for an annual review of the incentives and rewards programme and adheres to the fact that information security policies are a requirement of employment (terms and conditions).

Influencing Behaviour Through Raising Awareness

Awareness programmes have their place, but they are insufficient by themselves. More than just being aware of information security, people need to be educated about security and their role in it. The different management levels in an enterprise can raise awareness through the following means.

Information security management may organise awareness training on information security topics, supported by regular update sessions, and ensure that policies are readily available (e.g., through Internet publication). The CISO/CISM is also responsible for sharing knowledge regarding changes in the threat landscape, regularly communicating new ideas and outcomes, keeping track of market trends, and performing competitive analyses. **Business managers** regularly follow these awareness training events and are responsible for notifications or requests for comments on proposed changes. **Executive management** makes sure that information security incidents are communicated to the staff.

Page intentionally left blank

APPENDIX E
DETAILED GUIDANCE: INFORMATION ENABLER

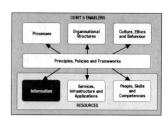

This appendix provides details regarding the use and optimisation of information security-related information types, based on the introduction of the information enabler in section II. An approach to map stakeholders involved in the use of information types is provided. In addition, all Information types are presented, including:
• Information security strategy
• Information security budget
• Information security plan
• Policies
• Information security requirements, which can include:
  – Information security configuration requirements
  – SLA/OLA information security requirements
• Awareness material
• Information security review reports, which include:
  – Information security audit findings
  – Information security maturity report
  – Information security-related risk management
    · Threat analysis
    · Vulnerability (information security) assessment reports
• Information security service catalogue
• Information risk profile, which includes:
  – Information risk register
  – Breaches and loss reports (consolidated incident report)
• Information security dashboard (or equivalent), which includes:
  – Information security incidents
  – Information security problems
  – Information security metrics

For each of the information types, more detailed guidance is provided, including:
• **Goals**—This describes a number of goals to be achieved, using the three categories defined in the information model. For these information types, goals for information are divided into three dimensions of quality:
  – **Intrinsic quality**—The extent to which data values are in conformance with the actual or true values
  – **Contextual quality**—The extent to which information is applicable to the task of the information user and is presented in an intelligible and clear manner, recognising that information quality depends on the context of use
  – **Security/accessibility quality**—The extent to which information is available or obtainable
• **Life cycle**—A specific description of the life cycle requirements
• **Good practices for this type of information**—A description of typical contents and structure

E.1 Information Security Stakeholders Template

A template to map the stakeholders for information security-related information types is described in **figure 38**, which contains:
• Stakeholder description—Based on the generic list of organisational structures of COBIT 5 (also used in the RACI charts in the process descriptions) and complemented with a number of additional external stakeholders for this specific domain
• Information types—As described in appendix B. Detailed Guidance: Information Enabler

Identifying the stakeholder of information is essential to optimise the development and distribution of information throughout the enterprise. The template in **figure 38** can assist in the identification exercise. The table needs to be adapted to the specific environment by translating the example information types and generic stakeholder descriptions.

An indication of the nature of the relationship of the stakeholder for each information type can be used such as (see the example in **figure 17**):
  – A—Approver
  – O—Originator
  – I—Destination for information purposes
  – U—Destination: information consumer

Figure 38—Information Related to Stakeholders for Information Security Template	Information Type									
Stakeholder	Information Security Strategy	Information Security Budget	Information Security Plan	Policies	Information Security Requirements	Awareness Material	Information Security Review Reports	Information Security Service Catalogue	Information Risk Profile	Information Security Dashboard
Internal: Enterprise										
Board										
Chief executive officer (CEO)										
Chief financial officer (CFO)										
Chief operating officer (COO)										
Chief risk officer (CRO)										
Information security steering committee (ISSC)										
Chief information security officer (CISO)										
Business executive										
Business process owner										
(Project and programme) steering committees										
Architecture board										
Enterprise risk management (ERM) committee										
Head of human resources (HR)										
Compliance										
Audit										
Programme and project management office (PMO)										
Value management office (VMO)										
Internal: IT										
Strategy (IT executive) committee										
Chief information officer (CIO)										
Head of architecture										
Head of development										
Head of IT operations										
Head of IT administration										
Service manager										
Information security manager (ISM)										
Business continuity manager										
Privacy officer										
External										
Investors										
Insurers										
Authorities (law enforcement)										
Regulators										
Business partners										
Vendors/suppliers										
External auditors										

E.2 Information Security Strategy

Goals

Information security strategy should strive to be state-of-the-art and in line with generally recognised principles. Furthermore, the architecture and design should be aligned to the organisation's enterprise architecture and specific situation, be comprehensive and complete, and contain all required information at the appropriate level of detail to be actionable. The information security strategy should be accessible only by those who need the access (i.e., the stakeholders).

These goals can be measured by metrics such as the:
• Percentage of information security activities that follow a recognised framework or that are benchmarked against peers
• Number of mismatches between information security strategy and architecture and enterprise architecture
• Percentage of stakeholders without access to information security strategy
• Number of information security violations

Life Cycle

Typically, an enterprise defines a strategy and architecture for the medium term to support achievement of the desired future state, but allowing for short-term (e.g., yearly) updates. In addition, the information security strategy should be made available to all relevant stakeholders.

Good Practice

The CISO/ISM is responsible for developing the information security strategy for the enterprise. The purpose of the information security strategy is to provide the enterprise with adequate direction on the matter of information security; this includes the entire enterprise, for example, senior management, audit, business management, IT development and IT operations.

The development of the information security strategy is described as follows:

> The business strategy provides a road map to achieving the business objectives. In addition, it should provide one of the primary inputs into the information security strategy. This flow serves to promote alignment of information security with business goals. The balance of inputs comes from determining the desired state of [information] security compared to the existing, or current, state. Business processes must also be considered, as well as key organisational risk, including regulatory requirements and the associated impact analysis to determine protection levels and priorities.

> The objective of the [information] security strategy is the desired state defined by business and [information] security attributes. The strategy provides the basis for an action plan comprised of one or more [information] security program that, as implemented, achieve the [information] security objectives. The action plan(s) must be formulated based on available resources and constraints, including consideration of relevant legal and regulatory requirements.

> The strategy and action plans must contain provisions for monitoring as well as defined metrics to determine the level of success. This provides feedback to the CISO and steering committee to allow for midcourse correction and ensure that [information] security initiatives are on track to meet defined objectives.[8]

In this development process, a CISO/ISM should take into account constraints that may influence the information security strategy:
• Legal and regulatory requirements
• Culture
• Organisational structure
• Costs
• Resources
• Capabilities
• Time
• Risk acceptance and tolerance

---

[8] ISACA, *CISM Review Manual 2012*, USA, 2012, section 1.9, page 47

The information security strategy should address the following topics, amongst others:
• Alignment of the information security activities with the overall enterprise objectives
• Information risk management—A description of the information risk management system that will be implemented throughout the enterprise. Such a system requires:
  – An enterprise view on strategic objectives and risk
  – Definition of enterprisewide risk appetite
  – An enterprisewide policy on risk response options and selection
  – Monitoring risk
• Overall principles and approach towards governance and management, describing:
  – Principles and policies
  – Organisational structures
  – Processes and practices
  – Skills, culture elements and behaviours

  These are needed to set direction and monitor information security so it is aligned with enterprise objectives and risk appetite. Governance defines, amongst other elements, accountability, responsibility and decision making.
• Information security architecture—A description of the major logical grouping of capabilities that manage information security. Capabilities include information, applications, technology and how these relate to the business processes.
• Compliance—Describes all applicable rules and regulations throughout the enterprise, and the system of policies, procedures and all other measures that the enterprise requires to comply with these regulations and to monitor compliance on a continuous basis
• Information security operations—The information security-related operational processes and procedures, including information security administration, information security monitoring and incident response
• Information security road map—The secure desired state, including people, processes, technologies and other resources

E.3 Information Security Budget

Goals
The information security budget should be adequate (ensuring appropriate resources), accurate, and contain correct and realistic amounts for all budget items. Furthermore, the budget should be comprehensive, complete and aligned to the organisation's enterprise security requirements and overall risk appetite. The information security budget should be available on a timely basis and accessible only to those who need access (i.e., stakeholders).

Examples of metrics for the budget area include the:
• Number of additional budget requests after the yearly budgeting cycle to review the budgeting evolution
• Number of discrepancies between the information security budget and needs in general (e.g., a budget vs. actual review)
• Difference between budget and actual costs
• Percentage of stakeholders without access to the information security budget

Life Cycle
Typically, enterprises have a yearly budget cycle. Budgets for information security-related costs and investments should follow this cycle.

Good Practice
Budgeting for information security is dependent on where the accountability and responsibility over information security reside within the enterprise. In this publication, the assumption is that the information security function is empowered to develop its own information security budget (which is the most effective method for ensuring that adequate information security resources are provided). In that case, the CISO/ISM has the responsibility of developing a budget for the information security function, as part of the budget cycle of the organisational entity to which the information security function reports, applying the enterprisewide budget processes. In addition, there should be an overview of information security-related investments and expenditures across the enterprise.

The purpose of the information security budget is to provide funding for the information security programme and enable appropriate information security support of the business. The information security programme contains all required investments to execute the information security strategy and architecture. In this context, it is important to have a proper budget allocation process in place. In accordance with the APO06 *Manage budget and costs* process of COBIT 5, the information security budget needs to be developed based on a BIA and consequential business requirements that are translated into information security requirements and initiatives. The actual definition of information security requirements is discussed in subsection E.6 Information Security Requirements.

The information security-related budget can include the following items:
• Budget for operating the information security function (staff cost, infrastructure, technology, projects)
• Budget for the information security programme, which can include:
  – One-off costs and investments to set up the information security function and related processes to execute information security-related projects
  – Recurring costs for operational information security measures (information security administration, monitoring, reporting, compliance)
  – Security awareness programme costs
  – Continuous improvement of security skills (security expert training, certifications, travel, conferences)
  – Corporate security certifications and external security audit costs
  – Outsourcing costs
  – Preparation for incident response costs

Information security budgets also are subject to regular follow-up (actual vs. budget, variances) according to the enterprise's policies and processes.

E.4 Information Security Plan

Goals
The information security plan should be accurate, comprehensive and complete, and contain correct and realistic actions based on the information security strategy. Furthermore, it should be aligned to the enterprise architecture and specific situation, and should be in line with overall risk appetite (i.e., there is enough money in the budget).
The information security plan should be available on a timely basis and accessible only to those who need access (i.e., stakeholders).

These goals can be measured by metrics including the:
• Number of actions that could not be implemented or executed
• Number of mismatches between the information security plan and enterprise architecture
• Percentage of stakeholders without access to the plan
• Number of violations against the plan

Life Cycle
An information security plan is created and then regularly followed up and updated as needed by the ISSC, synchronised with the budget cycle.

Good Practice
The CISO/ISM has the responsibility of developing an information security plan.

The information security plan is based on an information security strategy, which includes a sound risk analysis/ management plan, and addresses all information risk that exceeds the risk appetite. It also covers all risk response types (avoid, mitigate, transfer, accept), particularly addressing risk mitigation and risk transfer (insurance).

The information security plan defines all required investments to execute the information security strategy and architecture. The information security plan is defined in terms of all enablers:
• Processes that need to be defined, implemented or strengthened
• Organisational structures that need to be set up or strengthened
• Information flows related to information security management that need to be implemented
• Policies and procedures that need to be defined and put in practice
• Information security culture that needs to be adjusted or maintained
• Skills and behaviours that need to be built up or changed
• Capabilities that need to be acquired, for example, technology for information security, information security-specific applications and services

2

E.5 Policies

Policies are an important type of information for information security governance and management. Policies and principles are also one of the enablers for governance and management in the COBIT 5 framework. For that reason, it may be useful to refer to the more detailed discussion on policies in section II, chapter 2 of this publication.

E.6 Information Security Requirements

Goals

Information security requirements should be accurate, realistic, and aligned to business and regulatory needs. Furthermore, the requirements should be made available on a timely basis and be accessible only by stakeholders (i.e., those who need access).

Examples of metrics for this area include the:
• Number of projects with information security requirements reviewed by the information security function
• Number of requirements that are not met
• Number of requirements that are delivered in organisational projects or that are missing from delivered projects
• Number of signed acceptances by end users, indicating their receipt and acknowledgement of the latest security requirements

Life Cycle

Information security requirements are defined at several trigger points:
• At the beginning of new business projects, as part of the overall business and functional requirements—Information security is a business requirement; information security requirements are followed up throughout the life cycle of the initiative.
• During contract development/agreements with third parties
• When investigating company acquisitions/merging (putting requirements in place for managing brand name threats)

Good Practice

Information security requirements are part of the overall requirements for any type of enabler. They typically apply to new capabilities (applications, infrastructure), but they can also apply to the other enablers. Information security requirements are the responsibility of the final and/or main user, for example, the business process owner (for applications) or IT management (for IT infrastructure).

Information security requirements are defined relative to the business impact, goals and criteria in terms of:
• **Availability**—When the enabler needs to be available, to whom, to what extent, etc.
• **Integrity**—What the integrity requirements are for the enabler. This applies to specifications for information (application controls for information/transactions), policies (integrity of policies), etc.
• **Confidentiality**—Who can and cannot have access to the enabler. Typical questions include:
  – Who has access to information, on the basis of what job needs?
  – Who has access to organisational structures (decisions) and who does not?

E.7 Awareness Material

Goals

Awareness materials should be accurate and contain correct and realistic statements on risk and practices. Furthermore, awareness materials should be understood and tailored to most job functions (based on cost considerations). General and role-based awareness training is required for employees and employee incentives should be tied to information security awareness. Information security awareness training should be provided to all relevant target groups and employees and be made accessible only to those who need access (i.e., stakeholders).

Metrics for these goals may include the:
• Number of updates to information security awareness materials
• Percentage of employees passing certain levels in tests
• Percentage of employees with performance plans incorporating information security goals
• Number of participant postings providing answers to a pop quiz on awareness materials

These metrics can be used for administrative purposes; however, it should be noted that awareness can only be measured through behaviour and the consequences of that behaviour in terms of, for example, breaches and incidents.

Life Cycle
The awareness material should be updated periodically and/or when a specific event has occurred (event-driven).

Good Practice
The awareness material can help to change the mindset and behaviour of people, which improves overall information security. Awareness encourages correct behaviour and compliance with policies, and minimises information security-related non-compliance or unconscious risky behaviour.

Awareness material should take into account all of the following:
• The design and implementation of an effective information security awareness programme are aided by executive management commitment.
• The mandatory set of information is composed of the:
  – Business drivers for information security
  – Information security policy
  – Acceptable use policy
  – Consequences of non-compliance or dangerous behaviour for the enterprise and the individual
• The programme should aim to achieve the desired information security culture based on the enterprise goals. In enterprises operating internationally, the programme should also take into consideration local cultural aspects and allow for adjustments when required. However, a baseline for a minimum acceptable level should be established based on common values and principles in the enterprise.
• People are the main target group. They may be internal employees and can also be external workforces supporting the enterprise. Awareness material should be developed for specific functional and hierarchical target groups.
• The enterprise should define and implement repeatable awareness processes that will aid business stakeholders in accomplishing day-to-day business requirements. Means and content should be identified.
• Managers are responsible for supporting the awareness programme by ensuring employee participation. HR is responsible for on-boarding procedures and providing awareness material. Information security experts are responsible for providing content on which the awareness material is based. The CISO/ISM is responsible for the information security programme being carried out.
• Technology provides the means by which information security awareness material is distributed. For example, distribution methods may include communication channels, active content and e-learning, surveys and assessments. The material should be broadly accessible through multiple channels, for example, intranet, documents and video.
• The awareness material is prepared with support from information security experts, HR and business management. It can take form in on-boarding and exit material as well as continuous awareness programmes. Some training may be specific to targeted groups.
• It is used as input for the risk profile, information security design and the information security management programme.
• The awareness programme should be monitored and reported on through the:
  – Testing for proof of comprehension, with completion and pass dates, and exception reporting (non-completion of tests)
  – Monitoring of behaviour that may drive changes in the awareness material: changing threats, business, policies, procedures and incidents that may drive changes in the awareness material.

The metrics described previously will provide an indication of the quality of the products included in the awareness programme deployed within the enterprise. However, the efficiency of awareness initiatives should be measured in a different way. As noted previously, measuring awareness in an organisation requires measurement of the behaviours of the enterprise, not merely compliance with administrative goals.

E.8 Information Security Review Reports

Information security review reporting requires many types of reports, including, amongst others:
• Information security audit findings
• Information security maturity report
• Information security-related risk management
  – Threat analysis
  – Vulnerability (information security) assessment reports
  – BIA

In this section, threat analysis is described in detail as an example.

Goals

Information security review reporting should be accurate and complete, with spending targeted to areas of identified risk and a focus on reducing expenditures required to recover from exploits or incidents (including minimising revenue losses). Furthermore, threat analyses should identify all relevant and important threats to the business and should develop an appropriate action and risk response. Dashboards for key stakeholders should be updated on a timely basis and the dashboards should be accessible only to those who need access (i.e., stakeholders).

These goals can be measured by metrics such as the:
- Number of threat analyses presented per year
- Number of threats identified
- Percentage of threats addressed with information security practices
- Percentage of updates performed as scheduled
- Percentage of stakeholders without access
- Number of information security violations

Life Cycle

The threat analysis should be updated periodically and when specific events occur (event-driven). Examples of events that might necessitate an update of the threat analysis include new projects or a change in business initiatives.

Good Practice

To stay current on threats, the CISO and IT and business managers should frequently read information security-related news articles and research papers, and periodically connect with vendors.

Internal and external loss data provide information to enable the creation of scenarios that can be used to further analyse threats.

Threat analysis should focus on the following areas:
- A high-level threat analysis should be conducted to identify strategic information risk. For example, if a bank does not comply with information security requirements driven by a local financial supervisory authority, it may lose its license to operate.
- People need the appropriate functional skills and know-how to perform threat analyses. People are also one of the sources for violations and thereby contribute to the materialisation of threats. The human factor should always be considered when a threat analysis is done.
- The ERM function should define and implement the threat analysis as part of the risk management process that will aid business stakeholders in identifying, assessing, mitigating and predicting threats (to information security and other threats) in a preventive way.
- To some extent, technology can assist with threat analysis by gathering information. For example, technology may assist with log correlation and analysis using security information and event management (SIEM) systems, using data mining or business intelligence for pattern recognition, utilising data loss tools to identify data leakage, and detecting fraud.
- The high-level threat analysis should be created by the business managers, IT managers and the CISO/chief security officer (CSO).
- The detailed threat analysis should be performed by experts within their respective areas.
- The threat analysis is a confidential document that should be restricted to the relevant business, IT and information security managers. It should be stored and updated by the CSO/CISO.
- It serves as input for the risk profile, information security design and information security management programme.

E.9 Information Security Dashboard

Goals

Information security dashboards should contain all events and additional information as stated in the information security requirements, and the required information should be at the appropriate level of detail to be actionable. Dashboards for key stakeholders should be updated on a timely basis and should be accessible only to those who need access (i.e., stakeholders).

Examples of metrics for these goals include the:
- Number of problems with dashboard accuracy and completeness
- Number of mismatches between information security dashboard contents and information security requirements
- Time needed to analyse dashboards to obtain required information

• Percentage of updates performed as scheduled
• Percentage of stakeholders without access to information security dashboards
• Number of information security violations against information security dashboards

Life Cycle

Dashboard components should be renewed on a regular basis. The frequency for updates depends on the data type and criticality. For example, information relating to information security incidents may carry a requirement of immediate online updates, whereas other components, such as information security action plan status, may call for a monthly update.

The reports should be stored centrally and made available to all stakeholders in the form of a dashboard. Extracts or summaries can be produced, depending on the need or level of interest of the specific stakeholder.

Good Practice

Building and operating an information security dashboard should take the following into consideration:
• Dashboards should contain operational information as well as information on information security threats, threat levels and vulnerabilities.
• People are the greatest asset of any enterprise and integral to the successful implementation of the SIEM architecture; however, they need the appropriate functional skills and know-how.
• The enterprise should define and implement repeatable SIEM processes that will assist business stakeholders in accomplishing day-to-day business requirements.
• The following information should be part of the dashboard and reported:
  – The effectiveness and efficiency of information security activities
  – Areas where improvement is required
  – Information and systems that are subject to an unacceptable level of risk
  – Actions required to help minimise information risk (e.g., reviewing the enterprise risk appetite, understanding the information security threat environment, and encouraging business and system owners to remedy unacceptable risk)
  – Details of progress made since previous monitoring reports
  – Financial information regarding the cost of information security controls and the financial impact of information security incidents

Page intentionally left blank

APPENDIX F
DETAILED GUIDANCE: SERVICES, INFRASTRUCTURE AND APPLICATIONS ENABLER

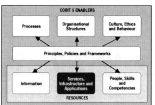

This appendix provides details regarding services, infrastructure and applications within information security based on the introduction of the services, infrastructure and applications enabler in section II. The following list contains some examples of potential security-related services, as they might appear in a service catalogue:
• Provide a security architecture.
• Provide security awareness.
• Provide secure development (development in line with security standards).
• Provide security assessments.
• Provide adequately secured and configured systems, in line with security requirements and security architecture.
• Provide user access and access rights in line with business requirements.
• Provide adequate protection against malware, external attacks and intrusion attempts.
• Provide adequate incident response.
• Provide security testing.
• Provide monitoring and alert services for security-related events.

For each of these service capabilities, the building blocks of services are described in this appendix:
• **Detailed description** of the service, including business functionality
• **Attributes**—The inputs, supporting technologies (including applications and infrastructure)
• **Goals**—The quality and compliance goals for each service capability and the related metrics

F.1 Security Architecture

Description of the Service Capability
Figure 39 describes the service capability for plan services.

Figure 39—Plan Services: Description of the Service Capability	
Service Capability	**Description**
Include information security in architecture.	Ensure inclusion of information security requirements when analysing gaps and selecting solutions for the enterprise.
Maintain security architecture.	Maintain an architecture repository containing information security-related standards, reusable components, modelling artefacts, relationships, dependencies and views to enable uniformity of architectural organisation and maintenance.
Set up and maintain asset inventory.	Provide a detailed inventory of information and physical assets with proper classification, ownership, location, maintenance type, value and criticality.
Provide information security configuration management.	Configuration management provides the data used to identify and progress information security incidents. Use the configuration management system (CMS) to assess the impact of an incident and to identify the users affected by potential problems. The CMS also contains information about categories of incidents. Leverage the CMS as a proactive approach to prevent an incident due to unknown configurations and to reduce costs by maintaining a standardised configuration.
Set up and maintain infrastructure discovery.	Enable discovery of new assets and entities that are provisioned or deployed to a given environment.

Attributes

Figure 40 describes attributes for plan services.

Figure 40—Plan Services: Attributes		
Service Capability	**Supporting Technology**	**Benefit**
Include information security in architecture.	N/A	
Maintain security architecture.	N/A	
Set up and maintain asset inventory.	• Configuration management database (CMDB) • Asset management systems • Simple Network Management Protocol (SNMP) • Reporting agents	• Identification of assets based on data type • Protection of desired IT assets • Clear picture of the scope that is susceptible to external attacks • Clear knowledge of the entry/exit points of the network • Inventory accuracy • Facilitation of configuration management • Stewardship of cost-benefit analysis
Provide information security configuration management.	• CMDB • Vulnerability scanners • Real-time database activity monitoring solutions • Policy auditing solutions	• Enablement of configuration standards to be tracked and enforced • Identification of exceptions to configuration standards • Reduction in vulnerabilities
Set up and maintain infrastructure discovery.	• CMDB • Network discovery tools • Asset management systems • SNMP • Reporting agents	• Identification of new assets • Protection of desired IT assets • Clear picture of the scope that is susceptible to external attacks • Clear knowledge of the entry/exit points of the network • Inventory accuracy • Facilitation of configuration management • Stewardship of cost-benefit analysis

Goals

Figure 41 describes goals for plan services.

Figure 41—Plan Services: Goals		
Service Capability	**Quality Goal**	**Metric**
Include information security in architecture.	Information security requirements are embedded within the enterprise architecture and translated into a formal information security architecture.	Number of exceptions to information security architecture standards
Maintain security architecture.	Information security architecture is aligned and evolves with changes to the enterprise architecture.	Date of last review and/or update to information security practices applied to the enterprise architecture
Set up and maintain asset inventory.	• All assets have been inventoried completely and accurately, and are up to date. • New assets and entities can be discovered on an accurate and timely basis.	• Number of assets not in inventory • Number of inaccuracies in inventory • Number of out-of-date entries in inventory • Total cost of ownership (TCO) • Number of copies of illegal software in use • Cost reduction/avoidance • Number of unidentified assets/entities • Time delay for discovery of new asset/entity

DETAILED GUIDANCE: SERVICES, INFRASTRUCTURE AND APPLICATION ENABLER

Figure 41—Plan Services: Goals *(cont.)*		
Service Capability	**Quality Goals**	**Metric**
Provide information security configuration management.	There is an accurate, complete and up-to-date configuration of all assets and entities under configuration management.	• Percent of changes withdrawn or rolled back • Accuracy of configuration items and associated attributes • Recovery testing efficiency • Percent of authorised vs. unauthorised changes • Number of configuration errors • Accuracy of configurations maintained for desired configurations • Number of standard configurations supported and the frequency of configuration drift from standards • Number of configuration item variances identified • Time it takes to change a configuration item • Accuracy of changes in specific change windows to specific configuration item types • Number of configuration item changes that are unplanned during a given time frame • Number of configuration item changes that have to be withdrawn or rolled back • Total number of configuration items managed • Completeness of configuration item attributes related to detail and depth
Set up and maintain infrastructure discovery.	New assets and entities can be discovered on a accurate and timely basis.	• Number of unidentified assets/entities • Time delay for discovery of new asset/entity

F.2 Security Awareness

Description of the Service Capability
Figure 42 describes the service capability for security awareness services.

Figure 42—Security Awareness Services: Description of the Service Capability	
Service Capability	**Description**
Provide information security communications (enabling awareness and training).	Provide the content, delivery and analysis of information security-related training, education, news, events, and the necessary correlation to a given entity or enterprise group.

Attributes
Figure 43 describes attributes for security awareness services.

Figure 43—Security Awareness Services: Attributes		
Service Capability	**Supporting Technology**	**Benefit**
Provide information security communications (enabling awareness and training).	• Training courses (internal and external) • News feeds • Knowledge bases (KBs) • Training tools • Social media • Email • Collaboration tools • Vendor and industry advisories • CERT advisories	• Increased information security awareness throughout the enterprise • Reduced risk of social engineering attacks (e.g., phishing, identity theft)

Goals
Figure 44 describes goals for security awareness services.

Figure 44—Security Awareness Services: Goals		
Service Capability	**Quality Goal**	**Metric**
Provide information security communications (enabling awareness and training).	Timely, accurate, effective information security communications and effective training	• Quality of communications to meet information security awareness and training needs of the enterprise • Degree of completeness of awareness and communications against the defined targets

F.3 Secure Development

Description of the Service Capability
Figure 45 describes the service capability for secure development services.

Figure 45—Secure Development Services: Description of the Service Capability	
Service Capability	**Description**
Develop secure coding practices.	The design and delivery of coding practices, examples and content demonstrating secure coding and development (development of code that can withstand attacks) for a given set of languages and environments
Develop secure infrastructure libraries.	The design and delivery of language- and environment-specific information security modules that provide essential or critical information security functions

Attributes
Figure 46 describes attributes for secure development services.

Figure 46—Secure Development Services: Attributes		
Service Capability	**Supporting Technology**	**Benefit**
Develop secure coding practices.	• Compilers, linkers • Secure coding resources (books, courses, examples) • Static and binary analysis tools • Code scanners	• Decreased likelihood of vulnerabilities in code • Assistance in conforming with compliance standards
Develop secure infrastructure libraries.	• Development languages • Secure coding resources (books, courses) • Code scanners • Static and binary analysis tools • Compilers, linkers	• Protection of intellectual property • Decreased likelihood of vulnerabilities in software development

Goals
Figure 47 describes goals for secure development services.

Figure 47—Secure Development Services: Goals		
Service Capability	**Quality Goal**	**Metric**
Develop secure coding practices.	Accurate identification of all information risk and resulting business risk/effects to a given asset or entity	Number of new types of risk discovered via incidents not covered in report
Develop secure infrastructure libraries.	Improvements in information security configuration of systems in alignment with information security requirements	Number of information security issues discovered after an information security assessment of the hardened system

F.4 Security Assessments

Description of the Service Capability
Figure 48 describes the service capability for security assessment services.

Figure 48—Security Assessment Services: Description of the Service Capability	
Service Capability	**Description**
Perform information security assessments.	Performance of an information security assessment of a given entity, system, process, procedure, application or organisational unit for information security issues
Perform information risk assessments.	Process of providing identification, evaluation, estimation and analysis of threats to and vulnerabilities of an given entity, system, process, procedure, application or organisational unit to determine the levels of risk involved (potential for losses), and using the analysis as a basis for identifying appropriate and cost-effective measures as well as the determination of an acceptable level of risk

DETAILED GUIDANCE: SERVICES, INFRASTRUCTURE AND APPLICATION ENABLER

Attributes

Figure 49 describes attributes for security assessment services.

Figure 49—Security Assessment Services: Attributes		
Service Capability	**Supporting Technology**	**Benefit**
Perform information security assessments.	• Vulnerability scanner • Fuzzers, sniffers • Protocol analysers • Passive and active network analysers • Honeypots • Endpoint agents • Application scanners • Compliance management • Reporting tools • Remote access (if needed), network, side channels, virtual private networks (VPNs)	• Identification of information security vulnerabilities • Identification of gaps that could lead to compliance issues
Perform information risk assessments.	Same as above: • Vulnerability scanner • Fuzzers, sniffers • Protocol analysers • Log analyser • Passive and active network analysers • Honeypots • Endpoint agents • Application scanners • Compliance management • Reporting tools • Remote access (if needed), network, side channels, VPNs	• Provision of risk rating for information security practices • Help in prioritising vulnerabilities based on risk • Insight into ways to mitigate risk based on business needs

Goals

Figure 50 describes goals for security assessment services.

Figure 50—Security Assessment Services: Goals		
Service Capability	**Quality Goal**	**Metric**
Perform information security assessments.	Accurate identification of all information security weaknesses, deficiencies, exposures, vulnerabilities and threats to a given asset or entity	Number of items discovered via incidents not covered in report
Perform information risk assessments.	Accurate identification of all information risk and resulting business risk/effects to a given asset or entity	Areas of new risk discovered via incidents not covered in report

F.5 Adequately Secured and Configured Systems, Aligned With Security Requirements and Security Architecture

Description of the Service Capability

Figure 51 describes the service capability for adequately secured systems services.

Figure 51—Adequately Secured Systems Services: Description of the Service Capability	
Service Capability	**Description**
Provide adequately secured hardened and configured systems, in line with information security requirements and information security architecture.	Provide the information security-related configuration, settings and system hardening to ensure that the information security posture of a given system is based on a set of requirements or architectural designs.
Provide device information security protection.	Provide device-specific information security measures and activities.
Provide physical information protection.	Provide adequate, specific information security measures for data and information that exist in non-digital forms, including documents, media, facilities, physical perimeter and transit.

Attributes

Figure 52 describes attributes for adequately secured systems services.

Figure 52—Adequately Secured Systems Services: Attributes		
Service Capability	**Supporting Technology**	**Benefit**
Provide adequately secured hardened and configured systems, in line with information security requirements and information security architecture.	• File Transfer Protocol (FTP) • CMDB update methods • Signature verification solutions • File integrity monitoring • Kernel modules • Information security requirements and information security architecture • System management • Patch management • Virtualisation management • Cloud management	• Reduced unauthorised access to data • Reduced external and internal threats • Simplified compliance
Provide device information security protection.	• Device-specific platform OS • Platform management console/systems	• Confidentiality in case of theft • Prevention of unauthorised access to specific devices • More explicit information security for specific devices
Provide physical information protection.	• Closed-circuit television (CCTV) • Locks • Alarms • Access control • Vaulting • Intelligence reports • First responder interfaces • Facilities management solutions • Fire protection systems • Time locks • Physical access solutions	Protection of physical assets from external and internal threats

Goals

Figure 53 describes goals for adequately secured systems services.

Figure 53—Adequately Secured Systems Services: Goals		
Service Capability	**Quality Goal**	**Metric**
Provide adequately secured hardened and configured systems, in line with information security requirements and information security architecture.	Improvements in information security configuration of systems in alignment with information security requirements	Number of information security issues discovered after an information security assessment of the hardened system
Provide device information security protection.	Improvements in information security configuration of device in alignment with information security requirements	Number of information security issues discovered after an information security assessment of the secured device
Provide physical information protection.	Physical controls in line with information security requirements	• Number of incidents not discovered by review/assessment • Number incidents detected not addressed by existing controls

F.6 User Access and Access Rights in Line With Business Requirements

Description of the Service Capability

Figure 54 describes the service capability for user access and access rights services.

Figure 54—User Access and Access Rights Services: Description of the Service Capability	
Service Capability	**Description**
Provide authentication services.	Provide a set of capabilities for performing user or entity identification using a set of factors as determined by the information security policy or access control requirements.
Provide information security provisioning services.	Provide a set of capabilities for creating, delivering and managing the information security-enabling technologies to a given system, entity, application, service or device.

Figure 54—User Access and Access Rights Services: Description of the Service Capability *(cont.)*	
Service Capability	Description
Evaluate information security entity classification services.	Evaluate the categories, classification, information security level and sensitivity for a given entity, system, process, procedure, application, service or organisational unit.
Provide revocation services.	Provide a set of capabilities for cancelling, withdrawing or terminating information security rights or abilities for a given system, entity, application, service, process, procedure, organisational unit or device.
Provide user authentication and authorisation rights in line with business requirements.	Provide a set of capabilities and management practices for performing user identification using a set of factors as determined by the information security policy or access control requirements as defined by the business requirements.

Attributes

Figure 55 describes attributes for user access and access rights services.

Figure 55—User Access and Access Rights Services: Attributes		
Service Capability	Supporting Technology	Benefit
Provide authentication services.	• Biometrics • Certificates • Dongles • Smart cards • Embedded device IDs • One-time passwords (OTPs), fobs, cellular telephones • Username/passwords • Identity as a Service (IDaaS), barcodes, universal product code (UPC) • Certificate revocation list (CRL), ID federation • Root certificates • Key management services • Location services • Reputation services • Public key infrastructure (PKI)	• Prevention of unauthorised access to systems/data • Assurance that every entity has only the necessary level of access • Safeguarding of sensitive information • Verification of the identity of users accessing systems
Provide information security provisioning services.	• Open Mobile Alliance (OMA) Device Management (DM) provisioning • Subscriber identity module (SIM), certificates, root certificates • Local and remote encryption services • Key management services • Location services system and device Management solutions • Software distribution solutions • HR data feed	Appropriate and timely access to needed systems for employees
Provide information security entity classification services.	• Diagram and visualisation tools • Classification tools • CMDB • Enterprise architecture • Classification standards • Release candidate push solutions	Enables appropriate grouping and categorisation of information security entities to classify the appropriate level of risk
Provide revocation services.	• SIM, certificates, root certificates • Local and remote encryption services • Key management services • Location services • HR data feed • PKI	• Prevention of systems access by unauthorised users after their privileges have been revoked (due to termination or role change) • Reduced likelihood of an internal attack
Provide user authentication and authorisation rights in line with business requirements.	• SIM, certificates, root certificates • Local and remote encryption services • Key management services • Location services • PKI	• Verification that users have appropriate level of access to needed systems only • Reduced exposure of sensitive data • Reduced likelihood of internal attack

Goals

Figure 56 describes goals for user access and access rights services.

Figure 56—User Access and Access Rights Services: Goals		
Service Capability	**Quality Goal**	**Metric**
Provide authentication services.	Accurate, complete and timely authentication of all entities and/or services	• Number of entities or services not under the authentication service • Completeness of authentication factors supporting information security requirements
Provide information security provisioning services.	Accurate, complete and timely provisioning of all services and information security elements for entities, devices or services	• Number of incomplete provisioning transactions • Number of inaccurate provisioning transactions • Average delay in provision • Violation of maximum delay in provisioning
Provide information security entity classification services.	Accurate and complete classification of all entities	• Number of inaccuracies in classification • Number of classes not defined for entities discovered • Number of changes required to existing classifications
Provide revocation privilege services.	Accurate, complete, and timely revocation of all entities and/or services	• Number of failed revocations for targets • Completeness of revocations supporting information security requirements • Delay in revocation of entities and services for a given target
Provide user authentication and authorisation rights in line with business requirements.	Accurate, complete, and timely authentication and proper authorisation of all entities and/or services	• Number of entities or services not under the authentication or authorisation service • Completeness of authentication and authorisation factors supporting information security and business requirements

F.7 Adequate Protection Against Malware, External Attacks and Intrusion Attempts

Description of the Service Capability

Figure 57 describes the service capability for protection against malware and attacks services.

Figure 57—Protection Against Malware and Attacks Services: Description of the Service Capability	
Service Capability	**Description**
Provide information security and countermeasures for threats (internal and external).	Plan, implement, maintain and improve measures, countermeasures and activities including, but not limited to, actions, processes, devices or systems, addressing threats and vulnerabilities as identified in the risk assessments, information security policies and information security strategy. Remain up to date on emerging technologies.
Provide data protection (in host, network, cloud and storage).	Provide a set of capabilities and management practices for implementing protection, confidentiality, integrity and availability of data in all of their states including, but not limited to, at rest or in transit, locally and externally, short-term and long-term.

Attributes

Figure 58 describes attributes for protection against malware and attacks services.

Figure 58—Protection Against Malware and Attacks Services: Attributes		
Service Capability	**Supporting Technology**	**Benefit**
Provide information security and countermeasures for threats (internal and external).	• Encryption • PKI, deep packet inspection (DPI), sniffers • Firewalls • Packet analyser, sensors • Compliance management • Information security requirements and information security architecture • CMDB • System patch management • Virtualisation management • Cloud management • Vendor-supplied dashboards and management agents • Vendor-supplied updates • Open source software (OSS) repositories • Vendor information security advisories and KBs, honeypots, tarpits • Antimalware, antirootkit, antispyware, antiphishing • Browser protection, sandboxing, content inspection • Reputation services	• An up-to-date reference for remediating threats • Prevention of internal and external attacks
Provide data protection (in host, network, cloud and storage).	• PKI, sniffers, DPI • Encryption services • Data loss prevention (DLP) • System and device management solutions • Software distribution solutions • Remote management systems • Virtualisation and cloud management solutions • Document management • Data classification systems • Application-centric data management solutions • Data obfuscation solutions	• Ability for data to be stored and transferred securely • Confidentiality, integrity and availability

Goals

Figure 59 describes goals for protection against malware and attacks services.

Figure 59—Protection Against Malware and Attacks Services: Goals		
Service Capability	**Quality Goal**	**Metric**
Provide information security and countermeasures for threats (internal and external).	Maximised protection against known and unknown threats	Number of information security-related incidents
Provide data protection (in host, network, cloud and storage).	Maximised data protection for all data states	Number of data exposures

F.8 Adequate Incident Response

Description of the Service Capability

Figure 60 describes the service capability for protection against malware and attacks services.

Figure 60—Incident Response Services: Description of the Service Capability	
Service Capability	**Description**
Provide information security escalation service.	Provide a set of capabilities and management practices (including, but not limited to, functional and hierarchical escalations) to resolve information security-related incidents on time.
Provide information security forensics (analysis).	Provide a set of capabilities that enable forensics to be performed on a given entity, system, process, procedure, application, service, device, or organisational unit (or groupings thereof) to support investigations, electronic discovery and evidentiary collection. Ensure that the set of capabilities is performed to enable legal treatment and maintenance of chain of custody as required by relevant legal/governmental procedures.

Attributes

Figure 61 describes attributes for incident response services.

Figure 61—Incident Response Services: Attributes		
Service Capability	**Supporting Technology**	**Benefit**
Provide information security escalation service.	• Vulnerability management • Information security vendor advisories • Industry information security advisories • Escalation hierarchy system (organisationally based) • Information security policies	Timely resolution of information security-related incidents by establishing a hierarchical path for escalation
Provide information security forensics (analysis).	• Memory inspection tools • Network analysers • Log analysers • Application and data inspection tools • Reverse engineering tools • Malware analysis tools • Vendor and OSS forensic toolsets • Network traffic • Malware and code snippets • SIEM	Support of the investigation and discovery of information security-related incidents

Goals

Figure 62 describes goals for incident response services.

Figure 62—Incident Response Services: Goals		
Service Capability	**Quality Goal**	**Metric**
Provide information security escalation service.	Timely, accurate, effective, efficient and targeted escalation procedures	• Number of inaccurate, ineffective, inefficient or misdirected escalations • Delay in escalation communications
Provide information security forensics (analysis).	Accurate, complete and discoverable information gathering and analysis	Number of inaccurate, incomplete or inadmissible forensics artefacts

F.9 Security Testing

Description of the Service Capability

Figure 63 describes the service capability for security testing services.

Figure 63—Security Testing Services: Description of the Service Capability	
Service Capability	**Description**
Perform information security testing.	Provide information security-based testing and evaluation services including, but not limited to, testing for data protection and integrity validation, information security-based regression analysis, test harnesses and frameworks, and antagonistic quality assurance, with the end goal of maintaining information security functionality as intended.

Attributes

Figure 64 describes attributes for security testing services.

Figure 64—Security Testing Services: Attributes		
Service Capability	**Supporting Technology**	**Benefit**
Perform information security testing.	• Information security toolkits • Test scripts • Software development kits (SDKs) • Alternate boot methods/OSs • Regression analysis tools • Information security testing tools • Unit test tools and systems	• Increased information security awareness • Insight into information security vulnerabilities into the enterprise • Opportunity to reduce vulnerabilities in early stages

Goals

Figure 65 describes goals for security testing services.

Figure 65—Security Testing Services: Goals		
Service Capability	**Quality Goal**	**Metric**
Perform information security testing.	Improvements in information security configuration of device in alignment with information security requirements	Number of information security issues discovered after an information security assessment of the secured device

F.10 Monitoring and Alert Services for Security-related Events

Description of the Service Capability

Figure 66 describes the service capability for information security monitoring/improvement services.

Figure 66—Information Security Monitoring/Improvement Services: Description of the Service Capability	
Service Capability	**Description**
Provide monitoring service for information security processes and events.	Provide a set of capabilities to enable both real-time and offline monitoring and dashboarding that support necessary data and event correlation and integration.
Provide alerting and reporting service for information security practices, processes and events.	Provide a set of capabilities to enable both real-time and post-event altering, reporting and correlation of events, incidents, processes and ticketed actions, as well as support for proper escalation and remediation.
Provide information security measurements and metrics (key goal indicators [KGIs], key performance indicators [KPIs], etc.).	Provide a set of capabilities that deliver information security measurements, metrics and analysis in which information security practices and goals are measured against actual and desired performance criteria.

Attributes

Figure 67 describes attributes for information security monitoring/improvement services.

Figure 67—Information Security Monitoring/Improvement Services: Attributes		
Service Capability	**Supporting Technology**	**Benefit**
Provide monitoring service for information security processes and events.	• Logs • SNMP • Alerting systems • SIEM • Management dashboards • Network operations centers (NOCs)	Real-time monitoring of appropriate events
Provide alerting and reporting service for information security practices, processes and events.	• Logs • SNMP • Alerting systems • SIEM • Management dashboards • NOCs	Appropriate response to information security events
Provide information security measurements and metrics (KGIs, KPIs, etc.)	• Spreadsheets and metrics standards • SIEM • Management dashboards • Scorecards • Alerting systems • Incident response tools • Information security policies	• Performance measurement • Quantifiable data

Goals

Figure 68 describes goals for information security monitoring/improvement services.

Figure 68—Information Security Monitoring/Improvement Services: Goals		
Service Capability	**Quality Goal**	**Metric**
Provide monitoring service for information security processes and events.	Accurate and complete monitoring of all information security processes and relevant events	Number of inaccurate or incomplete events monitored/logged
Provide alerting and reporting service for information security practices, processes and events.	Accurate, complete and timely alerting of all relevant or critical information security events	• Number of inaccurate or incomplete events alerted • Delay in alerting of critical information security events
Provide information security measurements and metrics (KGIs, KPIs, etc.).	Accurate and complete information security measurements that align with information security strategy	• Quality and completeness of KGIs and KPIs against target • Number of measurement errors

APPENDIX G
DETAILED GUIDANCE: PEOPLE, SKILLS AND COMPETENCIES ENABLER

This appendix contains detailed information on a set of skills and competencies, based on the introduction of the people, skills and competencies enabler in section II:
• Information security governance
• Information security strategy formulation
• Information risk management
• Information security architecture development
• Information security operations
• Information assessment and testing and compliance

For each of these skills and competencies, the following attributes are described:
• Skill description and definition
• Experience, education and qualifications required for the skill/competency
• Knowledge, technical skills and behavioural skills
• Related structure (if relevant)

G.1 Information Security Governance

Skill Description and Definition
This skill establishes and maintains an information security governance framework and supporting processes to ensure that the information security strategy is aligned with organisational goals and objectives, information risk is managed appropriately, and programme resources are managed responsibly.

Experience, Education and Qualifications Required for the Skill/Competency
Figure 69 describes experience and qualifications for information security governance.

Figure 69—Information Security Governance: Experience, Education and Qualifications	
Requirement	**Description**
Experience	Several years of experience in information security and IT/business management (recommended) including experience in: • Creating, implementing and measuring information security policies • Information security compliance with external regulations • Aligning information security strategy with corporate governance • Creating information security policies that align with business needs and devising methods to measure the effectiveness of the policies • Communicating with executive leadership
Qualifications	CISM

Knowledge, Technical Skills and Behavioural Skills
Figure 70 describes knowledge, technical and behavioural skills for information security governance.

Figure 70—Information Security Governance: Knowledge, Technical Skills and Behavioural Skills	
Requirement	**Description**
Knowledge	Ability to: • Define metrics that apply to information security governance • Create a performance measurement model based on the information security governance metrics to ensure that organisational objectives are achieved • Develop a business case justifying investments in information security Knowledge of: • Legal and regulatory requirements affecting information security • Roles and responsibilities required for information security throughout the enterprise • Methods to implement information security governance policies • The fundamental concepts of governance and how they relate to information security • Internationally recognised standards, frameworks and best practices related to information security governance and strategy development

Figure 70—Information Security Governance: Knowledge, Technical Skills and Behavioural Skills *(cont.)*	
Requirement	Description
Technical skills	Good understanding of information security practices that apply to the specific business
Behavioural skills	• Proven leader with excellent communication skills • Process orientation

G.2 Information Security Strategy Formulation

Skill Description and Definition
This skill defines and implements the information security vision, mission and goals aligned to the corporate strategy and culture.

Experience, Education and Qualifications Required for the Skill/Competency
Figure 71 describes experience, education and qualifications for information security strategy formulation.

Figure 71—Information Security Strategy Formulation: Experience, Education and Qualifications	
Requirement	Description
Experience	Several years of experience in information security and IT/business management (recommended), including: • Experience in information security strategy and governance • Experience in creating and implementing strategies and information security principles, practices and activities • A broad understanding of all information security functions and how they relate to the business
Qualifications	CISM

Knowledge, Technical Skills and Behavioural Skills
Figure 72 describes knowledge, technical and behavioural skills for information security strategy formulation.

Figure 72—Information Security Strategy Formulation: Knowledge, Technical Skills and Behavioural Skills	
Requirement	Description
Knowledge	Ability to: • Understand the enterprise culture and values • Define an information security strategy that is aligned with enterprise strategy • Develop information security policies and devise metrics to effectively measure the policies Knowledge of: • Information security trends, services and disciplines • Legal and regulatory requirements affecting information security • Internationally recognised standards, frameworks and best practices related to information security strategy development
Technical skills	Broad understanding of identity access management, threat and vulnerability management, information security architecture, and data protection
Behavioural skills	• Proven leader with excellent communication skills and ability to interface with all levels of the enterprise • Business orientation • High-level strategic thinking • An understanding of the big picture

Related Role/Structure
Figure 73 describes related role/structure for information security strategy formulation.

Figure 73—Information Security Strategy Formulation: Related Role/Structure
Related Role/Structure
CISO
ISSC

G.3 Information Risk Management

Skill Description and Definition

This skill ensures that information risk is managed to comply with ERM directives.

Experience, Education and Qualifications Required for the Skill/Competency

Figure 74 describes experience, education and qualifications for information risk management.

Figure 74—Information Risk Management: Experience, Education and Qualifications	
Requirement	**Description**
Experience	Several years of experience in information security and IT/business management (recommended) including experience in: • Assessing the risk related to information security practices • Mitigating risk based on the business needs of the enterprise • Risk management, risk profiling and threat assessments
Qualifications	CRISC

Knowledge, Technical Skills and Behavioural Skills

Figure 75 describes knowledge, technical skills and behavioural skills for information risk management.

Figure 75—Information Risk Management: Knowledge, Technical Skills and Behavioural Skills	
Requirement	**Description**
Knowledge	Knowledge of: • Methods to establish an information asset classification model consistent with business objectives • Risk assessment and analysis methodologies • Business processes and essential functions • Information security industry standards (e.g., NIST, PCI) • Information security-related laws and regulations (e.g., national and regional privacy legislation) • Risk frameworks and models, risk quantification, risk recording and risk reporting
Technical skills	• An understanding of information security practices and activities and the risk associated with them • Risk analysis and mitigating controls
Behavioural skills	• Abstract thinker • Problem solving expertise • Process orientation

G.4 Information Security Architecture Development

Skill Description and Definition

This skill oversees the design and implementation of the information security architecture.

Experience, Education and Qualifications Required for the Skill/Competency

Figure 76 describes experience, education and qualifications for information security architecture development.

Figure 76—Information Security Architecture Development: Experience, Education and Qualifications	
Requirement	**Description**
Experience	Several years of experience in information security (recommended), including: • Experience working with hardware and software systems, including OSs, databases, applications and networks • Technical understanding of how various systems interconnect with each other
Education/Qualifications	• Good understanding of networking protocol, databases, applications and OSs, and how they are applicable to the business processes • CRISC, CISSP

Knowledge, Technical Skills and Behavioural Skills

Figure 77 describes knowledge, technical skills and behavioural skills for information security architecture development.

Figure 77—Information Security Architecture Development: Knowledge, Technical Skills and Behavioural Skills	
Requirement	**Description**
Knowledge	Knowledge of: • How all the technologies within the enterprise interact with the business and information security policies • Information security architectures (e.g., Sherwood Applied Business Security Architecture [SABSA], The Open Group Architecture Framework [TOGAF]) and methods to apply them • Application design review and threat modelling • Methods to design information security practices • Managing computer information security programs, policies, procedures and standards as they pertain to business activities • Information security industry standards/best practices (e.g., ISO/IEC 27000 series, ISF, NIST, PCI) • Information security-related laws and regulations • Emerging information security technologies and development methodologies
Technical skills	• Deep and broad knowledge of IT and emerging trends • Technical design capabilities • Strong subject matter expertise in computer operations
Behavioural skills	• Abstract thinker • Problem solving expertise

Related Role/Structure

Figure 78 describes related role/structure for information security architecture development.

Figure 78—Information Security Architecture Development: Related Role/Structure
Related Role/Structure
ISM
Information security architect

G.5 Information Security Operations

Skill Description and Definition

This skill manages the information security programme in alignment with the information security strategy. This includes:
• Planning, establishing and managing the capability to detect, investigate, respond to and recover from information security incidents to minimise business impact
• Performing user provisioning tasks for enterprise systems and application environments
• Assisting with the definition of roles and access models for various application and platform environments
• Monitoring and maintaining technology platforms and access management solutions that support the access management capabilities
• Managing network and connectivity information security
• Managing endpoint information security
• Protecting against malware
• Handling security incident and event management

Experience, Education and Qualifications Required for the Skill/Competency

Figure 79 describes education and qualifications for information security operations.

Figure 79—Information Security Operations: Experience, Education and Qualifications	
Requirement	**Description**
Experience	IT/information security experience (recommended), including: • Strong background in information security. • Working knowledge of all information security functions in an enterprise and understanding of how they align with the business objectives
Education/Qualifications	• Experience in implementing information security management programme directives to protect corporate assets while minimising corporate risk, liabilities and losses • CRISC, CISSP • Vendor- and technology-specific certifications

Knowledge, Technical Skills and Behavioural Skills

Figure 80 describes knowledge, technical skills and behavioural skills for information security operations.

Figure 80—Information Security Operations: Knowledge, Technical Skills and Behavioural Skills	
Requirement	**Description**
Knowledge	Knowledge of: • Managing computer information security programs, policies, procedures and standards as they pertain to business activities • Log monitoring, log aggregation and log analysis
Technical skills	• Strong subject matter expertise in computer operations • In-depth knowledge of Windows®/UNIX® operating systems, authentication methods, firewalls, routers, web services, etc.
Behavioural skills	• Proficiency in managing projects and staff • Analytical mindset, detail orientation • Strong communication and facilitation skills • Strong time management skills

Related Role/Structure

Figure 81 describes related role/structure for information security operations.

Figure 81—Information Security Operations: Related Role/Structure
Related Role/Structure
ISM
Information security administrator

G.6 Information Assessment and Testing and Compliance

Skill Description and Definition

This skill assures compliance of information handling and processing with internal and external laws, regulations, directives, and standards.

Experience, Education and Qualifications Required for the Skill/Competency

Figure 82 describes experience, education and qualifications for information security auditing and compliance.

Figure 82—Information Security Auditing and Compliance: Experience, Education and Qualifications	
Requirement	**Description**
Experience	Several years of experience in information security and auditing/compliance (recommended), including experience in: • Auditing, with exposure to the laws and regulations with which the enterprise must comply • Ensuring that the documented information security practices are effective and are being applied
Qualifications	Certification in auditing information security and compliance-related activities (CISA)

Knowledge, Technical Skills and Behavioural Skills

Figure 83 describes knowledge, technical skills and behavioural skills for information security auditing and compliance.

Figure 83—Information Security Auditing and Compliance: Knowledge, Technical Skills and Behavioural Skills	
Requirement	**Description**
Knowledge	Knowledge of: • IS audit standards, guidelines and best practices to ensure that business systems are protected and managed • Audit planning and audit project management techniques • Information security industry standards (e.g., ISO/IEC 27000 series, ISF, NIST, PCI) • Local information security-related laws and regulations (e.g., US Gramm-Leach-Bliley Act [GLBA])
Technical skills	Audit-related tools, broad knowledge about IT, gap analysis
Behavioural skills	• High ethical values • Process orientation • Excellent negotiation capabilities

Page intentionally left blank

APPENDIX H
DETAILED MAPPINGS

This appendix provides a high-level mapping between a number of other standards and frameworks in the area of information security and *COBIT 5 for Information Security*, focussing on the processes enabler (**figure 84**). Based on the requirements of the information security professional and the specific environment in which the enterprise operates, the enterprise can define whether a particular source of guidance is relevant, and whether the guidance has been applied or a gap exists.

The following standards are included in the comparison in this appendix:
• ISO/IEC 27000 series—The ISO/IEC 27000 series provides a model for establishing, implementing, operating, monitoring, reviewing, maintaining and improving an ISMS. The following *COBIT 5 for Information Security* areas and domains are covered by the ISO/IEC 27000 series, including the control objectives and controls of Annex A in ISO/IEC 27001:
  – Security- and risk-related processes in the EDM, APO and DSS domains
  – Various security-related activities within processes in other domains
  – Monitoring and evaluating activities from the MEA domain
• The ISF *2011 Standard of Good Practice for Information Security* is based on the ISF Information Security Model and consists of an overview of good practice business activities, which are grouped by area and divided into four main categories: information security governance, information security requirements, control framework, and information security monitoring and improvement.
• *Guide for Assessing the Information Security Controls in Federal Information Systems and Organisations*, NIST—The purpose of this guide is to provide direction with regard to information security controls for executive agencies of the US government. This exercise uses NIST Special Publication 800-53A Revision 1.

Figure 84—Mapping of *COBIT 5 for Information Security* to Related Standards

COBIT 5 for Information Security	ISO/IEC 27001	Relevant? / Applied?	ISO/IEC 27002	Relevant? / Applied?	ISF	Relevant? / Applied?	NIST	Relevant? / Applied?
EDM01 Ensure governance framework setting and maintenance	5.1 Management commitment A.5 Security policy		6.1.1 Management commitment to information security		SG1.1 Security Governance Framework			
EDM02 Ensure benefits delivery	7. Management review of the ISMS 8. ISMS improvement				SG2.2 Stakeholder Value Delivery SG2.3 Information Security Assurance Programme			
EDM03 Ensure risk optimisation	4.2.1 Establish the ISMS 4.2.2 Implement and operate the ISMS 4.2.3 Monitor and review the ISMS 4.3 Documentation requirements		14.1.2 Business continuity and risk assessment		SR1 Information Risk Assessment CF20 Business Continuity SI2.2 Information Risk Reporting			
EDM04 Ensure resource optimisation	5.2 Resource management A.6 Organization of information security						Planning	
EDM05 Ensure stakeholder transparency	A.10 Communications and operations management		6.1.1 Management commitment to information security 6.1.2 Information security co-ordination 6.1.3 Allocation of information security responsibilities 6.1.4 Authorization process for information processing facilities 6.1.5 Confidentiality agreements 6.1.6 Contact with authorities 6.1.7 Contact with special interest groups 6.1.8 Independent review of information security		SG2.2 Stakeholder Value Delivery			
APO01 Manage the IT management framework	5.1 Management commitment A.5 Security policy A.6 Organization of information security		Organisation of information security		SG1.1 Security Governance Framework			
APO02 Manage strategy	4.2.1 Establish the ISMS				SG2.1 Information Security Strategy			

Figure 84—Mapping of COBIT 5 for Information Security to Related Standards (cont.)

COBIT 5 for Information Security	ISO/IEC 27001	Relevant?	Applied?	ISO/IEC 27002	Relevant?	Applied?	ISF	Relevant?	Applied?	NIST	Relevant?	Applied?
APO03 Manage enterprise architecture							CF4 Business Applications CF7 System Management CF8 Technical Information Security Infrastructure			Configuration Management		
APO04 Manage innovation												
APO05 Manage portfolio												
APO06 Manage budget and costs												
APO07 Manage human resources	5.2.2 Training, awareness and competence A.8 Human resources security			Human resources information security			CF2 Human Resource Information Security			• Awareness and Training • Planning • Personnel Information Security		
APO08 Manage relationships	A.6.1 Internal organization						CF5 Customer Access					
APO09 Manage service agreements				10.2.1 Service delivery 10.2.2 Monitoring and review of third-party services 10.2.3 Managing changes to third-party services			CF7.7 Service Level Agreements SI2.1 Security Monitoring SI2.2 Information Risk Reporting			System and Services Acquisition		
APO10 Manage suppliers	A.6.2 External parties			6.1.5 Confidentiality agreements 6.2.1 Identification of risks related to external parties 6.2.3 Addressing security in third-party agreements 8.1.2 Screening 8.1.3 Terms and conditions of employment 10.2.3 Manage changes to third-party services 10.8.2 Exchange agreements 12.4.2 Protection of system test data 12.5.5 Outsourced software development 15.1.4 Data protection and privacy of personal information			CF16 External Supplier Management			System and Services Acquisition		

Figure 84—Mapping of COBIT 5 for Information Security to Related Standards (cont.)

COBIT 5 for Information Security	ISO/IEC 27001	Relevant?	Applied?	ISO/IEC 27002	Relevant?	Applied?	ISF	Relevant?	Applied?	NIST	Relevant?	Applied?
APO11 Manage quality	7. Management review of the ISMS 8. ISMS improvement						CF17.3 Quality Assurance					
APO12 Manage risk	4.2.1 Establish the ISMS 4.2.2 Implement and operate the ISMS 4.2.3 Monitor and review the ISMS 4.3 Documentation requirements			13.1.1 Reporting information security events 13.1.2 Reporting security weaknesses 14.1.1 Including information security in the business continuity management process 14.1.2 Business continuity and risk assessment			SR1 Information Risk Assessment SR2 Compliance CF1 Information Security Policy and Organisation CF10 Threat and Vulnerability Management CF20 Business Continuity SI2.2 Information Risk Reporting SI2.3 Monitoring Information Security Compliance			• Incident Response • Risk Assessment		
APO13 Manage security	Dealt with throughout this standard			Dealt with throughout this standard			Dealt with throughout this standard			Dealt with throughout this standard		
BAI01 Manage programmes and projects										Program Management		
BAI02 Manage requirements definition				10.1.1 Security requirements analysis and specification 10.3.2 System acceptance 11.6.2 Sensitive system isolation 12.1.1 Security requirements analysis and specification			SR1.3 Confidentiality Requirements SR1.4 Integrity Requirements SR1.5 Availability Requirements CF18.1 Specification of Requirements					
BAI03 Manage solutions identification and build	A.12 Information systems acquisition, development and maintenance			Dealt with throughout this standard			CF17 System Development Management CF18 Systems Development Lifecycle			• Access Control • Configuration Management • Maintenance • System and Services Acquisition		
BAI04 Manage availability and capacity				10.3.1 Capacity management						• Contingency Planning • Planning		
BAI05 Manage organisational change enablement												
BAI06 Manage changes				10.1.2 Change management 11.5.4 Use of system utilities 12.5.1 Change control procedures 12.5.3 Restrictions on changes to software packages 12.6.1 Control of technical vulnerabilities			CF7.6 Change Management CF10 Threat and Vulnerability Management					

Figure 84—Mapping of *COBIT 5 for Information Security* to Related Standards *(cont.)*

COBIT 5 for Information Security	ISO/IEC 27001	Relevant?	Applied?	ISO/IEC 27002	Relevant?	Applied?	ISF	Relevant?	Applied?	NIST	Relevant?	Applied?
BAI07 Manage change acceptance and transitioning				6.1.4 Authorisation process for information processing facilities 8.2.2 Information security awareness, education and training 9.1.6 Public access, delivery and loading areas 10.1.4 Separation of development, test and operational facilities 10.3.2 System acceptance 12.4.2 Protection of system test data 12.4.3 Access control to program source code 12.5.1 Change control procedures 12.5.2 Technical review of applications after operating system changes			CF7.6 Change Management					
BAI08 Manage knowledge	4.3 Documentation requirements			10.1.1 Documented operating procedures 10.3.2 System acceptance 10.7.4 Security of system documentation 13.2.2 Learning from information security incidents			CF3.2 Document Management CF6 Access Management			Access Control		

Figure 84—Mapping of COBIT 5 for Information Security to Related Standards (cont.)

COBIT 5 for Information Security	ISO/IEC 27001	Relevant? / Applied?	ISO/IEC 27002	Relevant? / Applied?	ISF	Relevant? / Applied?	NIST	Relevant? / Applied?
BAI09 Manage assets	A.7 Asset management		7.1.1 Inventory of assets 7.1.2 Ownership of assets 7.2.2 Information labelling and handling 10.7.4 Security of system documentation 11.4.3 Equipment identification in networks 12.4.1 Control of operational software 12.4.2 Protection of system test data 12.5.2 Technical review of applications after operating system changes 12.5.3 Restrictions on changes to software packages 12.6.1 Control of technical vulnerabilities 15.1.5 Prevention of misuse of information processing facilities		CF3 Asset Management CF19 Physical and Environmental Information Security		• Media Protection • Physical and Environmental Protection	
BAI10 Manage configuration			7.1.1 Inventory of assets 7.1.2 Ownership of assets 7.2.2 Information labelling and handling 10.7.4 Security of system documentation 11.4.3 Equipment identification in networks 12.4.1 Control of operational software 12.4.2 Protection of system test data 12.5.2 Technical review of applications after operating system changes 12.5.3 Restrictions on changes to software packages 12.6.1 Control of technical vulnerabilities 15.1.5 Prevention of misuse of information processing facilities		CF4 Business Applications CF6 Access Management CF7 System Management CF8 Technical Information Security Infrastructure CF9 Network Management CF12 Local Environments CF13 Desktop Applications CF14 Mobile Computing CF15 Electronic Communications		• Access Control • Configuration Management • System and Services Acquisition	

Figure 84—Mapping of COBIT 5 for Information Security to Related Standards (cont.)

COBIT 5 for Information Security	ISO/IEC 27001	Relevant?	Applied?	ISO/IEC 27002	Relevant?	Applied?	ISF	Relevant?	Applied?	NIST	Relevant?	Applied?
DSS01 Manage operations	4.2.2 Implement and operate the ISMS			Communications and operations management			CF6 Access Management CF7 System Management CF9 Network Management					
DSS02 Manage service requests and incidents	A.13 Information security incident management			Information security incident management			CF10 Threat and Vulnerability Management CF11 Incident Management			Incident Response		
DSS03 Manage problems				13.2.2 Learning from information security incidents			CF10 Threat and Vulnerability Management CF11 Incident Management			Incident Response		
DSS04 Manage continuity	4.2.4 Maintain and improve the ISMS 4.3 Documentation requirements 8. ISMS improvement A.14 Business continuity management			Business continuity management			CF20 Business Continuity			Contingency Planning		
DSS05 Manage security services	Dealt with throughout this standard			Dealt with throughout this standard			Dealt with throughout this standard			Dealt with throughout this standard		
DSS06 Manage business process controls	4.2.3 Monitor and review the ISMS			8.2.1 Management responsibilities 10.1.3 Segregation of duties 10.1.4 Separation of development, test and operational facilities 10.5.1 Information backup 10.6.1 Network controls 10.7.3 Information handling procedures 10.8.3 Physical media in transit 10.8.4 Electronic messaging 12.4.2 Protection of system test data 12.4.3 Access control to program source code			CF1 Information Security Policy and Organisation CF7 System Management			• Media Protection • System and Information Integrity		
MEA01 Monitor, evaluate and assess performance and conformance	4.2.3 Monitor and review the ISMS 4.2.4 Maintain and improve the ISMS 7. Management review of the ISMS			10.10.2 Monitoring system use 5.1.2 Review of the information security policy 6.1.8 Independent review of information security 10.10.2 Monitoring system use			SR2 Compliance SI1 Information Security Audit SI2 Information Security Performance			• Audit and Accountability • Information Security Assessment and Authorization		

Figure 84—Mapping of COBIT 5 for Information Security to Related Standards (cont.)

COBIT 5 for Information Security	ISO/IEC 27001	Relevant?	Applied?	ISO/IEC 27002	Relevant?	Applied?	ISF	Relevant?	Applied?	NIST	Relevant?	Applied?
MEA02 Monitor, evaluate and assess the system of internal control	4.2.3 Monitor and review the ISMS 6. Internal ISMS audits A.15.2 Compliance with security policies and standards, and technical compliance			5.1.1 Information security policy document 5.1.2 Review of the information security policy 6.1.8 Independent review of information security 6.2.3 Addressing security in third-party agreements 10.2.2 Monitoring and review of third-party services 10.10.2 Monitoring system use 10.10.4 Administrator and operator logs 15.2.1 Compliance with security policies and standards 15.2.2 Technical compliance checking 15.3.1 Information systems audit controls			CF1 Information Security Policy and Organisation SI1 Information Security Audit			Audit and Accountability		
MEA03 Monitor, evaluate and assess compliance with external requirements	6. Internal ISMS audits A.15.1 Compliance with legal requirements A.15.3 Information systems audit considerations			6.1.6 Contact with authorities 15.1.1 Identification of applicable legislation 15.1.2 Intellectual property rights (IPR) 15.1.4 Data protection and privacy of personal information			SR2 Compliance					

ACRONYMS

Term	Definition
CCTV	Closed-circuit television
CGEIT	Certified in the Governance of Enterprise IT
CIA	Confidentiality, integrity and availability
CISA	Certified Information Systems Auditor
CISM	Certified Information Security Manager
CISSP	Certified Information System Security Professional
CMDB	Configuration management data base
CRISC	Certified in Risk and Information Systems Control
CRL	Certificate revocation list
DLP	Data loss prevention or data leak prevention
DPI	Deep packet inspection
ERM	Enterprise risk management
FTP	File Transfer Protocol
IDaaS	Identity as a Service
NIST	U.S. National Institute of Standards and Technology
NOC	Network operations center
OMA DM	Open Mobile Alliance Device Management
OSS	Open source software
OTP	One-time password
PCI DSS	Payment Card Industry Data Security Standards
PKI	Public key infrastructure
PMO	Project management office
SIEM	Security information and event management
SIM	Subscriber identity module
SNMP	Simple Network Management Protocol
UPC	Universal product code
VPN	Virtual private network

Page intentionally left blank

GLOSSARY

Term	Definition
Accountable party (RACI)	The individual, group or entity that is ultimately responsible for a subject matter, process or scope In a RACI chart, answers the question: **Who accounts for the success of the task?**
Activity	In COBIT, the main action taken to operate the process. Guidance to achieve management practices for successful governance and management of enterprise IT. Activities: • Describe a set of necessary and sufficient action-oriented implementation steps to achieve a governance practice or management practice • Consider the inputs and outputs of the process • Are based on generally accepted standards and good practices • Support establishment of clear roles and responsibilities • Are non-prescriptive, and need to be adapted and developed into specific procedures appropriate for the enterprise
Alignment	A state where the enablers of governance and management of enterprise IT support the goals and strategies of the enterprise
Architecture board	A group of stakeholders and experts who are accountable for guidance on enterprise- architecture-related matters and decisions, and for setting architectural policies and standards
Authentication	The act of verifying the identity of a user and the user's eligibility to access computerised information Scope note: Assurance: Authentication is designed to protect against fraudulent logon activity. It can also refer to the verification of the correctness of a piece of data.
Availability	Ensuring timely and reliable access to and use of information
Benefits realisation	One of the objectives of governance. The bringing about of new benefits for the enterprise, the maintenance and extension of existing forms of benefits, and the elimination of those initiatives and assets that are not creating sufficient value.
Business continuity	Preventing, mitigating and recovering from disruption. The terms 'business resumption planning', 'disaster recovery planning' and 'contingency planning' also may be used in this context; they focus on recovery aspects of continuity, and for that reason the 'resilience' aspect should also be taken into account.
Business goal	The translation of the enterprise's mission from a statement of intention into performance targets and results
Business process control	The policies, procedures, practices and organisational structures designed to provide reasonable assurance that a business process will achieve its objectives
Certification (general)	An independent assessment declaring that specified requirements pertaining to a product, person, process or management system have been met
Competence	The ability to perform a specific task, action or function successfully
Confidentiality	Preserving authorised restrictions on access and disclosure, including means for protecting privacy and proprietary information
Consulted party (RACI)	Refers to those people whose opinions are sought on an activity (two-way communication) In a RACI chart, answers the question: **Who is providing input?** Key roles that provide input. Note that it is up to the accountable and responsible roles to obtain information from other units or external partners, too; however, inputs from the consulted roles listed should are to be considered and, if required, appropriate action has to be taken for escalation, including the information of the process owner and/or the steering committee.
Context	The overall set of internal and external factors that might influence or determine how an enterprise, entity, process or individual acts Scope Note: Context includes: • Technology context—Technological factors that affect an organisation's ability to extract value from data • Data context—Data accuracy, availability, currency and quality • Skills and knowledge—General experience, and analytical, technical and business skills • Organisational and cultural context—Political factors, and whether the organisation prefers data to intuition • Strategic context—Strategic objectives of the enterprise
Control	The means of managing risk, including policies, procedures, guidelines, practices or organisational structures, which can be of an administrative, technical, management, or legal nature. Also used as a synonym for safeguard or countermeasure.
Culture	A pattern of behaviours, beliefs, assumptions, attitudes and ways of doing things
Driver	External and internal factors that initiate and affect how an enterprise or individuals act or change
Enterprise goal	See Business goal

Term	Definition
Enterprise governance	A set of responsibilities and practices exercised by the board and executive management with the goal of providing strategic direction, ensuring that objectives are achieved, ascertaining that risk is managed appropriately and verifying that the enterprise's resources are used responsibly. It could also mean a governance view focussing on the overall enterprise; t. The highest-level view of governance to which, all others must align.
Fob	Information security access device with built-in authentication used to control and secure access
Fuzzer	Software that performs a vulnerability testing technique, often automated or semi-automated, that involves providing invalid, unexpected or random data to the inputs of a computer program or system. Vulnerabilities identified using this technique could lead to system compromise.
Good practice	A proven activity or process that has been successfully used by multiple enterprises and has been shown to produce reliable results
Governance	Governance ensures that stakeholder needs, conditions and options are evaluated to determine balanced, agreed-on enterprise objectives to be achieved; setting direction through prioritization and decision making; and monitoring performance and compliance against agreed-on direction and objectives.
Governance/management practice	For each COBIT process, the governance and management practices provide a complete set of high-level requirements for effective and practical governance and management of enterprise IT. They are statements of actions from governance bodies and management
Governance enabler	Something (tangible or intangible) that assists in the realisation of effective governance
Governance framework	A framework is a basic conceptual structure used to solve or address complex issues; an enabler of governance; a set of concepts, assumptions and practices that define how something can be approached or understood, the relationships amongst the entities involved, the roles of those involved, and the boundaries (what is and is not included in the governance system). Examples: COBIT and Committee of Sponsoring Organizations of the Treadway Commission's (COSO's) *Internal Control—Integrated Framework.*
Governance of enterprise IT	A governance view that ensures that information and related technology support and enable the enterprise strategy and the achievement of enterprise objectives. It also includes the functional governance of IT, i.e., ensuring that IT capabilities are provided efficiently and effectively.
Honeypot	A specially configured server, also known as a decoy server, designed to attract and monitor intruders in a manner such that their actions do not affect production systems
Information	An asset that, like other important business assets, is essential to an enterprise's business. It can exist in many forms: printed or written on paper, stored electronically, transmitted by post or electronically, shown on films, or spoken in conversation.
Information security	Ensures that within the enterprise, information is protected against disclosure to unauthorised users (confidentiality), improper modification (integrity) and non-access when required (availability)
Informed party (RACI)	Refers to those people who are kept up to date on the progress of an activity (one-way communication) In a RACI chart, answers the question: **Who is receiving information?** Roles who are informed of the achievements and/or deliverables of the task. The role in 'accountable', of course, should always receive appropriate information to oversee the task, as do the responsible roles for their area of interest.
Inputs and outputs	The process work products/artefacts considered necessary to support operation of the process. They enable key decisions, provide a record and audit trail of process activities, and enable follow-up in the event of an incident. They are defined at the key management practice level, may include some work products used only within the process and are often essential inputs to other processes. The illustrative COBIT 5 inputs and outputs should not be regarded as an exhaustive list since additional information flows could be defined depending on a particular enterprise's environment and process framework.
Integrity	Guarding against improper information modification or destruction, and includes ensuring information non-repudiation and authenticity
IT service	The day-to-day provision to customers of IT infrastructure and applications and support for their use. Examples include service desk, equipment supply and moves, and security authorisations.
Management	Management plans, builds, runs and monitors activities in alignment with the direction set by the governance body to achieve the enterprise objectives.
Model	A way to describe a given set of components and how those components relate to each other to describe the main workings of an object, system or concept
Objective	Statement of a desired outcome
Organisational structures	An enabler of governance and of management. Includes the enterprise and its structures, hierarchies and dependencies. Example: steering committee.
Output	See Inputs and outputs
Owner	Individual or group that holds or possesses the rights of and the responsibilities for an enterprise, entity or asset, e.g., process owner, system owner
Policy	Overall intention and direction as formally expressed by management

Term	Definition
Principle	An enabler of governance and of management. Comprises the values and fundamental assumptions held by the enterprise, the beliefs that guide and put boundaries around the enterprise's decision making, communication within and outside the enterprise, and stewardship—caring for assets owned by another. Examples: ethics charter, social responsibility charter.
Process	Generally, a collection of practices influenced by the enterprise's policies and procedures that takes inputs from a number of sources (including other processes), manipulates the inputs and produces outputs (e.g., products, services). Scope note: Processes have clear business reasons for existing, accountable owners, clear roles and responsibilities around the execution of the process, and the means to measure performance.
Process goal	A statement describing the desired outcome of a process. An outcome can be an artefact, a significant change of a state or a significant capability improvement of other processes.
Programme and project management office (PMO)	The function responsible for supporting programme and project managers, and for gathering, assessing and reporting information about the conduct of their programmes and constituent projects
Quality	Being fit for purpose (achieving intended value)
Resource	Any enterprise asset that can help the organisation to achieve its objectives
Resource optimisation	One of the governance objectives. Involves effective, efficient and responsible use of all resources—human, financial, equipment, facilities, etc.
Responsible party (RACI)	Refers to the person who must ensure that activities are completed successfully In a RACI chart, answers the question: **Who is getting the task done?** Roles taking the main operational stake in fulfilling the activity listed and creating the intended outcome.
Risk	The combination of the probability of an event and its consequence (ISO/IEC 73)
Risk management	One of the governance objectives. Entails recognising risk; assessing the impact and likelihood of that risk; and developing strategies, such as avoiding the risk, reducing the negative effect of the risk and/or transferring the risk, to manage it within the context of the enterprise's risk appetite.
Role	Prescribed or expected behaviour associated with a particular position or status in a group or organisation. A job or position that has a specific set of expectations attached to it.
Services	See IT service
Skill	The learned capacity to achieve predetermined results
Sniffer	Also known as packet analyser, network analyser or protocol analyser. Computer software or hardware that can intercept and log traffic passing over a digital network.
Stakeholder	Anyone who has a responsibility for, an expectation from or some other interest in the enterprise, e.g., shareholders, users, government, suppliers, customers and the public
Tarpit	A service on a computer system (usually a server) that delays incoming connections for as long as possible. Developed as a defence against a computer worm, with the idea that network abuses such as spamming or broad scanning are less effective if they take too long.
Test harness	Environment or system that provides the ability to perform tests against an entity with an expected set of results
Value creation	The main governance objective of an enterprise, achieved when the three underlying objectives (benefits realisation, risk optimisation and resource optimisation) are balanced

Page intentionally left blank